BEYOND HEAVING BOSOMS

The Smart Bitches' Guide
to Romance Novels

Sarah Wendell
and Candy Tan

Illustrations by Joanne Renaud and Carol Main

A FIRESIDE BOOK
Published by Simon & Schuster

New York   London   Toronto   Sydney

Fireside
A Division of Simon & Schuster, Inc.
1230 Avenue of the Americas
New York, NY 10020

First Fireside trade paperback edition April 2009

FIRESIDE and colophon are registered trademarks of Simon & Schuster, Inc.

For information about special discounts for bulk purchases,
please contact Simon & Schuster Special Sales at
1-800-456-6798 or business@simonandschuster.com.

The Simon & Schuster Speakers Bureau can bring authors to your
live event. For more information or to book an event contact the
Simon & Schuster Speakers Bureau at 866-248-3049 or visit our
website at www.simonspeakers.com.

Manufactured in the United States of America

10 9 8 7 6 5 4 3 2 1

Library of Congress Cataloging-in-Publication Data
Wendell, Sarah.
    Beyond heaving bosoms: the smart bitches' guide to romance novels/
Sarah Wendell and Candy Tan.
        p.   cm.—(A fireside book)
    1. Love stories—History and criticism.   I. Tan, Candy.   II. Title.
    PN3448.L67W46 2009
    809.3'85—dc22   2008037578

ISBN-13: 978-1-4165-7122-3
ISBN-10:   1-4165-7122-1

CANDY'S DEDICATION
To my sister, Honey, the original smart bitch who loves trashy books

SARAH'S DEDICATION
To my husband, Adam, for being my romance, every day

CONTENTS

BEYOND
HEAVING
BOSOMS

Chapter Cleavage

An Introduction to Romance
and to the Smart Bitches

Welcome!

No, no, don't hide your romance novel. You don't have to wrap it in a quilted cover or slide it in between the pages of *The New Yorker*. We know you're smart. We also know you like romance novels.

Your romance novels are welcome here. Celebrated. Loved. Cuddled, even, if they're particularly good. Adorned with man titty and paraded up and down the street to acclaim, applause, and perhaps stray dollar bills. We'll occasionally poke—with savage abandon, even—at the more ludicrous aspects of the genre, but we kvetch because we love. Our point is:

Welcome.

This is *Beyond Heaving Bosoms: The Smart Bitches' Guide to Romance Novels*. We're not egomaniacal enough to think it's *the* Definitive Guide to Romance Novels, but guides written for readers by readers are few and far between. There are plenty of articles and books that dismiss the genre, and some excellent academic examinations that subject the genre to a long-overdue analysis. Us? We're here to throw a party for the genre—to celebrate its soaring successes as well as its appalling excesses, and to raise a beverage to the continued health and happiness of our favorite reading material.

And yes, we're here to throw a drunken yet solidly comforting arm around your shoulders and say, "Oh, yes! We read them! We love them! Even the awful ones, them, too. And people who think we're dumb for reading them? Screw 'em! What the hell do they know?"

There are some things only a reader of romance can understand and appreciate. The bemulleted cover models. The alpha hero whom you love to read about but who'd be fodder for *COPS* episodes in real life. The heroines who are either so feisty they make your teeth hurt, or the embodiment of every virtue known to man, dog, and Chthonic deities. Deep tongue kissing first thing in the morning after a long night of bonkety-bonk, because romance protagonists do not *ever* have morning breath.

Then there are the fun parts of romance novels: the escape into a story that's happy and satisfying, but won't insult your intelligence. The spicy passages that feature . . . spicy passages. The characters you befriend and revisit when you're feeling down or in need of comfort reading. The stories that unabashedly depict love, relationships, and happiness.

There's nothing quite like a beautifully executed romance novel or the afterglow upon finishing an especially good one, and that's why we Smart Bitches are celebrating them.

If you were to gather romance readers into one room, that room would circle the earth seventeen times and do the hokey-pokey while it turned itself around. Most likely we'd all get seasick. But while we fought for the Dramamine, no doubt we'd notice that romance readers represent an astonishing cross section of political, social, religious, and economic groups. According to the oft-quoted statistic from Romance Writers of America (RWA), one out of every five people reads romance. This is, in mathematically correct notation, "a shitfuckton of people." A quick examination of the highlights of those statistics yields numbers with decimal points that are necessary only because that many zeroes become tiresome to type out. In 2006, romance accounted for $1.37 billion in sales, and 64.6 million Americans read at least one romance in 2005. No matter what you do to those numbers, whether you divide them or watch them do a tango, those numbers are freaking huge.

And yet, despite the millions of dollars and those millions of readers and that (quivering alabaster) mound of books sold in every language known to print, romance is easily the most well-hidden literary habit in America. Millions of dollars are spent on romance novels, yet few will admit to reading them. We Smart Bitches, we know you read romance.

In fact, we'll come right out and say five out of five readers have read romance—they just didn't know it. Think about it: just about every work of fiction has a romantic element in it. The love, sex, or attraction part might not be the primary focus, but they're almost always there. What would the *Iliad* be without Paris and Helen, or the *Odyssey* without Odysseus and Penelope? What would a story of danger and intrigue be without sexual attraction and tension? What would horror be without some damn fool woman running around so that some muscled hero could rescue her scantily clad ass? Love stories, from epic poems to schlocky bestsellers, form the backbone of our storytelling tradition.

So tie another ribbon around the What-the-Fuck tree: a staggering number of people read romance, few admit to it, and romantic elements are ubiquitous, but when that romance stands on its own two glass-slippered feet as the focus and driving element of the plot, then it's craaaap. No one who is anyone likes romance novels.

But somehow, everyone has a very firm idea of what the average romance reader is like. We bet you already know her. She's rather dim and kind of tubby—undereducated *and* undersexed—and she displays a distressing affinity for mom jeans and sweaters covered in puffy paint and appliquéd kittens. So even though repeated surveys conducted by independent research reveal that an astonishingly diverse and often affluent population reads romance novels, in popular depictions, we're all the same.

"In all honesty, the dichotomy inherent in the conflicting nobility and morality of the duke is quite a fascinating subject to analyze."

Here she is: meet Mavis. She's not only a romance reader, she's *the* romance reader, the image everyone pictures when they discuss the romance novels those bored housewives love so much. Funny thing about Mavis, and you, and us, and everyone else who read romance: our love of romance novels is probably all that we have in common, but because of this shared interest, we're transformed from women of all walks of life to storm troopers: not very bright, evidence of the triumph of the Evil Empires of Bad Taste and Degraded Literature, and impossible to tell apart from one another.

Maybe you're already familiar with the genre. Maybe your budget is earmarked for romance novels, then rent, then food. Maybe your bookcases look like ours, and there are paperback romance novels wedged two deep on each shelf. Or maybe you're curious why romance is so popular, and why the otherwise-intelligent women in your life enjoy this cultural blight. Or perhaps you know us from our site, and you're just wondering how many times we're going to say expletives like "fuck" or "shit" or "holy cuntmonkeys" in this book.*

Maybe you're just curious why women proclaiming themselves to be "Smart Bitches" would spend time, effort, and adoration on a genre that everyone else dismisses as tawdry, smutty, and lame. Sit down. We will explain—or at the very least provide a profanity-filled précis.

So Who Are You, and Where Did You Come From?

When people ask us why we started Smart Bitches, we usually have a hot pink list of reasons we trot out. The Internet was riddled with romance Web sites whose grading curve wasn't curvy enough for our tastes, and we figured we could help change that. Or: we wanted the freedom to provide honest, no-holds-barred commentary on all aspects of romance novels. Or: we wanted a public venue

---

*The answer: many.

in which we could use the words "cuntmonkey" and "dichotomy" in the same discussion as "man titty" and "Fabio," and make all the fart jokes we possibly could whenever we came across titles like *Savage Thunder* or *Brave the Wild Wind*.

But ultimately, it boiled down to this fact: the two of us, we're neither fish nor fowl nor meat—which would make us either TVP or tofu, but we digress. See, there tend to be two big camps in the discourse surrounding romance novels:

Camp Number One consists of those Who Just Don't Get It. They've either never read a romance novel before, or they picked one up, discovered it was awful, experienced permanent retinal scarring from the terrible cover, and wrote the entire genre off— and the readers, too. The people in this camp are fond of accusing romance readers of being intellectually lazy, or hopelessly addicted to emotional porn. When the people in this camp find out they have friends—friends whose tastes they trust, even—who read and enjoy romance novels, their reaction is usually incredulousness, fol- lowed up by some variant of this backhanded compliment: "But you're so smart!" they cry out. "How can you possibly read that tripe?"

Unfortunately, it often feels as if Those Who Just Don't Get It outnumber the ones who do. Those Who Just Don't Get It are the readers and critics who object strenuously to the idea of romance novels being reviewed in the *New York Times Book Review*. They're the ones who, feeling defensive after having their media habits thor- oughly scrutinized, say, "Well, at least I don't read romance novels." They're the people who don't know nearly as much as they think they do; they often end up making ludicrous flubs, such as mistak- ing Harlequin romances for erotica. But then, it's difficult to prop- erly criticize a genre when one hasn't read extensively in it, and let's face it: romance novels, with their titty-licious covers, overwrought cover copy, and genre constraints are an easier piñata to smack around than most. But because most of the people in this camp don't know the genre, most of them don't suspect that the best is on par with the best books in any genre, and that the worst books are even more vile than they could've imagined.

Camp Number Two is the cheerleader camp. Almost everything is at least four stars, or throbbing hearts, or fluffy kittens, or calling birds (partridge in a pear tree not included). Their attitude seems to boil down to: "Romance is awesome, and if you don't have a nice word to say then you should just shut up. Bless your heart." One of the signature arguments of this camp involves a contradiction that, to be honest, drives us a little bugfuck. On one hand, they would've made Rodney Dangerfield proud with the way they growl about how romance novels get no respect, no respect at all. On the other hand, when reviewers point out some romance novels are about as substantial as a house built entirely of meringue and dandelion down, or attempt to figure out what the fuck is up with the excess of abusive alpha "heroes" in the genre, these people are often the same ones who claim that romance novels are escapist fun, and somehow exempt from rigorous literary examination.

It's odd to be in disagreement with both camps, but here we are, setting up a Bitching picnic. But the points we make aren't that revolutionary, even if they give the Know It Alls and the Love It Alls a tweak in the nose.

Point the first: Romance novels aren't all inconsequential bits of fluff.

Point the second: Many romance novels offer complex, nuanced stories.

And heads up and break out your red pen and your English degree! While it's undeniable that romance novels are great fun, they should absolutely be subject to rigorous examination. We lit nerds say so.

Moreover, and worst of all, some romances are utter fucking crap. Complete, utter shittastic fuckcakes of crap with a side order of "How in the world did I pay actual money for this?"

When we started our site, we felt like we were two of only a few on the Internet who wanted to give romance a close examination.

We looked around for a community of smarter-than-average romance readers who spoke their minds as they saw fit, and weren't afraid to unleash their inner George Carlin when the occasion called for it; a community that was unabashedly geeky, and would get references that run the gamut from 1980s one-hit wonders to jokes about Leibniz and Newton without our having to explain who either person was. There were a few sites, such as All About Romance, that fit most of our criteria, but salty language was frowned on, and frankly, we wanted the freedom to say whatever the hell we wanted. We knew we were odd ducks, but we weren't *that* weird—we are, after all, talking about the Internet. If the sneeze fetishists and furries and Armin Meiwes, the Rotenburg Cannibal, could find people on the same wavelength online, there had to be other people out there whose interests intersect with ours. Nathaniel Hawthorne would blanch at how big those damned mobs of scribbling women have grown. Tens of millions of people read this stuff—and we're not all cretins. So we set about creating our own community.

TODAY'S MENU: ROMANCE! ROMANCE FOR ALL!

Saying that you read romance novels is like saying you like food. Just as there's a world of difference between homemade panang curry and an Egg McMuffin, there's mind-boggling variety in the romance genre. It's huge. Huge like Fabio's pectorals crossed with Diana Gabaldon's total word count. Consider the types of books that can fall under the heading "Romance":

There's historical romance—but what kind of historical romance? A traditional Regency, in which the hero and heroine barely kiss? A novel set in the Victorian era, featuring bondage and anal sex? A story about lovers in ancient Rome? Colonial American? An American western? How about something set in Revolutionary France, or fourteenth-century Florence?

And contemporaries: is it a category romance or a single title? Is it a mystery or romantic suspense? (For the record, "romantic suspense" does not mean that the romance is in doubt and must be investigated. It does, however, mean that there is an 87.6 percent likelihood that the cover will feature two people running.) Is it a comedy? An ensemble of women that could be "women's fiction" or chick-lit? (We'd just like to note for the record that that's one of the worst terms ever to hit the genre since "bodice ripper.") A wrenching story of emotional recovery, complete with a winning, adorable rescue dog?

And then we get to the landscape of paranormals: Vampires! Werewolves! Vampire werewolves! Mummies! Psychics! The undead! The reanimated! The demonic and the celestial! The slayers, the fey, the wee folk, the fairies, trolls, and selkies. They all fall under "paranormal," which has its roots in an ancient Greek word meaning "overcrowded genre."

And then there's that scary place, the crossroads of romance, fantasy, and perhaps even science fiction, where the puffy-paint sweatshirt-clad stereotypical romance readers meet the stock sci-fi readers, complete with Spock ears and communicator pin, and they all do the hora with the fantasy readers who have d20s in their pockets and long sword replicas strapped to their backs. In fantasy or science-fiction romance, the fate of *the entire fucking universe* can depend on the Happily Ever After of the hero and heroine. No pressure or anything. It's a scary mixture, but it works. Why? Because romance deals with one of the most elemental blocks of human relationships. Just as any work of fiction can have a romantic element, any romance can include the elements of other popular fictional genres. The genre is huge, creative, evolving, and a multiavenue crossroads of just about every other type of fiction. And it has been ignored for far too long. Conveniently, that's why we're here.

Chapter Petticoat

A BRIEF HISTORY OF
THE MODERN ROMANCE NOVEL

Some of the misconceptions about romance novels are, unfortunately, all too understandable. Take, for instance, the reputation that they're all bodice rippers. Just look at the covers they've been inflicted with: a woman with quivering mounds one button away from a wardrobe malfunction being held up by a male specimen whose quivering mounds of man titty are even larger and firmer than hers. The woman looks either orgasmic or nauseated—hard to tell sometimes. The man's face is usually clenched in masculine determination, as if attempting to hold Montezuma's revenge at bay, with limited success. Unfortunate hand or body placements can give the pained expressions new meaning entirely, making us wonder why so many romance novel heroes are being presented as ad hoc proctologists.

Here's a shocking revelation: the content of the book is rarely reflected in the cover.

But what are the romance novels about, then, if not about a man's tender voyage into the most secret depths of a woman's bowels to study the proliferation of rectal polyps?

Don't get us wrong: some romance novels are full of assholes—but not in quite the way the covers would have us think. The basic formula is deceptively simple:

Boy meets girl.

Holy crap, shit happens!

Eventually, the boy gets the girl back.

They live Happily Ever After.

One would almost think that we could tell the story once and be done with it. But we've written and read countless thousands of variations of this story, and we show no signs of being sick of it.

The romance tradition goes all the way back to the oldest myths, and we could wank on and on about medieval courtly love, the rise of the gothic tradition (which marked some of the first popular novels written by and for women), and the influence that people like the Brontë sisters and Jane Austen have had on the various elements of romance, but that could easily take up a book in and of itself. We're just going to cut right to the chase and talk about the clearest predecessor we can find for the modern romance novel: *The Flame and the Flower* by Kathleen E. Woodiwiss.

The Flame and the Flower was first published in 1972, and it's one of the most famous in the bodice-ripper tradition. These books are typically set in the past, and the hero is a great deal older, more brutal, and more rapetastic than the heroine—but then, despite the way more and more romances push the envelope, we've yet to encounter one in which the heroine plunges the depths of the hero's dark tunnel of muddy love against his will.

But back to *The Flame and the Flower*. This novel is, in many ways, the Platonic ideal of the bodice ripper. The heroine's bodice is, in fact, ripped; the hero is appropriately arrogant and hard-edged before being brought low by the power of love; swashes are buckled; buckles are swashed; villains are suitably hideous; and the adventure runs at quite the fever pitch. No noun or verb is left unmodified, and Woodiwiss works simile and metaphor to limp exhaustion. It was a runaway bestseller and spawned countless books that followed, with various degrees of success, that particular formula, such as Rosemary Rogers's infamous *Sweet Savage Love* (which, if nothing else, is probably the most-parodied romance novel title of all time).

And honestly, "sweet, savage love" serves as a neat encapsulation of the older style of romances. The turmoil and violence, they runneth over in torrents as mighty as the hero's seed. And speaking of mighty torrents of heroic seed, it was well-nigh de rigueur for the heroine to be raped by the hero in those novels. The rape would be justified in any number of ways within the framework of the story (something we'll discuss in much more detail later). Sometimes, the heroine was the spoils of war, so clearly, it was acceptable to rape her. Other times, the hero would assume the heroine was sexually experienced, and as we all know, rape counts only if the rapist knows the victim is a virgin. Other times, the allure of the heroine was too much for the hero to take, and his penis took over—and what can a man do, really, once his Privy Counselor demands he invade the heroine's inner sanctum?

And oh lawdy, the sexual euphemisms. Romances like *Sweet Savage Love* and *The Flame and the Flower* were a great deal more humpy than any of the other mainstream love stories at the time, and there was a veritable arms race to see who could come up with the moistest grottoes and the most potent (and jutting) spears of manhood so they could titillate without being considered obscene.

They were discreet enough at first. They danced the dance as old as time, culminating in explosions of ecstasy. Then quivering mounds and flowers of femininity—and the feasting on thereof—started making an appearance. Steely shafts with throbbing veins quickly followed suit. Honestly, with all the rearing stallions, jutting man staffs, and tall soldiers everywhere, one would be hardpressed to decipher how the men hid their tumescent towers.

By the late 1980s, oral sex scenes were practically a requirement (as was the accompanying fluttering distress and confusion of the heroine the first time her hey-nanner-nanner made the acquaintance of the hero's mouth), and we had the occasional startling turn of phrase, like the hero who "burst like a ripe melon" within the heroine, as recorded by Rebecca Brandewyne's deathless prose in *Desire in Disguise*. Then authors like Susan Johnson and Linda Howard showed us their heroes' rampant cocks—and we're not talking about a coat of arms or a rooster, if you know what we mean.*

The genre, however, has changed a great deal since those Old Skool romances were published. It's true: the covers haven't changed that much. There are still allusions to anal probing and buxom men grasping at equally buxom women. But though the covers may be similar, the content is different in some substantial ways.

In fact, we have a flowchart to help you tell the difference between Old Skool and New Skool romance on pages 14 and 15. The Old Skool, very roughly speaking, ran from the late 1970s through the '80s, while the New Skool started sometime in the late 1980s and continues to the present, but as with any attempts at categorization, there were some books published in the '80s that were in the New Skool mode, and Old Skool–style romances are still occasionally published. That's why the chart will serve as a handy-dandy guide.

Most Old Skool romances, from historicals to contemporaries to category romances, shared several elements in common, elements that don't necessarily hold true for the newer types of romances that now dominate the market. Some of them include:

BRUTAL HEROES

These heroes aren't just determined, assertive, and confident—they're hard, arrogant, and harsh, and the heroine is often afraid of him. He's a punisher as well as lover and protector, but he hurts her only because he loves her so much. Baby. Punitive kisses were dealt with abandon, and the heroine, after stiffening up and resisting, would eventually soften into his kiss—after all, who wouldn't love having their lips mashed hard enough to leave bruises? And speaking of bruises: grabbing the heroine by the arms so hard that they leave marks was another earmark of Old Skool heroes.

* And we think you do.

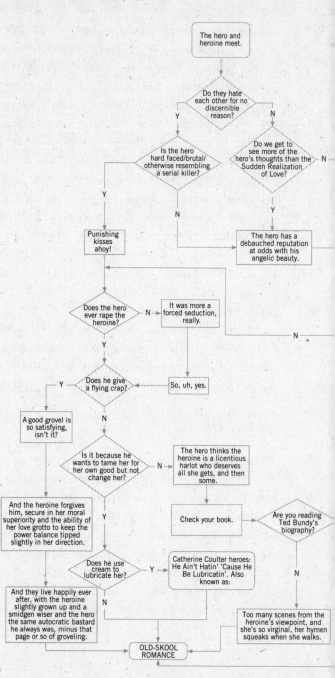

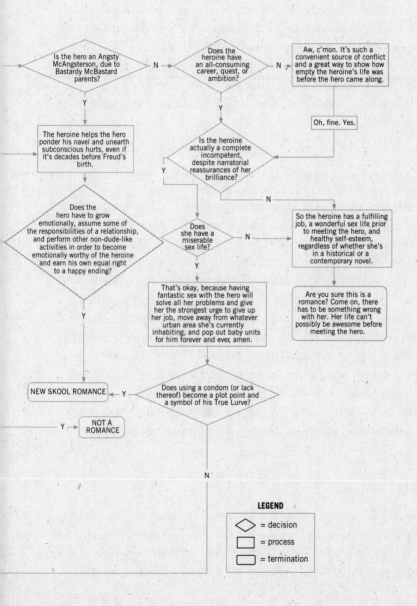

Is the hero an Angsty McAngsterson, due to Bastardy McBastard parents? — N →

Does the heroine have an all-consuming career, quest, or ambition? — N →

Aw, c'mon. It's such a convenient source of conflict and a great way to show how empty the heroine's life was before the hero came along.

Oh, fine. Yes.

Y ↓

The heroine helps the hero ponder his navel and unearth subconscious hurts, even if it's decades before Freud's birth.

Y ↓

Is the heroine actually a complete incompetent, despite narratorial reassurances of her brilliance?

Y

N →

So the heroine has a fulfilling job, a wonderful sex life prior to meeting the hero, and healthy self-esteem, regardless of whether she's in a historical or a contemporary novel.

Does the hero have to grow emotionally, assume some of the responsibilities of a relationship, and perform other non-dude-like activities in order to become emotionally worthy of the heroine and earn his own equal right to a happy ending?

Does she have a miserable sex life? — N →

Are you sure this is a romance? Come on, there has to be something wrong with her. Her life can't possibly be awesome before meeting the hero.

Y ↓

That's okay, because having fantastic sex with the hero will solve all her problems and give her the strongest urge to give up her job, move away from whatever urban area she's currently inhabiting, and pop out baby units for him forever and ever, amen.

Y ↓

NEW SKOOL ROMANCE — Y ←

Does using a condom (or lack thereof) become a plot point and a symbol of his True Lurve?

Y → NOT A ROMANCE

N ↓

LEGEND

◇ = decision

▭ = process

▱ = termination

RAPE

As we mentioned above, it was practically de rigueur Back in the Day, and, boy, did the critics have a field day with that particular aspect of romance novels. We won't go into the whys and wherefores at the moment, but just know that if it was a romance novel published between the 1970s and mid-'80s, and especially if it was a historical romance, you could usually count on some forceful plucking of the heroine's delicate bud of womanhood.

But never, ever doubt, dear reader, that they live happily ever after.

THE HEROINE: COMING-OF-AGE COMES EARLY

The heroines in Old Skool romances were often much, much younger than the hero. How much younger? Eighteen-year-old heroines were very, very common for a long time; they were often distressingly innocent—if they had been married before, the authors would often go through the most elaborate contortions to preserve her virginity, most of them centering on the erectile deficiencies of the first husband. But the innocence extended beyond the heroine not knowing her hoo hoo from a hole in a ground. One of the defining characteristics of the Old Skool romance is how most of them are coming-of-age stories for the heroines; the heroines are often incredibly sheltered and just starting to come into their own when they're thrown into a world full of high-finance hostile takeovers or cross-dressing adventure on the high seas.

THE CONFLICTS

The Big Secret was a staple of Old Skool romance novels. Ranging from "My brother is a spy for the enemy" to "I'm a maaaan, baby" to "I lied about something very small and extremely pointless at the beginning of the story, and now it's snowballed out of control because the author needs about twenty thousand more words' worth of conflict," Big Secrets littered the landscape of Romancelandia like dollar bills on a strip club stage.

And then there were the Big Arguments. Relationships were much more antagonistic in most of the romance novels Back in the Day—they were, in many ways, Fight 'em and Fuck 'em romances. The heroine usually hated the hero on sight, and they'd scrap and make up and scrap and make up again until the difference between fighting and fucking would be blurred into a roiling cloud, not unlike those cartoon clouds that indicated huge brawls, except with more pebbled nipples and turgid staffs.

And perhaps because knowledge is power, and the power struggle was more overt in the Old Skool, Big Misunderstandings would often be part of the romance landscape, too. The protagonists would have an exasperating knack of overreading or underreading a situation at just the wrong time, but if the two of them were locked in a room for five minutes with truth serum and a big stick for beating heads, all problems would be solved, but not only would that be too convenient, the book would also be over in a mere dozen pages. So, much like a soap opera, in which the happiness of the characters can last only an episode or two before Much Sadness-Soaked Angst and Drama must befall them again, the entirety of a Big Mis storyline was sustained not only by the Big Mis itself, but by the bullheaded idiocy of the protagonists.

Imagine the Big Mis romance confronting Judge Judy:

HEROINE: "Your Honor, the defendant's older brother looks just like him, and because I once took his arm at a masked ball following a musicale in the garden beneath a weeping willow tree, the defendant now thinks I am a cheating harlot. And really, he is an unfeeling callous monster who has a first wife he swears is dead, but is not!"

HERO: "Your Honor, the plaintiff is a cheating harlot."

JUDGE JUDY: "Sir, be quiet. It's not your turn."

HEROINE: "I am not a cheating harlot! And it's never my turn. You

only say I'm a harlot because you saw yourself in the mirror after
we . . . after we . . ."

HERO: "After you gave it up like the slut you are, spreading your legs
for anyone in the family, since you're desperate for a title and a
fortune, as I heard you whispering to your late father the day
before we were wed!"

HEROINE: "I have a title, numbnuts! I'm a princess, a duchess, and a
marchioness through my great aunt's half sister's dogwalker's
estate entailed through my mother, and I didn't tell you because
you're merely an earl and I thought it would hurt your pride!"

HERO: "You're a cheating harlot!"

HEROINE: "I am not! I've never had anyone in my tender river but
you!"

HERO: "Prove it!"

HEROINE: "Your brother has no man root—your father told me!
How could I . . . do that . . . with a man who has no manhood?
And speaking of things you never told me about, what about your
first wife? I've seen her everywhere! She's still alive, you
bigamist!"

HERO: "She's dead!"

HEROINE: "Oh, my stars, you killed her!"

HERO: "No, I was having her portrait cleaned and was moving it
about the house to make sure the surface was consistently pure so
I could—"

HEROINE: "You're still in love with her, you callous, heartless man!"

HERO: ". . . have it painted over with your image, since I love you so."

HEROINE: ". . . Oh."

HERO: "Oh, my darling Epistemologia, I do love you so."

HEROINE: "Oh, I love you, too."

JUDGE JUDY: *shoots self*

THE SUDDEN REALIZATION OF LOVE

Given the antagonistic nature of the lovers, resolving the tension
between their evident hatred for each other and their out-of-control

lust was quite the trick to pull. Thus was born the Sudden Realization of Love device. At some point, the hero and heroine realize: OH! All that hatred, and the fights, and the fear? All actually manifestations of love. Hey, Ike hit Tina because *he loved her*, okay? And when the hero hits her, it feels like a kiss, obviously.

We'd almost always witness this critical epiphany on the part of the heroine, inevitably followed by page upon page of angst about how the hero could not possibly love her back, so she'd act like even more of a spoiled buttnoid because it's not as if what she did mattered any more, anyway (cue the world's tiniest violin). And sometimes, we'd witness the hero being coldcocked by the brass-knuckled fist of love as well, but that was a relative rarity. It was much more common in Old Skool romances for heroes to relate to the heroine, in excruciating detail, about the Exact Moment the scales fell off his eyes—usually during the denouement at the end of the book. Why? Because of:

THE POINT OF VIEW

Most of these Old Skool romances were written solely or mostly from the heroine's viewpoint, though a few early authors started including the hero's point of view, too. This was sometimes a good thing, because it allowed us to experience the process of falling in love from both perspectives (and trust us, sometimes the readers needed all the explanation they could get about why and how the constantly warring factions could find enough time to fall in love). Sometimes, though, it wasn't so good, when the hero revealed himself to be an unrepentant rapist assclown.

Scholars have differing views as to why the viewpoints stayed so faithfully with the heroine for so long. Pamela Regis, in *A Natural History of the Romance Novel*, offers an analysis of how Old Skool romances followed the heroines partially because they had much more development to undergo than the hero, and the heroine's achievement of autonomy and self-actualization was the point of the narrative. This is borne out by the thirteen-item plot summary for the ideal Old Skool romance formulated by Janice Radway in *Reading the Romance*, published in 1982:

1. The heroine's social identity is destroyed.
2. The heroine reacts antagonistically to an aristocratic male.
3. The aristocratic male responds ambiguously to the heroine.
4. The heroine interprets the hero's behavior as evidence of a purely sexual interest in her.
5. The heroine responds to the hero's behavior with anger or coldness.
6. The hero retaliates by punishing the heroine.
7. The heroine and hero are physically and/or emotionally separated.
8. The hero treats the heroine tenderly.
9. The heroine responds warmly to the hero's act of tenderness.
10. The heroine reinterprets the hero's ambiguous behavior as the product of previous hurt.
11. The hero proposes/openly declares his love for/demonstrates his unwavering commitment to the heroine with a supreme act of tenderness.
12. The heroine responds sexually and emotionally.
13. The heroine's identity is restored.

In other words, the quest of the romance was the fulfillment of the heroine, and the hero was often a tool (in the construction sense, not in the dickhead sense, though often he could be both) in that fulfillment.

This idea has merit, but the fact that the hero was simultaneously villain and savior, punisher and lover, probably also dictated the choice of point of view. A lot of the central conflict and tension in Old Skool romances depended on the heroine and the reader not really knowing what the hell was going on in the hero's head— insofar as he showed any capacity for rational thought not dictated by his penis, that is, and given the priapic state of many romance heroes, that capability is somewhat in doubt. At any rate, despite the reassurance of the happy ending, not truly knowing what the hero is thinking or how he's going to react to situations lends a certain tension that wouldn't be there if the readers were inside his head.

But romances, as we've mentioned before, have undergone some fairly drastic changes over the past several decades, with trends visibly changing by the late 1980s and early '90s. In "Trying to Tame the Romance," an essay in *Dangerous Men and Adventurous Women*, massively bestselling author Jayne Ann Krentz attempted to pin the blame on a cadre of young editors, fresh out of "East Coast colleges" (one can't help but read that as some sort of coded term for "over-educated liberal arts major," but then, haven't editors been hired largely from that pool since, well, forever?). These college graduates, claimed Krentz, were trying to make romance more politically correct, and in those efforts systematically sought to destroy some cornerstones of romance, including the brutal heroes, the obsession with virginity, and rape (which she chose to describe as aggressive seduction, and we can buy that, sure—what's assault and battery if not an aggressive embrace?). She concluded that the changes wouldn't take, and that the editors had been largely unsuccessful.

That book was published in 1992. Now, whether or not Krentz was correct about the editors, or whether the market changed drastically when a new generation of readers grew into our own and had enough money to make our preferences known on the marketplace—and our Bitch money is on the latter scenario, since personally, we've never been very fond of many aspects of Old Skool romances, and neither are most of the people of our generation and younger—the fact remains that she was wrong about her predictions. The heroes softened and became less monolithic in their roles as symbols of love and fear; rape largely disappeared from the genre; and the heroine's sexual purity, while still an unhealthy indicator of moral integrity in many novels, is no longer clung to as stringently.

Just as Old Skool romance has several distinct distinguishing characteristics, New Skool romances tend to feature the following:

GENTLER HEROES

Romance heroes aren't wimpy, but there's a lot more room for the nice boys now—the ones Krentz denigrated as being sensitive and unaggressive (and therefore undesirable, unlike the iconic alpha males she described) in her essay. Vicki Lewis Thompson, for example, has been fairly successful with her series of books featuring nerd heroes.

Don't get us wrong; romance novel heroes are still, by and large, a testosterone-laden bunch, with tree-trunk thighs and a near-magical ability to vanquish villains with nothing more than the power of their utterly huge, utterly massive, utterly intimidating . . . guns, when a veritable army of people have failed. The heroes just aren't quite as shouty and grabby and punishy as they used to be.

We're not sure which came first: the not-quite-as-shouty-and-angry hero or the switch in point of view, but there's no question that many New Skool romances feature . . .

MORE SCENES FROM THE HERO'S POINT OF VIEW

According to Pamela Regis, the evolution of the romance novel led to the involvement of the hero in the narrative to the point where his story was "much more in evidence, much more a part of the action." Because modern heroines began in much more control of their lives politically, economically, and socially (having achieved, in Regis's words, affective individualism), contemporary retellings of the heroine's courtship began to show the emotional evolution of the hero, instead of having us view it through the (thoroughly unreliable but fetchingly bedewed) eyes of the heroine.

Why is seeing the story from both sides so satisfying? The fact is, affective individualism and autonomous heroines aside, books told from both points of view provide a stronger emotional punch, and we romance readers, we sure do love having our emotions thoroughly pummeled. Hey, if seeing the torments one party has to undergo for the sake of love is good, seeing two is even better, right?

THE RISE OF THE KICK-ASS SEXUALLY EXPERIENCED HEROINES

For all the derring-do and high adventure in Old Skool romances, it was relatively rare for the heroine to save the hero—or demonstrate much competence in anything, really. One of the classic peeves we have with Old Skool contemporary romance is how the author continually tells the reader how the heroine is the best in her field and an utterly ruthless career person, but continually shows instead what an incompetent dingbat she is. Negotiations with a rival company going badly? Instead of requesting arbitration or siccing the lawyers on them, let's do something that's *guaranteed* to work, like move into the smoking-hot company owner's house without warning and pester him until he gives in to your demands.

This lack of anything resembling common sense, coupled with the need to show us that the heroine has more than a limp noodle for backbone, often leads to annoyingly feisty heroines, who in turn are the precursors to the dreaded Too Stupid to Live heroine. You know her. She's the one who insists on facing down the bandits alone despite the lack of any sort of physical prowess whatsoever, other than the ability to stamp her foot very prettily, or on going to the unsavory parts of town unaccompanied (because what could *possibly* happen to a gently bred girl in the worst stews of London?), or on committing any number of other dangerous imbecilities— and all for no particular reason that we can discern other than so they can be very fetchingly caught and threatened by the villain.

Not that New Skool romances are perfect in this regard. Heroines still show a tendency to commit howlingly awful mistakes or make decisions that make absolutely no sense given the character setup provided. But they're no longer quite as young and naïve, and they're certainly not as virginal as they used to be. The population of heroines in contemporary romances who are beautiful, smart, and independent, yet for unfathomable reasons unacquainted with the existence of their womanly bud, much less somebody else's cock, has plummeted of late, and we can only cheer the attrition of their thoroughly odious ranks.

And can we have three cheers for birth control and prophylactics finally making an appearance in romance novels? Fantasies are all well and good, but given how slutty some romance novel heroes are, knowing that they're sensible enough to put a jimmy hat on their johnson before playing let's-make-a-pickle-sandwich at least alleviates the worry that all that burning the heroine feels in her loins might actually be due to gonorrhea, not runaway hormones.

Not only that, but romance novel heroines who are fully capable of saving themselves *and* the hero are becoming more and more common. These are romance heroines now who, if the rapist heroes of yore attempted to harvest the pure flower of their femininity, would've been able to kick those heroes into the middle of the next week. Which brings us to . . .

THE QUIET DEATH OF THE RAPIST HERO

The rapist hero went away by degrees. For a time, the rape scenes became somewhat more ambiguous, with the heroine telegraphing mixed signals (unlike the unambiguous rapes portrayed in books like *The Flame and the Flower*) and the hero showing more and more remorse for his acts. Thus was the era of the Forced Seduction born. Motto: If she kinda wants it, give it to her hard. Other motto: It's not rape if she comes!

But those sorts of encounters started slowly withering away, too. Now, when books featuring rape or forced seduction scenes rear their tumescent, purple-helmeted heads, Internet message boards on romance Web sites light up like Christmas trees, with the majority of people expressing indignation at the continued presence of this specter in our genre. This was amply demonstrated by the reaction many readers had to *A Well-Pleasured Lady* by Christina Dodd in the late 1990s, and the more recent kerfuffle involving *Claiming the Courtesan* by Anna Campbell. Much as Jayne Ann Krentz would like to say the editors dunnit—and editors could probably occupy the same niche as butlers did in murder mysteries set in British manors—cultural sensibilities have changed, and fictional rape, especially by the hero, is more likely to burn the average romance reader's biscuit than melt our butter. (But for the record, we would like to note that while we, personally, are glad that the rapist hero is no longer the default model in Romancelandia, we are fully in favor of writers writing whatever the hell they want, and readers enjoying the same.)

However, has rape really disappeared from the landscape? Perhaps not. The rape of the heroine may have shifted focus; instead of violating the heroine's hoo hoo, rape may be visited instead on her will. This sort of metaphorical breach is especially pervasive in paranormal romances, in which heroines are often changed or transformed without their consent, even against their express wishes, by the hero. Pity those heroines! Imagine the shock of waking up one day to discover that from that day forward, they'd have to suck blood down like rock stars chase beer with Vicodin, or that they'd spend a portion of every month sporting lush fur in parts of their body where no fur had ever been before and feeling overwhelmed with the urge to groom their own asses.

Rape in romance: it's magically delicious, whether real or metaphorical.

And there you have it: a quick and moderately dirty précis of the romance genre as we know it in the late twentieth and early twenty-first century. Let's get to the nitty-gritty details, shall we?

The Bitches' Dictionary
(With apologies to Ambrose Bierce)

We romance aficionados know that Romancelandia has its own dialect that may be unfamiliar to outsiders of the genre. Fear not, gentle reader, for we have here an extremely handy dictionary, composed with greatest care, that should hopefully eliminate any and all confusion you might have. We are, in fact, proud to present to you: **The Bitches' Dictionary**.

Hero. *n.* He who gets the milk for free only to find he *must* have the cow as well, for he cannot get it up for any of the other dairy maids.

Heroine. *n.* She who could be given a direct map to fulfillment and happiness, but would still find a way to get lost.

Kick-ass heroine. *n.* A heroine who allegedly knows how to handle herself in a dangerous situation, yet still shows the occasional distressing proclivity toward throwing her gun at the villain instead of shooting it.

Virginity. *n.* An oxymoronic state of physical and spiritual being. She who has it wants to lose it; she who has lost it needs it back.

Cabin boy. *n.* Often a heroine in boy's clothing; the hero's attraction to her will sometimes lead him to agonize over his masculinity and sexual proclivities, because it's not as if sailors have been known to engage in homosexual shenanigans after many months at sea. Never. Not once. Not known to happen. Ever.

Pirate. *n.* A seafaring criminal with a penchant for puffy linen shirts that are unbuttoned to the waist, yet still firmly tucked into trousers, thus rendering him irresistible to cross-dressing heroines. *See* CABIN BOY.

Viking. *n.* Another seafaring species, this one has a penchant for wearing furry vests and horned helmets and having their fingers pulled.

Rake. *n.* **1:** A sharp gardening implement used to comb through dense bushes, usually in the hopes of finding riches and security.

2: A species of attractive and sexually promiscuous male; scientists postulate that rakes exhibited strong antibacterial properties, as they were capable of copulating with anything and everything on two legs without falling prey to venereal disease.

Vampire. *n.* **1:** Immortal, soulless animate corpse that drinks the blood of the living. This is, for some reason, considered extremely sexy.

2: An excuse for authors to inflict their most Outrhageouz Nhames on the reading populace.

3: IS MORE EMO THAN YOU.

Werewolf. *n.* The only creature with hairy shoulders who is portrayed as sexually viable in romance novels.

Shapeshifter. *n. See* WEREWOLF.

Hymen. *n.* A membrane partially covering the vaginal opening, especially in females who haven't experienced penetrative sex. In romance novels, often located two to three inches inside the vagina itself, with the toughness and resiliency of a rubber sheet, though massaging it with fingers apparently can help relax it.

Sheikh. *n.* A swarthy, hard-edged playboy hero of Middle Eastern origin, though, oddly enough, rarely a devout Muslim who desires that the heroine convert to Islam.

Tycoon. *n.* A swarthy, hard-edged playboy hero, usually of Mediterranean origin who, oddly enough, has scads of free time to chase after the virginal heroine despite having billion-dollar business concerns to look after.

Cowboy. *n.* Always smells like horses, hay, and sweat. This is always a good comforting smell that never makes the heroine want to head for the nearest fire hose to bathe him forcibly.

Navy SEAL. *n.* Fearsome modern warrior of the deep who in real life smokes two packs a day and can be emotionally nonfunctioning, but in a romance has deep, rich, hidden, murky but not watery sensitive depths.

Mistress. *n.* **1:** A woman of ill repute who services the hero sexually in exchange for money and gifts before he meets the heroine. Her ability to enjoy orgasms without requiring a wedding ring of the hero is usually a sign of villainy, as is her use of makeup and nail polish.

 2: Harlequin romance only: A position the virginal heroine can occupy that doesn't actually require her to engage in sexual intercourse in any way, shape, or fashion.

Widow. *n. See* VIRGINITY.

Amnesia. *n.* A temporary but severe memory loss caused by head trauma that is rarely accompanied by the usual side effects of real-life amnesia, such as personality changes, loss of motor control, and incontinence. If amnesia helped mask heroine's former hatred of hero, another blow to the head or similar trauma will restore her memory and generate, at minimum, another fifty pages of conflict.

Secret baby. *n.* A stupid plot device by any other name would still smell as much like a used diaper and be full of too much screaming cluelessness to sue for child support.

Chaperone. *n.* A singularly ineffective guarding device, usually aged past its prime and sleeping on the job.

Corset/stays. *n.* **1:** Boned fabric meant to whittle a woman's waist to significantly unhealthy circumference, depending on the year and the style of that time.

 2: Item commonly not worn by heroine (*see above*), despite historical knowledge that indicates her dress would then look like a misshapen sack.

3. Historical equivalent of Barbie doll meant to contribute to intimidation and poor body image of reader. *See also* SIMULTANEOUS ORGASM.

Pelisse. *n.* Some kind of coat. Every historical heroine has one, and usually it gets wet or is in some way insufficient protection from the elements.

Riding habit. *n.* A jacket and skirt ensemble worn habitually by heroines in every novel for horseback riding, sidesaddle of course.

Musicale. *n.* Someone will be singing or playing an instrument, and the quality of the performance will be worse than dreadful.

Lady's maid/Abigail. *n.* Servant who assists independent, autonomous, and individually feisty heroine with washing, bathing, drying, dressing, hairstyling, wiping, chamber pot emptying, bed making, and just about every other domestic task known to woman.

Simultaneous orgasm. *n.* Everyone has them but you.

Dog. *n.* Companion of hero or heroine (*see above*) used as foil to highlight presence or absence of loyalty, faithfulness, and devotion in owner.

Hedgehog. *n.* Most awesome sidekick animal ever in the history of the world, bar none.

Chapter Corset

An In-Depth Investigation of the Romance Heroine, Emphasis, Obviously, on "Depth"

The Heroine

Can't make a soufflé without breaking a few eggs. Can't make romance novels without breaking a few heroines.

The heroine is a difficult beast to create. She has gorgeous hair, fine eyes, a mouth that usually begs to be kissed or at least gazed at while thinking of kissing, and a plucky, demure, yet saucy and seductive personality—all housed in a perfectly perfect character that drives the hero wild, and perhaps annoys the ever-living shit out of the reader. Like it or not, romance readers are oftentimes harder on the heroine than they are on the hero, and managing the hero isn't exactly an easy job for the heroine, either, especially if she has to deal with an Old Skool alpha hero, full of rape and fury, signifying imminent assault.

The readers (and the hero) often demand impossible things of her. First of all, we prefer a heroine who's drop-dead gorgeous—but she has to be completely unaware of that beauty. We want her to be intelligent, independent, brave, and strong—but we don't want her to outshine the hero. We want her to have a stellar sex life and the ability to experience multiple orgasms with the hero—but be demure and sexually unawakened prior to knowing him; a heroine having multiple lovers and enjoying the experience the way the hero enjoys sex with his bevy of mistresses and former lovers would be about kosher as a bacon cheeseburger. If she's a paragon, we want to shake up that perfection; if she's less than perfect, we often find her flaws annoying. The hero, however, can't resist her. She drives him crazy; she oftentimes drives the readers crazy, too.

And what would a Smart Bitch guide to romance be without an exhaustive list of the various flavors of Heroine Sauce available on the market? Here are the different types of heroines we've been able to discern using our patented Detect-a-Magic-Hoo-Hoo technology:

Too Stupid to Live: *Unfortunately, not extinct, but potentially endangered. At every moment.* This heroine archetype was first recognized and the term coined at romance supersite All About Romance. She runs down dark alleys and wonders why each and every time she meets up with danger. She challenges at the wrong moment, fights when everyone, including the reader, can see her cause is lost, and generally makes an annoying, whiny nuisance of herself. This heroine, more than any other, has the greatest potential to cost you thousands of dollars in dental work as you grind your teeth in frustration. Last seen: Old Skool romance. Prototype: *Shanna* by Kathleen E. Woodiwiss; Cathy from *Island Flame* by Karen Robards.

Spoiled Hoyden of Historical Inaccuracy: *Unfortunately, not extinct, but seen less lately, thank heavens.* She's in your face. She's in the hero's face. She thumbs her nose at social mores; she bites her thumb at you. She wants a job at a time when employment was Not for Gently Bred Ladies. She wants autonomy before the word had been invented yet. She's utterly anachronistic, spoiled, and irritating, and if she lived in contemporary times, she'd drive you up a wall if she were your coworker, what with her petulant demands. Last seen: Old Skool romance. Prototype: Whitney, who is not our love, from *Whitney, My Love,* by Judith McNaught; Genny from Catherine Coulter's *Night Storm.*

Doormat: *Still out there, waiting for you to wipe your shoes on her.* She's malleable, weak, and an utter bore. She doesn't stand up to anything, much less her own desires, and can be found swooning on the nearest sofa, or lying on the bed while she's ravished with pleasure that she so does not deserve. Might be seen swooning, wringing her hands, whining, or otherwise worrying about something. Any resistance she might mount against the hero is ineffectual, and she couldn't find her own backbone if you showed her an X-ray and counted each vertebrae. Last seen: freaking everywhere, dammit, especially in older Harlequins as the victim of punishing kisses. Current idol: Marissa from *Lover Revealed* by J. R. Ward; Bella from the Twilight series by Stephanie Meyer. Former all-time greats: Sarah from Linda Howard's *Sarah's Child*; Marlie from *Dream Man,* also by Linda Howard.

Plain and Strong: *If you find her, and she's well written, she's wonderful.* One of our favorite types of heroines: she's nothing extraordinary, but she's a marvelously good person. No fiery hair, no flashing eyes, no outlandish adventures or daring feats of iconoclastic inappropriate behavior. But being around her makes the hero happy. Maybe she cooks well, or she's caring and warm in a way that reaches him, but she's the lighthouse in his storm, and while superficially she's not spectacular, her determination, honor, sense of humor, and strength can make for a marvelous story. Last seen: making us happy. Prototype: Honoria Anstruther-Wetherby from *Devil's Bride* by Stephanie Laurens; Folie from Laura Kinsale's *My Sweet Folly*; Leda from *The Shadow and the Star* by Laura Kinsale; Sara from *Dreaming of You* by Lisa Kleypas.

Antiheroine: *Her mantra as coined by Jorge Luis Borges: "To fall in love is to create a religion that has a fallible god."* First identified by former English professor Robin L. Harders (writing under the pseudonym Janet) at Dear Author, this heroine may eventually fall in love with the hero—but she's definitely not crazy about the idea of being in love. She genuinely and consistenly resists committing to the relationship, sometimes because of the nature of the conflict in the book, sometimes because she wants to maintain her independence—true independence of the self-sufficient sort, not the "I'm going to stamp my foot prettily, run away, and promptly be caught by the bad guys" variety. When written clumsily, she veers dangerously close to Too Stupid to Live territory, basing her resistance on some thin reasoning. When written well, however, her integrity and consistency provide a refreshing change from the bevy of heroines in Romancelandia whose loudly proclaimed resistance collapses like a soggy pile of cards in the face of the heroes' masculine wiles, or the heroes' masculine chests. However, many readers often perceive the resistance as insufferable stubbornness or selfishness—after all, *they* can see how wonderful the hero is, so why can't the heroine? Last seen: a sparse smattering throughout contemporary romance, paranormal romance, and historical intrigues. Prototype: Eve from J. D. Robb's In Death series; Merlin from Laura Kinsale's *Midsummer Moon*; Tessa from Kathleen O'Reilly's *Shaken and Stirred*; Meriel from Mary Jo Putney's *Uncommon Vows*.

Ingénue: I'm just beginning to show my utter awesomeness. Stay tuned. She's young, innocent, and a tender flower, but what she lacks in experience, she more than makes up for in good humor and a surprising resiliency. She can be clueless at times, but she differentiates herself from the Too Stupid to Live heroine by displaying flashes of good sense. Books featuring the Ingénue are often coming-of-age tales as well as love stories; heroines who start out as ingénues are often strong, capable women by the end of the story. Last seen: books that straddle the Old Skool and the more current paradigm, as well as many traditional Regencies. Prototype: any heroine in any Laura London novel, but especially Merry from *The Windflower*; innumerable Georgette Heyer heroines.

Alpha Heroine: Kicking ass, can't be bothered to take names. The magnificent bitch of Romancelandia; you can try to cross her, but before you do, try to determine which part of your body you can best live without. Alpha heroines are probably one of the newest species of heroine, and they're becoming more popular with time. They break certain cardinal rules of romance novel heroine behavior. First of all, they're usually one of the few heroines who are allowed to outrank the hero in significant ways, such as in social standing, political power, or firepower. Second of all, they will not put up with any shit from anybody, much less the hero. Third of all, they're often unabashed about the measures they must take in order to save their loved ones and themselves. Snuff a villain? Scheme and skullduggery? Hurt the hero where it counts, when it counts? They'll do it, and do it *well.* They fight to the finish, they probably eat their spinach, and they can rescue themselves, thanks very much. But a hero for that soul-deep completion and unbearably supernatural orgasms? That'd be great. They sometimes rub readers the wrong way because they come across as hard, manipulative, and selfish. The best ones, however, are magnificent, if just a little bit terrifying. Last seen: queening it over the masses in the occasional paranormal, romantic suspense, and historical. Prototype: Eve (again) from J. D. Robb's In Death series; Melanthe of *For My Lady's Heart* by Laura Kinsale; Lady Lyssa from Joey W. Hill's *The Vampire Queen's Servant*; Kaderin the Coldhearted, from Kresley Cole's *A Hunger Like No Other*; Jaz Parks, from the Jaz Parks series, by Jennifer Rardin.

Wounded (and Occasionally Soiled) Dove: These heroines are Hamletesque in their angst and tormented psyches—and, occasionally, their tiresomeness. The Wounded Dove usually comes from some sort of horrific past and, in a rather neat role inversion, puts the hero in the position of being the nurturer and healer. Her actions are often driven by fear and distrust; any conflicts in the story are often exacerbated because she refuses to completely trust the hero to help her. Former prostitutes and rape victims in historicals are especially ripe candidates for Wounded Doves—because who better than a hero to provide her with some sexual healin'? Last seen: in every other Mary Balogh novel. Prototype: Zenia from *The Dream Hunter* by Laura Kinsale; Viola from Mary Balogh's *No Man's Mistress*; Leigh from Laura Kinsale's *The Prince of Midnight*.

Smart-Mouthed Cynic: *Jaded, cautious, and funny as hell.* Life isn't a bed of roses. Wait, maybe it *is* a bed of roses: intensely prickly, nourished by piles of crap, and potentially crawling with aphids. Whatever. In any case, life isn't easy, and nobody knows this better than the Smart-Mouthed Cynic. She approaches life and love with caution, though without the same level of reluctance to commit as the Antiheroine, and she copes with her disillusionment and pain by being funny. Really, really funny. Last seen: many modern romantic comedies. Prototype: Just about any Jennifer Crusie heroine you'd care to name, but especially Min from *Bet Me*.

Airhead: *It's like, totally cosmic, man, like, how annoying this heroine can, like, be, you know?* The good-natured airhead is much less common than she used to be, but for a while, authors seemed to think it was a great idea to use ditzy heroines as foils for tough-talking, hard-living, uptight heroes. The idea was, we think, that the heroes would ground the heroines, and the heroines would, like, teach the totally uptight hero how to loosen up a little. This sometimes worked, when the characters found just the right balance with each other. More often than not, however, the chemistry was painful and the comedy ham-handed. To add insult to injury, these heroines, if present in contemporary novels, were almost always New Age dipshits who believed in a dizzying array of woo-woo crap. Just kill us now. By destroying our heart chakra. Which you can achieve if you can focus your energy on that crystal. Last seen: in the mid-to-late 1990s. Prototype: Gabrielle from Rachel Gibson's *It Must Be Love*; Leda from *Charms* by Kathleen Kane.

TEN COMMANDMENTS OF HEROINE CONDUCT

1. Thou shalt not lust in thy panties for any male's mighty wang due to normal sexual horny pants. Thou shalt lust in thy panties only for the mighty wang of the hero. There is no "ho" in heroine.

2. Thou shalt not offer an accurate representation of the financial insecurity of women at the time period by actively looking for a hero of wealth and reputation, and admitting that thou art doing so without remorse. Just because every unmarried woman at that time actually was doing so is no excuse for similar behavior in a romance heroine.

3. If thou art in a historical, thou shalt not be without a loyal, trusty servant, even though trusting the servant put the servant in a complicated position of power over her mistress, and really, a heroine who is blackmailed by her servants is scarcely a noble prototype of admirable behavior.

4. Thou shalt not be aware of your beauty. Every villain, sleazy uncle, and otherwise able-bodied male who has ever clapped eyes on thee may make sexual overtures on thee, but thou shalt remain in blissful oblivion.

5. Thou shalt have a nurturing streak larger and warmer than the South China Sea. Thy desire for children shall be unquestioned and unperturbed by real-life concerns such as the cost of child rearing, reproductive choice, and child-support payments (in contemporaries), or the dangers of childbearing (in historicals). And shouldst thou choose to remain child-free, thou freak of nature, verily thou shouldst display your nurturing streak with animals. Preferably cute, neurotic ones.

6. If thou shalt have a baby with the hero prior to getting together with him, thou shalt keep this baby a secret. See also commandment 5.

7. Thy amnesia shalt be sexy and not be complicated by distinctly unsexy side effects such as loss of motor control, speech impediments, loss of cognitive skills, and inability to control bodily functions.

8. Thou shalt not win against the hero in any significant way. A few moral victories shall be thine; all other substantive victories shalt lie with the hero, for yea, his wang is mighty.

9. If in a historical, thou shalt desire escape from the domestic sphere. If a contemporary, thou shalt desire escape from a soul-sucking career. If in a paranormal, thou shalt desire escape from the superpowers and eternal life that have been foisted unwillingly upon thee.

10. Thou shalt not kill, unless it be accidental or under extremely limited circumstances. Thou especially shalt not be an efficient killer, unless thou art in a paranormal and thou killest mostly nonhuman bad guys who verily had it coming to their asses.

VIRGINITY AND THE HEROINE: LESS FILLING, TASTES GREAT

One of the more peculiar constants of most romance novels, from historicals to contemporaries to paranormals to even erotica, is the sexually unawakened state of the heroine. She's relatively innocent, as proven by her inexperience or her outright virginity. No matter what type she is, she is definitely not the ho-type.

Therein lies the deep, humid, dark, and somewhat curious den that is home to the two sacred mythical beasts beloved to Romancelandia. They're interconnected, if you know what we mean (and we think you do): the Unawakened Woman and the Heroic Wang of Mighty Lovin'. They are the plague and the backbone of romance. No other genre is as obsessed with the heroine (a) having excellent sex, and (b) not having sex at all unless it's with the One True Love, who's also usually the sole person who can make her come. Got orgasm? Got true love! The heroine's sexual inexperience remains intact only until the hero's wang of mighty lovin' introduces her to the wonderment of the fizznuckin'. It's part and parcel of the fantasy: the awakening to love is that much more powerful when it's accompanied by a sexual awakening as well.

Everything about the love has to be superlative, and on the

heroine's part, it's easiest to use an association we're already comfortable with: sexual purity. The sexually experienced woman in fiction still raises hackles and creates uncomfortable associations with uncleanness, the threat of infidelity, and moral degeneration. Interestingly enough, the sexual experience is also superlative for the hero, but authors choose to portray it using, not inexperience (which would ruin the fantasy, because we're not necessarily interested in reading about lovers who come a little bit too fast and use a little bit too much tongue when kissing), but what we and many others online refer to as the Magic Hoo Hoo. The Magic Hoo Hoo does it all: it heals all ills, psychic and sexual. It provides unparalleled pleasure to the hero, despite the heroine's reluctance, inexperience, and awkwardness. It's capable of experiencing (and inducing) earth-shattering multiple orgasms on its first outing. It also creates an instant emotional bond that's even more irrational and persistent than a newly hatched chick imprinting on the first living thing it sees. All that, *and* it makes you coffee in the morning. One taste of the Magic Hoo Hoo is all it takes; the hero won't be satisfied with anything else, physically or emotionally.

Single virgin women in historical romances are somewhat more coherent constructs than their counterparts in other subgenres, especially if they're from respectable families. A sheltered eighteen-year-old virgin debutante in Regency England—or even a twenty-six-year-old virgin bluestocking—doesn't overtax the gentle reader's credulity, though it makes a body wonder how so many of these creatures went through all their lives feeling nary a tingle in their nethers, not even when faced with a handsome footman, or the flirtatious squire's son. Horny teenagerhood didn't exist back in Merry Olde Englande, apparently. If the virginity stopped there, that'd be fine, but the fact is, virgins predominate to this day, no matter what the period setting or subgenre. This state of overwhelming heroine virginity was especially true of most books published prior to the mid-1990s. Didn't matter who the heroine was, or what time period she lived in. A glamorous international spy? A brilliant scientist? A nurse? A boardroom mistress? An amnesiac heiress? A widow of many years? A time-traveling scientist who used to be a glamorous international spy in twentieth-century America but is now an amnesiac heiress in fifteenth-century France? Somehow, some way, her Hymen of Steel will be preserved in all its stalwart glory.

A Hymn to the Hymen

Without including a picture that would make this book NC-17 and more controversial than Harry Potter, we'd like to share a word or two about hymens. Specifically, where they are and what they're made of.

Time and again we Smart Bitches read romance novels, particularly historical novels, wherein the hero readies his sword of plenty to invade the delicate virgin passage of the heroine. And it goes a little something like this: Hit it!

Gulfvar's man root trembled with barely leashed passion. Eleanora's moist love grotto beckoned to him, glistening with her ardor, and he could tell from the mewling sounds coming from the pursed bow of her mouth that she was ready, ready to receive him at last.

He positioned the head of his engorged staff while he kissed away her protests that it certainly would never fit, and slowly slid his aching rod into her tender valley. Gods, but she was tight!

Suddenly he felt the tip of his eager manhood brush against her maidenhead. He pushed her hair back from her face, and whispered to her gently.

"It will only hurt but a moment, and then it will be gone," he said. Then he reared back as if he and his man-staff were jumping hedges at full gallop, and thrust himself deep within her.

Eleanora screamed as if she'd been impaled upon a pikestaff, beating his shoulders with her fists and crying out from the pain. Gulfvar struggled to hold himself still within her, as the tightness of her tender virginal womanhood cradled him, increasing his aching need to thrust within her again and claim her as his own. But first she needed to feel pleasure, not the pain of her first experience with love.

He reached down, found her tender love nubbin, and stroked her until she quieted, until her gasps of pain became moans of pleasure. As she reached her peak of pleasure, and cried out his name, he allowed himself to crest within her, and spilled his seed within her aching, tender passage.

Can you root through the purple prose to find the fallacy? Not the phallus. The fallacy.

Her maidenhead? Up the vaginal canal by an inch or two? NOT POSSIBLE.

This biological inaccuracy is passed on from novel to novel like e-mail hoaxes that tell you Microsoft will give you a dollar every time you forward a message. The mystery of the hymen remains intact, impervious to the throbbing staff of truth.

Here's the truth about the hymen. Are you sitting down? Good, grab a mirror and play along.

The hymen is external. That's right. It's outside the vagina. Let us say it again: it is external. It is not located up the vaginal canal. It's a fold of membrane that partially covers the external vaginal opening. And most of the time it's receded or stretched by the time a woman experiences sexual intercourse, so it's usually not a bloodbath or a profoundly painful experience. There are exceptions to that rule, but even still, those exceptions of the hymen still rest on the scientific goddamn fact that the hymen. Is. External. For. The. Love. Of. All. That. Is. Holey.

Some historical novelists research down to the types of feathers on the costumes, the decor, even the language of their protagonists, and still have the hero battering his manly ram against the heroine's poor hymen. Nothing says, "I couldn't be arsed to even look at Wikipedia," better than having a hero encounter a brick wall of a maidenhead up the heroine's vaginal canal.

Sometimes, a mucous membrane covering the vaginal opening isn't just a mucous membrane covering the vaginal opening. Some other inexperience supplements or substitutes for that virginity. For example, she may be unfamiliar with his world, his profession, or the town to which she's just moved. Either way, virginity and inexperience are extremely common methods to establish an imbalance of power between the hero and the heroine, without the need for whips, chains, and ball gags—unless one or both parties are into that kind of thing.

The power imbalance becomes one of the crucial conflicts of a romance, as the characters seek to rebalance that power, either with the heroine gaining the required experience, or by making peace with the fact that her power will stem from other sources. Either way, the happy resolution of the relationship needs to restore balance in the world after its deliberate disruption in the beginning. But the fact that it's overwhelmingly the chick who is in a position of virginity, inexperience, or limitation says something about how comfortable romances are with depicting women at an advantage over the hero, and how readers perceive a power deficit on the hero's side as an emasculation. The heroine is pinned down by her own hymen, the poor dear, because otherwise the alternative—that the hero has a (metaphorically) tiny wang—disrupts the fantasy world unacceptably.

This run of either no sex or incredibly bad sex has to leave its mark somehow, and it is a truth universally acknowledged that a single romance novel heroine seeking a hero must be in want of a good neurosis. So we'll take you through in a game we like to call "Oh, Honey, What's Your Problem?" You choose your neurosis and your form of virginal inexperience to craft the perfect heroine—though never fear, even with all that imperfection, you're still perfect. Mix and match, Chinese Family Dinner style, or just close your eyes and point with one erect finger (or something else that's erect—we won't stop you).

Virginity	Neurosis
You're a virgin.	You're not a werewolf, which the hero will eventually fix with a blood-swapping ritual and

(continued on next page)

Virginity	Neurosis
	copious amounts of doggy-style sex.
You're a widow and a virgin.	You need to sell your virginity to the highest bidder.
You're a widow and never had an orgasm.	You don't feel like people can see see the "real you," so you move to a tiny town in the middle of nowhere with a name like Tiddlywinks-on-the-Santorum, because if there's anyone who can see the real you, it'd be the citizens of a claustrophobically tiny hamlet in the verdant English or Adirondack countryside.
You've been married more than twice, still no orgasm.	You have self-esteem issues.
You've never had an orgasm, despite being a courtesan.	You have self-esteem issues manifested in body-image problems.
You're a virgin and a courtesan.	You have self-esteem issues and body-image problems but you're otherwise a perfect height and weight.
You're a virgin, but you dress provocatively and everyone thinks you're a dirty hooooor.	You have self-esteem issues and body-image problems and you need to lose some weight.
You've been promoted to a new job, but while the cover copy and descriptions indicate you're a professional, in every scene you act like a moron. Because competence is boring when compared to wacky hijinks at the	You have self-esteem issues and body-image problems, and with the help of Photoshop and/or a carnival funhouse mirror you know what you'll look like fifty pounds lighter.

Virginity	Neurosis
expense of your professional image.	
You're psychic with powers that are untrained and oh-so-dangerous.	You're not a vampire, which the hero will eventually fix with a blood-swapping ritual and copious amounts of doggy-style sex.
You're a witch with a deep fear of your magic heritage.	You're not a selkie, which the hero will eventually fix with a blood-swapping ritual and copious amounts of doggy-style sex.
You're an emo-superhero who doesn't want her superpowers.	You're not psychic, which the hero can't fix, but since *he's* psychic, he can assure you that simultaneously experiencing two orgasms during doggy-style sex is every bit as amazing as he thought it'd ever be.
You're a werecod. Or a wereslug.	Your parents were mean to you.
You're a demon with a heart of gold. Literally.	Your parents were Satan. Literally.

EXPERIENCE: HEROINES DO NOT HAVE IT

The more progressive romance novels allow the heroines to experience some sweet, sweet lovin' prior to the hero, but these concessions have been grudging. Sure, she was allowed to have sexual experiences, but they had to be either stunningly mediocre or downright awful. It was the Curse of the Bad Wang, and its blight affected both virgin and nonvirgin women in Romancelandia. Rapist Wang; Abusive Wang; Overly Massive Wang; Teeny-Tiny Wang; Evil Homosexual Wang (and its close relative, Evil Bisexual Wang); Drug-Addicted Wang; Wang That Died Before It Could Do Its Duty; Utter Lack of Wang Due to Overprotective

Top Ten Reasons Behind the Creation of a Virgin Widow

10. The late husband was old. Really, really, flaccidly old.
9. He loved his horses more than he loved her. And, yes, this does occasionally mean what you think it does.
8. A sad preference for opium created a little matchstick that would not light, if you catch our drift.
7. He was a soldier who shipped overseas right after the wedding, and some time in the chaos forgot to make love to his newlywed bride, because it's not as if young soldiers about to go to war have sex on their minds, or anything like that.
6. She can't speak of it. It is too horrible.
5. Lord Floppebottom married her by proxy, and never came to claim his bride.
4. The sweaty temptations of the flesh were nothing but a trifle when compared to spending long evenings reading aloud the works of great philosophers.
3. She *really* can't speak of it. It's too horrible.
2. She was too perfect for him to touch. (Oh, for God's sake.)
1. Three words: He was gay. Gay as a three-dollar bill. A three-dollar bill that really enjoyed cock sucking and bad house music.

Male Relatives; Incompetent Wang That Couldn't Find the Clitoris with a Flashlight, a Magnifying Glass, and a Pair of Bomb-Sniffing Dogs: you name it, and some incarnation of Bad Wang has been invoked in a romance novel. For a long time, it was almost like an episode of *Scooby-Doo*—you knew some crotchety (or crusty) wang was behind the heroine's virginity or frigidity; you just had to figure out why.

If the heroines weren't virgins and had, by the grace of a merciful author, experienced orgasms some time in the past, you can bet your virgin widow's stipend that it was due to the hero. The hero, you see, possesses the only thing that can break the Curse of the Bad Wang: the Heroic Wang of Mighty Lovin'. And if the romance novel is in any way a love reunited story, then you can bet that wheresoever goeth the Heroic Wang, there followeth the sex life. The poor heroines are generally left in a holding pattern until the hero returns. Do not pass Go, do not find another orgasm, do not collect two hundred dollars. Yea, though the heroine may walk in the valley of the shadow of the death of her sexuality, she shall find no vibrator or removable showerhead, nor figure out what her fingers can do, nor meet a remotely competent lover.

The apotheosis of the Bad Wang can be seen in the fabled virgin widow, a creature unique, as far as we know, to the romance genre. When you see a virgin widow, you can be assured that acrobatic feats of storytelling will ensue in an effort to explain why her cinnabar cavern has remained unspelunked.

THE MAGIC HOO HOO

We understand the appeal of the Unawakened Woman. We do. There's a lot of cultural significance attached to first times, whether it's your first love, first sexual experience, or first orgasm. It's appealing for the first love also to be the forever love. However, part of the fantasy of romance novels is that the *hero* is equally floored when he encounters the heroine, and sexually unaware men are in extremely short supply in Romancelandia. How do authors achieve this emotional intensity on the hero's part?

By capitalizing on the Magic Hoo Hoo, of course. The chemistry is hotter than the fire of a thousand blazing suns, and the hero is often left at a loss for what to do. It's not just the physical experience that's different; it's a different emotional experience as well. The sex is so good, it's completely overwhelming. That relatively few romance novels use this method of making the sexual experience special for the heroine is probably a testament to the tenacity of the idea that a woman who enjoys sex for sex itself is morally suspect.

The explanations for virgin widows and Bad Wang can be so ridiculous that we have, in the past, suggested a rating system to judge these poor orgasmless creatures. We call it the Bitch, Please

The Hymen: Definitive Proof in the Court of Love

Misunderstandings can be rife in any romance novel, and chief among these is the assumption by the hero that the heroine is a slut, a dirty, dirty slut. Reasoning previously used by actual heroes in actual romance novels to definitively prove that the heroine is a Slutty McSlutterson includes:

- She flirts with other men.
- She was out walking alone, at night.
- She's too beautiful.
- She's too unconventional.
- Look, other people said so, all right? Christ, if you can't believe in gossip and hearsay, what can you believe in?
- She's a widow.
- She's an heiress.
- She's his housekeeper.
- She's his maid.
- She's his secretary.
- She's a romance author.
- She works in a whorehouse.
- She was born to a beautiful mother.
- Who was an actress.
- And also, you know, a whore.
- Who owned her own whorehouse.
- And auctioned off the heroine to the hero.

The hymen, however, provides proof of the heroine's purity and allows her to hold her head high despite the slings and arrows of outrageous misunderstandings, and should the hero choose to divest the heroine of her virginity via rape, not only does her hymen prove him wrong, it can actually inspire regret—possibly even contrition.

But Wait! There's More!

The postrape regret hangover brings up a rather sticky question: How does a hero adequately express the regret and sorrow raging in his breast? It is, at the very least, a tremendously awkward situation.

Well, wonder no longer! Behold our new Smart Bitch line of "Holy Crap, I Raped a Virgin!" greeting cards. With sentiments like:

- "Sorry I Raped You . . . Again. And Again. And Again."
- "I Thought You Were a Whore, Not a Real Person . . . Please Forgive Me?"
- "Mom Was an Evil Slut and I Assumed You Were, Too . . . But Your Hymen Proved Me Wrong."
- "Sorry I Raped You. I Thought You Were Your Mom."

Heroes will be sure to find the appropriate card for every occasion.

scale; individual units of measurement are BPs. The rating is obtained by how often the setup makes you think or say out loud "Bitch, please!" For example, Amanda from *The Real Deal* by Lucy Monroe is a sexually unawakened woman because not only is her husband an emotionally abusive pig, he's a bisexual emotionally abusive pig who is willing to fuck anything that moves other than the heroine. That heavy-handed, clichéd approach (the Insta-Gay method of creating a villain merits multiple BPs alone) earned at least 50 BPs. On the other hand, Daphne from Loretta Chase's *Mr. Impossible* earned only 2 or so BPs. Even though ultimate angelic-choirs-bursting-forth-in-song orgasms were reserved for the hero, Daphne actually enjoyed sex in the past, but was left unfulfilled by her inept older husband, who was mildly appalled that a gently bred woman would enjoy sex so much. The more nuanced take on sexual pleasure and the convincing historical attitude lessened the BP rating drastically. We'll let you know if the International Bureau of Weights and Measures accepts the BP as part of the International System of Units anytime soon.

FEMME VILLAINY

Heroes don't face quite the same constraints as the heroine. For one thing, the Heroic Wang works on all and sundry. His jealous ex-mistresses would (and frequently did attempt to) kill to preserve their access to the Boner o' Gold. And speaking of jealous ex-mistresses, one of the most bizarre elements to romance novel stereotyping? The villainous sexy woman. If there's a woman who likes sex, who likes sex a lot, who likes it so much that she knows how to capitalize on it, she's a villain without a heart. Woe betide you if you're a woman who enjoys sex for its own sake and knows your way around a manicure, because as far as we can tell, snappy, immaculately applied fingernail polish combined with an ability to experience orgasms while not madly in love are two sure signs of a fatal degeneration in feminine virtue. Being a native of some sort of glamorous foreign country (Greece, Italy, France, the Upper East Side of Manhattan) only makes it worse. Sexual ignorance is the same as moral purity; sexual experience or knowledge, even in some contemporaries, is treated the same as moral turpitude.

Why the contrast? Generally speaking, the heroine in the vast majority of romance novels is an Unawakened Woman in every way, not merely sexually. If she's a raving beauty, she has no idea whatsoever about her physical attributes—this sort of heroine was the staple of Old Skool romances, and her lack of awareness was often part and parcel of her youth. She's usually mousy, or brash, or tomboyish, or just plain oblivious. She's a modern-day Snow White. She's the prettiest one of all, but she'll never know it—she will, in fact, happily cohabitate in platonic bliss with a group of short, non-sexually threatening men until some dude on a horse shows up and French-kisses her corpse into sexual awakening and a realization of the power she holds.

This is in direct contrast to the villainess. If the heroine is Snow White, the villainess is the pre—old-hag wicked stepmother. She's sharp, she's sophisticated, she's unafraid to wield her sexuality as a weapon, and damn, she looks good in black. She also has a tendency to be psychotically pissed off when she finds out she's not the most beautiful of all. This species of villainess is usually the woman who is in direct competition with the heroine. She's the ex-mistress, the former girlfriend, the horrible ex-wife who died some appropriately gruesome death. In short, she's the rival.

The other type of villainess is usually old and ugly, and is presented as either grossly obese or grotesquely gaunt. These tend to be the people who can exert immediate power of the heroine: the evil stepmother, the vicious aunt, the harsh housekeeper. She is the heroine's captor. In this sort of villainess, the threatening sexuality of the heroine's rival is removed almost entirely because it's completely irrelevant; the cautionary aspect of what beauty and sex can lead to when untempered by the Powah of Lurve is unnecessary. Instead, the focus switches to using physical appearance instead of sexual experience to denote villainy. Here, as in many fairy tales, you can literally see the person's soul made flesh. Outward markers of hideousness often correspond to internal character flaws.

The preoccupation with moral purity through sexual (in)experience doesn't just play into the fantasy of Sleeping Beauty being woken with love's first kiss; it expresses societal anxieties about sexually available females who aren't affiliated with a culturally sanctioned protector or mate. The simple fact is, widespread acceptance of women as fully actualized human beings with rights equal to those of men is only a handful of decades old in many industrialized nations and barely in its nascent stages in most parts of the world. Old attitudes about women as property are bound to crop up in fiction, and author Lilith Saintcrow, in the essay "Half of Humanity Is Worth Less Than a Chair" published in the *Nothing But Red* anthology, calls it the problem of the wandering vagina. Because of the vagina's lack of ownership, the woman is quite literally a walking property crime waiting to happen, not simply because she doesn't have an owner, but because she can potentially bear a bastard son.

Interpreted through this lens, the root cause for the sexy villainesses beyond the "oh, it's the sexual double standard" dismissal begins to emerge. A woman using her sexuality for her own ends and deriving sexual pleasure independent of love and reproduction isn't just party to a property crime—she's about as natural as a chair suddenly getting up and wanting to sit on a person. People react similarly to slave uprisings, and it's no coincidence that black male slaves were also often portrayed as sexually voracious predators who had to be restrained whenever possible—and fictionally, the villainesses' ultimate fates aren't much better. The villainess also lessens the potency of the male: by reclaiming her body via her sexuality, she rejects the power of the male, and if there's one thing that's unacceptable in the romance genre, it's a hero with an inferior wang.

Conversely, says Saintcrow, demonstrating a heroine's virginity is a way of reinforcing the order, because the sexually active woman who gets to choose her partner (for rather liberal interpretations of "choose," since the choice is quite literally forced on the heroine in many Old Skool romances) is turned into a safe figure. The woman reclaims her sexuality, but with the hero as a necessary and sufficient condition. Her vagina, if it ever wandered, finds a steady home in short order.

Sex Is Natural, Sex Is Good

All this analysis aside, however, we do have to give romance novels their due: no other fiction genre focuses sexuality in general and female sexuality in particular in the context of happy romantic relationships. Not that we're aiming to comprehensively summarize the sexual mores of Western civilization via an examination of its literary canon, but generally speaking, the wages of Unmarried Nookie seem to be death, even if the woman didn't consent to the nookie (see *Tess of the D'Urbervilles*), while the wages of Extra-marital Nookie is fleeting pleasure followed by lifelong repentance (see: *The Scarlet Letter*), death (see: *Madame Bovary*) or grinding misery (good Lord, take your pick). We're not attempting to dismiss these works as somehow unworthy, and Lord knows we loves us the canon, but let's be honest: the portrayal of sex skews toward the grim. Sex, and especially female sexuality and sexual pleasure, is by and large treated with distrust and viewed as a destructive force, with relatively little acknowledgment of its redemptive and constructive powers. This isn't particularly surprising; narratives tend to conform to the cultural space of the times. Looking back, it makes sense that the sagas full of virgins in imminent peril of being constantly raped were prevalent in the 1970s and '80s, as modern feminism and the sexual revolution struggled and screamed into existence. The historical romances published today are considerably different beasts from the Old Skool novels in structure and sensibility; if nothing else, the conflicts regarding women's bodies are no longer being visited in quite so literal fashion on the heroine.

In contemporary romance, virginity is treated differently. The heroine can be:

A. A bona fide virgin, for any number of reasons, many of them completely neurotic and serving as backstory for why the heroine doesn't believe in herself.

B. Sexually experienced—but it's never been like it is with the hero, because she has been cursed by Bad Wang. The hero's sexing is the pinnacle of all sexual experiences, and he has a heroine who was previously convinced she's frigid yodeling in happiness within fifteen minutes of the application of his Heroic Wang. It's almost like a box cake recipe: to make happy heroine, remove pants, add cock, and stir until creamy consistency is achieved.

C. Sexually experienced and perfectly happy with her past orgasms, so much so that it's a nonissue, but inexperienced in some other, very significant way.

Most contemporary romance novels published after the early 1990s allow the heroines to have sex. They have sex before marriage with somebody who isn't the hero. They aren't presented as pure, pristine vessels of womanhood to make their bows before a monarch (well, most of them are not, anyway) and they may have even had (Gasp!) enjoyable nonhero-bestowed orgasms (though this particular heroine is still a relative rarity—it's difficult to give up the fantasy of the completely Unawakened Woman being woken by the One True Love).

So how to create that imbalance of power? What can substitute for virginity?

Ignorance and inexperience, of course! And maybe life-threatening danger.

Many a contemporary heroine finds herself a fish out of water in the plot of a romance. The city girl moves to the small town in the country. The country girl moves to the city and impresses everyone with her down-home wisdom and guileless charm. The mailroom clerk finds herself advising the CEO. The daughter of the CEO finds herself in control of a company she knows nothing about. The heroine discovers that many parts of her former life (usually her career and fiancé) have stifled her to the point that she might as well be stumbling around in a zombie state moaning that she wants brains, sweet sweet brains, so she goes on a tear: quits her job, breaks up with her lover, moves to another town, adopts a dog even more neurotic than her, whatever. The list could go on and on—situations ripe for misunderstanding and the education of the ignorant heroine substitute for that pesky virginity, and really, the contemporary heroine's inexperience is much more satisfying because you can lose your virginity only once. But you can make a fool of yourself and charm or fight your way out time and again—it never gets old!

Paranormal romances have a different spin on the virginity angle. Not only is there a chance for an otherwordly protagonist and an innocent human becoming mixed up in each other's worlds, but there's always the question of whether he will change or turn her into whatever creature he is. Lilith Saintcrow theorizes that the "changing" or "turning" motif of paranormal romances is the new virginity, and we Bitches think she's on to something. How many conflicts in paranormal romances are created because he bites her and turns her into a vampire or were-[insert sexy mammalian predator here]? Rarely is there a cure. Instead, the happy ending hinges on the communion and then a new community—the heroine becomes like the hero after he initiates her into his world.

Saintcrow traces the modern origins of the virginity/paranormal change parallel to Anne Rice and the first several books of Laurell K. Hamilton's Anita Blake series. Rice's "florid descriptions of teeth puncturing the skin in her vampire series are downright erotic, code-talk for sex." As Saintcrow tells it, among a generation of women who had grown up in a time when unprecedented developments in birth control finally allowed women largely to avoid the risk of pregnancy, and record numbers of women were graduating from college, in swaggered Anita Blake, a gun-toting vampire hunter who was not only strong and competent, but "morally and ethically ambiguous," in a way mostly allowed in male characters at the time. The mix of unwilling penetration and transformation with strong female characters led to a transgressive space in which a woman is allowed to own her own body and sexuality, but lingering cultural anxieties about ownership over the wandering vagina meant the "metaphor of 'contamination' by werewolf, vampire, etc., takes the place of the defloration."

Saintcrow also points out that the language between the heroine's unwilling loss of virginity and the unwilling change is startlingly similar. As she wrote in an interview with us:

The heated descriptions of breaking the hymen can, with very little trouble, be transferred over to the male vampire/werewolf biting the female human to transform her. Through this agency of contamination the female human is initiated into the world of sex or "darkness" and discovers sexual autonomy/Phenom Cosmic Power. It's simply not workable to have a believable female virgin over thirty anymore. Not because it's socially impossible anymore, but because the women shelling out the dough to buy the romances won't buy it the way they would in the seventies. . . .

And really, that's the basic plot of any virginity loss: he initiates her into his experience, and includes her in his world. The variations of that paranormal sexual transformation range from biting fangs and scratching claws to, in the case of Kresley Cole's Immortals After Dark series, lightning: the Valkyrie are created when Woden and Freya send lightning down, and in one case, through a maiden warrior who cries out for strength and courage in battle. Stir that box cake mix of sexual empowerment metaphors with your nearest wooden cock, I mean, spoon, for a while, and see what pastry of leavened sexual mores you get out of the oven. And save us a slice. We won't lie: we love cake.

OTHER FORMS OF LOSING YOUR FLOWER, AND YOUR CHERRY

There's more than one way to lose your virginity—and we're not necessarily talking about the myriad of organs, limbs, and orifices made available by paranormal erotica. Sexual defloration is the most obvious way for a hero to claim the heroine for his own, and so is the transformation of the heroine into something supernatural. But there's another way heroines are rendered extraordinary. Presenting: the Color Wheel of the Heroine.

Heroines—especially Old Skool heroines—are colorful, colorful creatures. Hair of titian, flax, honey, deepest auburn . . . no heroine ever has plain old brown hair. Or plain old blond. Or black. Heroines can have raven tresses, or shiny mahogany. Nothing is ever plain about a heroine.

Most heroines fall into three distinct physical types, which are different from the personality types we discussed earlier.

The Swan: This sort of heroine was de rigueur in Old Skool romances. They had it all: winged eyebrows, tumbling tresses, heart-shaped faces, creamy skin, full mouths, glorious alabaster mounds, impossibly tiny waists, and large sparkling orbs worthy of any anime character (take your pick between sapphire, emerald, amethyst, morning mist, or chocolate). Her beauty was usually obvious to everybody except herself. The hero certainly noticed, and so did the villains, because Lord knows the urge to pluck her flower ran strong in all and sundry. The villainesses (both the rivals and captors) couldn't help but see her blazing beauty and feel jealous. The few heroines who were allowed to be aware of her effect on men were usually presented as self-centered and vain—something that the hero would eventually fix, of course.

Romance novels with a more modern sensibility still feature the raving beauty, but she's no longer quite as young or quite as clueless, and when they do, the authors sometimes have fun with the archetype. Judith Ivory's *Beast,* for example, is in many ways a deconstruction of a vain Swan and pits her against a hero who is, in his way, every bit as narcissistic as she is.

The Ugly Duckling: This is the heroine who was, at one point in time, less than the epitome of fashionable beauty, usually in some superficial, fixable way. She's tomboyish and awkward, for example, or she's overweight and pimply. Her coming of age, however, reveals the Swan who was underneath all along. The hero may or may not notice her beauty prior to her transformation. In Jude Deveraux's *Wishes,* for example, the hero finds the overweight heroine delicious and desirable, a regular peach, even before she loses weight due to (we shit you not) a *Cosmo*-reading fairy godmother, and becomes a more conventional beauty. The fairy godmother, a modern selfish woman doing penance in the afterlife by fixing the heroine's multiple miseries, assumed that being thin would solve all the heroine's problems. The hero liked her no matter what she looked like, and her relative size had nothing to do with her happiness. The heroine, Nellie, like many romance heroines, may become beautiful, but the moral journey and improvement are just as important. Suddenly becoming hot isn't the express route to a happy ending.

Other heroes, such as Jordan from Judith McNaught's *Something Wonderful*, catch a small glimpse of the heroine's quirky charm pre-transformation, but it takes a long separation and a transformation from gamine to gorgeous to really knock them on their asses.

The Plain Jane: These heroines truly came into their own in the mid-to-late 1990s, and many of the most beloved heroines of this era are plain Janes. They're nothing remarkable to look at—sometimes even dumpy—or they don't conform to the standards of beauty of the times, but something about her grabs the hero and doesn't let go. Sara from *Dreaming of You* by Lisa Kleypas, Olympia from *Seize the Fire* by Laura Kinsale, Min from *Bet Me* by Jennifer Crusie (or just about any Crusie heroine): all of them are presented as distinctly ordinary-looking, and the hero is often the only one who can discern their true beauty, who notices the sexy quirk everybody else has overlooked.

The Ugly Duckling and the Plain Jane are now probably the more prevalent type of heroine, and this has provided many opportunities for the hero yet again to be first at the gate. One of the more interesting—and frequently appearing—secret beauty surprises of heroines that rise up and smack the reader in the ass is the "other color" that lurks in the heroine's hair. Somehow, the hero will see her backlit by some powerful ray of sunlight, or a stray glimmer of candlelight will caress her noble, virginal head, and the hero will see the auburn that lurks within her brown hair, the gold within her blond that only waited for his attention to show itself. If the back-cover copy hadn't alerted you to the identity of the heroine already, the sunlight-produced color effects and the fragments of that color that are noticed only by the hero are a sure sign that she is The One.

Only the hero can truly identify and appreciate her and rectify the torment of being denied acknowledgment for the special, unique, and oh-so-colorful snowflake she really is. Just as her hymen may be intact as she waited for his special attention, her beauty is unmined like a fat, conflict-free diamond, and only the hero has the tool needed to unearth her true potential.

Yeah, that's a little sexist. Okay, a lot sexist. But the truth is, for every heroine who wallows in the maudlin confines of mediocrity until Sir Hero storms the castle of her love and decorates the whole place with the banners of her beauty and accomplishments (wow, did that metaphor ever collapse under its own weight), there are plenty of heroines who are just fine at the start of the story, but who become something more—more themselves, more special, more admirable—with the addition of that special person. It's almost a second virginity, if you will, that only the hero can see, nurture, and appreciate. Thus yet again the female is captured in the male gaze, and he is the owner of the special love-tinted glasses that see her true form, and in effect the hero can "own" her in yet another way. That traffic of ownership and experience, be it piercing the hymen or seeing her highlights or slurping on her neck, is a constant undercurrent to the creation of any heroine, and the hero who defines her, deflowers her, or devours her.

Some heroines are beautiful but dismissed as shallow or stupid in the beginning of the story. Some are plain and brilliant: but the plainness is part and parcel with the intelligence and cannot be separated. Some are marvelous in their own right. However, the hero always brings that "something more" that dips the heroine in the color palette of love and renders her breathtaking, not just to the hero but often to the entire known world in the context of the novel. Screw light curves and color histograms. Love: it is the powerful addition to your Photoshop toolbox, and a powerful addition to your everyday romance heroine.

THE NEW ALPHA HEROINE

So if the heroine of the current mode of historical novel and of some contemporary novels is a middle-of-the-road testament to perfection, what about the alpha heroine? As we've noted in the heroine breakdown, she's a relatively recent creation, and we Bitches theorize she is the product of all the heroine archetypes who came before her (literally). Is she a popular romance heroine? Sort of. As usual, readers are picky—most alpha females are not beloved by other females. That's part of what makes them alpha. Think about it: Margaret Thatcher? Anna Wintour? No one would accuse either of being cuddly. Not unless you like snuggling with barracudas. In *Novelist's Boot Camp,* writer Todd A. Stone outlines the top six characteristics required for an alpha female:

1. An iron will that demands action (up with no shit will she put).
2. A true understanding of right and wrong (aka a moral compass. One that works. This is in contrast with many heroes in the same mold).
3. A connection to her feelings, her family, and her community (aka not a sociopath. Again, this is in contrast with many heroes in the same mold).
4. A clear and usually accurate ability to assess and evaluate people.
5. Grace under fire, courage under pressure (she'll say no, and follow it up with a punch to the groin if necessary).
6. A sex drive (she'll say yes, and mean it).

A sex drive? Yes, it's true: only when embracing the moral and character strengths of heroes can a woman embrace her sex drive as well. The alpha female—who you can identify by the cover of the book, because usually she's pictured with a weapon, a gigantic schlonglike weapon—is a character infused with power, sexuality, confidence, and ass-kicking prowess, which might explain why she's so popular in fantasy, science fiction, urban fantasy, paranormal,

contemporary, and historical romance. Regency women band-
ing together as spies on the home front? Yup: Jenna Petersen's
Lady M series. Investigating forensic accountants blowing the whis-
tle on corporate malfeasance and outright crime? Yup: Stephanie
Feagan's Pink Pearl series. Sword-wielding, ass-kicking heroines
battling evil? Christ on a cracker, take your pick. The alpha female
is abundant when the plot calls for battling evil.

The alpha female essentially takes the lioness aspect of the female personality and wraps her entire character within it. It's acceptable for a woman, socially, to be outspoken and rude when
defending her children—everyone knows not to get between a
mother bear and her cub. But what about when defending the innocent people trapped inside the gas station as the vampire has a
hissy fit out front? Or when the corporate giant bankrupts the employee pension fund to fuel their next manager's executive retreat?
There are plenty of occasions when a kick-ass female is needed, and
the alpha heroine is a fascinating method through which to explore
the courage of women, both in combat and in everyday spine-filled
behavior.

So what does she need the hero for? Instead of Old Skool
romance's conquering of the heroine's will or forcing her adoption
of his worldview, the alpha heroine goes head-to-head with the
hero, and in battle of one form or another, be it verbal, literal, or
sexual, they come to a compromise that ultimately elevates them
both. With the alpha heroine, love doesn't just conquer all. Love
kicks ass.

IDENTIFICATION: I'M THE HEROINE, THAT'S WHY

Romance readers, probably more than the readers of any other fiction genre, are the subject of all sorts of speculation about how and
why we read what we read. The default assumptions tend to be un-
charitable: we're reading because we're love-starved. We're reading because we are weak-minded ninnies who require undemanding,
simplistic fiction that reinforces our unrealistic worldview. Ro-

mance novels, say the critics, offer false comfort in a cold, complicated world with few easy answers.

Underlying these assumptions is the certainty that readers universally identify with the heroine, and that we're desperate to find the perfect man in fiction that we're unable to find in real life. The heroines in a romance novel are wish-fulfillment placeholders, reinforcing the idea that we women want nothing more than to be swept off our feet by the fine, fine lovin' and limitless financial resources of the nearest Viscount Tycoon Billionaire Pirate Lord Rake Navy SEAL P.I. Cowboy.

Fantasy wish fulfillment? Not entirely, at least, not where we are concerned. The condescending attitude is always enjoyable to savor for its overdone assault on the senses, like when you've added too much sweetener to your coffee, but we tire of the accusation that we are too dim, too dippy, we women, to differentiate between reality and fiction, and that we read romance only to indulge our innermost (virginal) fantasies.

But putting aside the insult of wish fulfillment, the question of identification with the heroine is a curious one, and setting further aside the condescending assumptions as to what we want to read about when we strum our own lutes and who we want to be in our fantasies, whether the heroine is a placeholder in the imagination of the reader is a matter of some debate.

Lisa Kleypas, for example, firmly believes, based on her own experience, that the heroine is indeed a placeholder for the reader:

> I believe the heroine is the placeholder—I once read a really fascinating article by Laura Kinsale arguing that the HERO is the placeholder for the reader, but even though I admired the idea, I wasn't convinced. It's the heroine.
>
> I've gotten so many comments throughout my career from readers who complain about the heroine's actions in terms of "I wouldn't have made the choice she did . . . she didn't react like I think she should have . . . why didn't she just . . ." and all of these comments are evidence to me that the reader generally experi-

ences the story from the heroine's POV even when the hero's POV
is strongly represented.

And it's the trickiest part as an author to create a heroine that
most readers will like, and it's not always possible. As you know,
readers seem to allow a MUCH broader spectrum of behavior for
the hero than for the heroine. A hero can be a complete jerk as
long as he grovels proportionately at the end. But a heroine cannot
be a bitch and be afforded the same forgiveness. I still haven't decided why—it's possible that most readers like the heroine to be
an idealized version of themselves? I really don't know why heroines seem to be held to a higher standard of behavior.

Kleypas's experience leads her to believe that readers engage in
a symbiotic role-play with the heroine to the point where decisions
made by the heroine that the reader disagrees with take on a very
personal tone; the rigid code of conduct enforced on heroines hints
at the level to which readers put themselves in the heroine's place,
whether or not they actually identify with that particular heroine
herself. When the heroine behaves in ways that the reader approves
of, she is able to immerse herself as the heroine, and the world of
the story is smooth. When the heroine behaves in a way the reader
finds unacceptable, however, that particular heroine suddenly stops
being strictly a placeholder, and instead becomes a rival for the
hero's affections.

It's a strong argument for placeholder status of the heroine, and
the level to which readers identify with the heroine that there is
such a rigid code of conduct enforced on heroines. Women are, of
course, their own worst critics, and enforce upon each other the
cultural and stylistic requirements of the time, whether it's 1811 or
2009. Do you think men notice hemlines, inseam length, zipper
length, or the type of sleeve a woman wears? Not a damn chance in
hell.

The heroine, she is a tricky woman to be. Look at the plethora of
women operating in isolation in historical romances. Look at the
number of contemporary romance heroines who have a saucy side-

kick best friend who is a foil or even a villainess in disguise more than an actual best friend. Kleypas agrees, especially regarding her Wallflower Quartet books, which featured interconnected stories of four heroines who were very close friends:

> The more I thought about it, the more I became convinced that I could really do something with a female-based series. At that time, I had gotten involved with a group of writer friends who became a powerful force in my own life. . . . I adore each of them individually, but also the group dynamics were amazing. Women together as a group can be more than the sum of their parts—the creative energy, the humor, the personal and professional insights, were sort of stunning to me.
>
> And I realized as I considered the wallflower idea, that the heroine in historical romance novels is often remarkably isolated. Which was not true at all in real life . . . back then, women could not survive without each other, and women's friendships were deep and lifelong and essential. So the idea of a romance novel heroine having a problem or question, taking it back to her friends, getting their take on it, or at least getting their emotional support, was very exciting. (And so natural!) My publisher expressed some doubt about the viability of a female-oriented series, but they did let me go through with it. And I think it surprised a lot of people that I would write something like this, because I've sort of become known for writing strong heroes.
>
> There's no way of knowing for sure, but I think the wallflower readers really seemed to feel that these heroines were their friends, too, and they had the sense of familiarity and comfort of "visiting" with them. It made the placeholding "bigger" in each subsequent wallflower novel, because readers had the experience of living each heroine's story and also experiencing her as a friend.

The isolation of the heroine may contribute to the degree to which readers identify with her, but the clichéd degree of the heroine's isolation is almost comical. The variations are numerous:

she's an iconoclastic bluestocking historical miss who wants autonomy in a world that won't permit it. She's miserable for personal/
family reasons, regardless of time period. She's a contemporary
heroine who wants home and hearth when the urban pressure is to
Be Something (not Someone) and Have a Career, etc. She's a paranormal heroine who is Set Apart by Superpowers or an Insatiable
Need to Get It On Till the Break of Dawn. Whatever the reason,
heroines are often all by themselves.

But then, consider the lukewarm twinkle of the average romance heroine. Kleypas calls her a "creature of moderation." A romance heroine is like the ideal porridge for Goldilocks, if Goldilocks
is a romance reader and the porridge is the heroine's role as placeholder. Not too hot, not too cold, not too tall, not too fat, not too
smart, certainly not stupid, not driven by greed, not driven by any
historical accuracy as pertains to gender politics, not at all sexually
aware, and a perfectly nice, vanilla creation of moderation and perfection that easily enables the reader, if the reader identifies with
the heroine, to slip into her role and embark upon her own romance, again and again and again.

Kleypas adds:

I've heard some readers comment that they adore it when a
heroine's flaws match their own, but everyone seems to get a little
"itchy," so to speak, when we get a little too close to reality. The
fairy tale, and therefore that necessary touch of idealization, can't
be threatened. Or else the whole point of the romance is lost. And
then that leads to the question of how realistic you can be without
breaking the spell. No one wants to read about a woman's hairy
legs, or morning breath, or what the Victorians politely called
"bodily exhalations." Sweat seems to be okay, but it is often described as "clean sweat."

What I do rather like is that when a modern woman reads a
historical romance, she gives herself "permission" to experience
being protected, pampered, even sexually dominated without any
guilt. The historical context sort of lets us relax and enjoy the

"I don't select my books based on placeholder heroines. I'm more
likely to seek a dynamic interplay of theories of sexual agency,
autonomy, and dichotomous evolution."

ride, correctness be damned. A historical heroine is never responsible for her own orgasm. That is truly nice, isn't it?

This sort of escape is hardly unique to women-centered fiction.
Readers engage in a similar species of escape when they pick up a
military thriller, in which the grizzled hero performs physically impossible feats of badassery, totes around more firepower than all the
countries ending in -stan put together, and gets a nubile young thing

(or twenty) along the way. And yet women take all kinds of crap and heat, or heated crap, for the escapist elements of romance fiction, as if men reading military thrillers or folks reading mysteries don't escape into a world where the bad guy gets it in the end, or in the head, or both, and the whodunnit becomes a matter of the butler doing it (not in the erotica sense, in the felonious sense).

Discussions of romance reader identification become a minefield, simply because they open the door for people to discredit our intelligence, to accuse women of needing that emotional escape from their fiction because they have to *be* the heroine in order to merely enjoy the story. This ignores the different ways other readers respond to the texts, because while it seems clear that many readers do identify strongly with the heroine, some readers identify with the hero, while others identify with both while simultaneously remaining removed.

However, examining how readers react to fiction is particularly prescient when examining romance simply because women buy millions of goddamn dollars' worth of it, despite being denigrated for doing so, despite the accusations that it's all the same pornography in the end, etc. Serious questions about what attraction romance holds for readers are as valid as any other examination, so onward we go.

Nora Roberts discussed this in an interview with us.

NORA ROBERTS: I really think it just depends on the reader. I'm trying to think if, as a reader, I identify more with either of the mains, and I don't think I do. For me, it's the couple and the relationship—so as a reader and a writer—I identify with both. Or don't if the book doesn't grab me.

I think, if I had to do a sweeping generalization, I'd say most female readers ID with the heroine, but want to fall in love with—or at least feel attracted to—the hero. He is absolutely essential for the reader's enjoyment and emotional investment of the book. She is essential as, I think, the reader must understand and respect her, even if they don't identify with her.

SARAH: But if the reader, in your sweepy generalization, identifies
with the heroine but falls in love with the hero, that would make
the heroine more of a placeholder for the reader, unless I'm
reading you wrong.

I'm a weird reader, I've decided. I don't identify with the
heroine much, though I empathize with her. Mostly I start
rooting for the both of them, and look for that emotional pull (if
the book has grabbed me) that makes me care and cheer on both
of them. I hover over the action like a benevolent nosy ghost.

NORA ROBERTS: Exactly how it is for me. I guess, in my sweeping
generalization, "empathize" is a better word indeed than
"identify." I think as women, most will FEEL more what the
writer causes the heroine to feel. Understand it more, maybe. I
know, absolutely, some readers need to BE the heroine. I had a
reader (who regularly wrote many of us the same thing) who
asked, month after month for a "black-haired virgin heroine." She
preferred it when she was paired with a blond hero. And, of
course, explained that she had black hair, had been a virgin on
her wedding night, and her husband was blond.

She took it way over the top.

While Sarah "hovers like a benevolent ghost," Candy dubs her
particular reading style the Homunculus Theory of Reader Identification: she inhabits both the hero and heroine's spaces while remaining somewhat separate from them. However, when reading
Old Skool romances, this ceases to be true because she identifies
more with the heroine. As she was trying to figure out why—it's
not as if she likes these heroines very much, because she doesn't—it
hit her: it's because the hero's worldview is presented as the implicitly correct one, and the implicit worldview in Old Skool romances,
especially as embodied by the hero, is one she finds repugnant.

So who does she end up rooting for and identifying with? The
character who's struggling against the worldview, the one who's
actively trying to defy it: the heroine. Unfortunately, the heroine
inevitably succumbs to the hero's normative view, and it's part of

the reason why Old Skool romances, more than just about any other type of literature, infuriate Candy. The worldview she despises is affirmed as being dominant and right and just, over and over and over again—and not only that, but ideal and desirable as well. Her frustration with the characters goes beyond not liking them because they don't behave in ways that she thinks a heroic character should—because she's able to tolerate considerable variation in heroic behavior, running from genuinely sweet protagonists such as Christy Morrell from *To Love and to Cherish* or Sara Fielding from *Dreaming of You* to darker, more complicated characters like Sheridan Drake from *Seize the Fire* and Sebastian Verlaine from *To Have and to Hold*. Her rejection of the characters is rooted in her distaste for the fictional universe and the real-world values they represent.

Sebastian from *To Have and to Hold,* in particular, illustrates how a rapist hero can eventually be redeemed. When Sebastian forces Rachel to have sex with him, he's dissolute and bored, but his conscience already bothers him somewhat. The cognitive dissonance eventually becomes too loud to ignore when he sees one of his friends treating her the way he has, and he genuinely reforms his attitude and behavior toward Rachel. In *To Have and to Hold*, while the hero still holds considerably more power than the heroine, his actions are not implicitly endorsed by the worldview presented in the book.

In Old Skool romances and people who love Old Skool romances, the readers may not necessarily be identifying with the hero, thereby making his actions palatable; the readers may be buying into the idea that his worldview is correct, and therefore assuring themselves that everything will turn out for the best even when he treats the heroine with brutality. The power of the Happily Ever After allows readers to put up with a lot of bad behavior because it's ultimately all for a good cause. The readers, from their superior vantage point, can interpret the hero's actions as evidence of his love/attraction for the heroine, even when the heroine, from her limited point of view, misinterprets the signals egregiously and acts accordingly. These readers may identify with the heroine, but they are at the same time separate from her by virtue of their superior knowledge.

All this talk of reader identification has to separate Old Skool romances from the newer forms, however, because the heroines and the range of acceptable behavior are so different. Identification with the Old Skool heroine is, in some ways, easier, because she's often quite clearly set up as the more vulnerable party, and it's often easier to identify with the victims than with predators or people in positions of power. Perhaps part of the reason why the heroines are so tooth-hurtingly feisty in the Old Skool novels is to lessen the victim dynamic somewhat, to make it seem as if they're giving as good as they get, and that the hero's acts in taming and dominating her are justified. This dynamic—whether consciously created or not—comes across especially strongly in books like *Island Flame* by Karen Robards, in which the heroine is extremely combative and shrill.

But then Susan Elizabeth Phillips's "The Romance and the Empowerment of Women" in *Dangerous Men, Adventurous Women* demonstrates just how very subjective the reader experience can be. Phillips argues that Old Skool romance novels portray the heroines giving as good as they get; Candy views their struggles as futile because in most of the ways that matter, the hero gets to win after a token resistance from the heroine. Phillips sees the Old Skool romances as empowering; Candy sees them as reinforcing the old order. And there's plenty of room for both interpretations in the text.

Chapter Codpiece

THE ROMANCE HERO

It's not easy, being a romance novel hero. An ever-changing multi-faceted depiction of manhood, the hero is a male specimen designed to ignite the fantasies and flame the undying passions of all females within his vicinity. Heroes have a hard row to hoe (if you know what we mean, and we think you do), and that's before they get around to tackling the heroine, both literally and figuratively. All that, and they have to get the readers' motors running.

Our Top Favorite Heroes

SARAH:

Lyon, *The Lion's Lady*, Julie Garwood. Julie Garwood's older historicals give me the happy shivers. I love them like I love icing on cupcakes. Lyon in particular is tormented, and has been betrayed deeply by his first wife. And when the heroine, Christina, starts lying left and right to him and he knows it, he doesn't immediately cast her in the exact same mold as his first wife (thus giving himself an excuse to be a complete douche bag). He's driven to understand why she won't trust him and, in doing so, earns her trust while giving her his own.

(continued on next page)

Grayson Thane, *Born in Ice*, Nora Roberts. Misanthrope ahoy! Grayson Thane is a curmudgeonly and very successful mystery writer who, when in the throes of a really solid story idea, hides away in his room and growls and throws things at anyone who dares interrupt him. Intelligent intensity = hawwt.

Ethan Quinn, *Rising Tides*, Nora Roberts. Another Roberts hero. I love them. A quiet yet deeply intense man who hides turbulent and overwhelming emotions, Ethan is ferocious about a very specific group: those people whom he considers his family. Again, that intensity, plus healing and recovery from deep emotional harm, creates a deeply memorable hero.

Hawk, *Midsummer Magic*, Catherine Coulter. It's not just that this is the first romance I ever read, though that nostalgia is part of the allure. Hawk is autocratic, somewhat cruel to his new bride, and I won't mention the cream factor, but Coulter involves the reader in Hawk's backstory enough that the reader sees he's trying his best to live up to expectations, and at heart is a noble, caring person who doesn't want to love his wife but ends up doing so. I'm a total sucker for the "I don't wanna love you. I don't wanna like you. I can't stop thinking about your hair, dammit!" storyline.

CANDY:

Christy, *To Love and to Cherish*, Patricia Gaffney. Christy is incredibly sexy because he's that rarest of creatures in modern fiction: a hero who's good-hearted to the core while never being preachy, boring, or a paragon of every holy virtue envisioned in the fevered dreams of Christian saints. He's sincere, he's funny, he writes the most hilariously atrocious love poetry to show his devotion to Anne, and he looks like an angel. How can I not love him? Plus, there's that edge of "Woo, forbidden sex with the pastor."

Michael, *Wild at Heart*, **Patricia Gaffney.** Part of the reason Michael is on this list is because he fulfills all of my "I want to marry Mowgli when I grow up" fantasies. Part of it's also because I have a hard-on the size of Alpha Centauri for virgin heroes. But if I had to give the core reason why Michael appeals to me that much, it's because nobody knows how to combine sweet and sexy the way Gaffney can; Michael's sweetness is tempered by his wildness, and Gaffney makes it clear that he *can* be dangerous—he just chooses, almost every time, not to be.

Justin, *Only with Your Love*, **Lisa Kleypas.** Justin is my favorite guilty pleasure. He's an Old Skool hero, except he's also written by Lisa Kleypas, which means all his infuriating, rapey, alpha bits are more than compensated for by his angsty, sensitive, nurturing side. He's my ultimate fantasy hero, and by that, I mean he's someone I desire strictly as a fantasy. If I met him in real life, I'd be running for a restraining order. If he were a contemporary hero, he'd probably be a rock star, fucking groupies, guzzling red wine and Vicodin, and trashing hotel rooms. Instead, he's a Louisiana pirate with a tormented soul, which is miles more appealing to read about.

Sheridan, *Seize the Fire*, **Laura Kinsale.** Sheridan Drake is the perfect example of a hero I enjoy reading about, and whom I find completely compelling, but whom I don't desire in the least—he's the only hero on this list I don't have a bit of a crush on. He's extremely damaged, what with his awful father and his experiences in the Navy, and God knows nobody writes appealing damaged protagonists better than Laura Kinsale, but more than that, he's incredibly self-aware, and his deeply (and I mean *deeply*) buried gallant streak shows up at just the right times.

(*continued on next page*)

> **Alex, *Anyone But You*, Jennifer Crusie.** Alex seems to be,
> at first blush, a fairly typical contemporary hero specimen: he's
> good-looking, he's a doctor, he's crazy about the heroine. What
> makes him stand out, however, is his lack of ambition to be the
> Most Bad-Ass Surgeon Ever in Some Impossibly Difficult and
> High-Demand Specialty. He's an ER doctor, he's really good at
> it, and he's happy and satisfied with that. After an overdose of
> angsty heroes who have to dominate in every way and in every
> aspect of their lives, Alex is a startling (and really sexy) breath
> of fresh air. *And* he loves *Mystery Science Theater 3000*. For that
> alone, he deserves a spot on the list.

The romance novel hero is subject to many conflicted interpretations and misunderstandings more than other types of genre
heroes because not only is he rewarded with the girl, he's often held
up as the ideal man for a romantic relationship as if the fiction were
a template for reality. For example: the über-alpha hero, who is so
alpha it's a wonder he doesn't gnaw on parked cars. Why is it that
romance readers can tolerate any number of crazed behaviors from
a romance hero, whereas if a real-life dude did one-tenth of a hero's
dastardly deeds, not the least of which is raping the heroine, she'd
be calling 911 faster than you can say "restraining order"? What is it
about the hero who fascinates us enough that we'll forgive him anything?

First, there's the fantasy element. Women are not dumb. We
know we're reading fiction, so the supposition that we're not able
to separate fantasy from reality and that we'd tolerate in reality
what we enjoy in fantasy is somewhat insulting. There's a certain
amount of enticing power in the man so manly, his own shadow
takes a dump in fear of him. Considering the multiple roles modern
women can embrace in a given twenty-four-hour period—mother,
wife, daughter, manager, administrator, chauffeur, employee, em-
ployer, lover, chef, parent, partner, volunteer, breadwinner, bread

**The Three Most Fucked-Up Things
Heroes Have Done and Gotten Away With; or,
You Think We're Joking, But Holy Shit, We So Are Not**

It's sometimes difficult to tell the difference between the hero and the villain in a romance novel. Near as we can tell, the most reliable indicator seems to be dental hygiene. (The motto of the International Coalition of Villains: Flossing Is for Pussies!) That, and the fact that the hero actually gets away with his stunts instead of being killed in some horrible fashion by the end of the book. Some romances push the envelope a lot harder than others, though, and here are three we've stumbled across in real novels that made our jaws drop:

1. Deliberately seducing (or raping—hard to tell the difference sometimes) the heroine, marrying her, and then abandoning her, all because her father wronged the hero or the hero's family in the past. (The only thing more fucked-up than this storyline is how popular they used to be—they popped up with strange regularity in old Harlequin novels.)
2. Marrying the heroine to another man, only to dismiss the erstwhile groom on the wedding night so he could rape the heroine.
3. Kidnapping the heroine on the day before her wedding to another man and raping her so that she'd have no choice but to marry him.

maker, bread toaster, bread eater—the fantasy of an overbearing hero can represent for some women devotion, attraction, and protection instead of bullying. As Lisa Kleypas remarked to us, there's something incredibly seductive about a man saying, in all respects, from the management of the home to the management of her orgasm, "Don't worry about a thing. I'm on it."

The romance novel heroes' attempts at control and domination, in Old Skool romances especially, usually result in antagonism, not happiness—at least, not until the end of the book. Part of the heroic association with control can be explained by the nature of storytelling. Conflict is by far more interesting to read and vicariously experience than quiet contentment. If the hero wrenched control from the heroine by, say, forcing her to sit and relax with a good book while he vacuumed and did the dishes, there wouldn't be much of a story there, even if these sorts of partners are highly valued in real life.

But the other part has its roots in the hypertrophied masculinity exhibited by many romance novel heroes. Romance novel heroes must have the Biggest and Best Schlong of All in both figurative and literal terms. In many ways, the violence and wrenching of power away from the heroine in Old Skool romance novels function not only to drive the conflict, but to pump up the cock. Once his cock is metaphorically big enough, we begin to see the restoration of power toward the heroine, and the subjugation and taming of the hero that, while complete, never hints at emasculation. Romance novel heroes often show how much they care in big, showy gestures, like saving the heroine from certain death; small domestic gestures that might come across as womanish, such as cleaning the house after she's had a difficult day, will rarely show themselves.

Additionally, power and an edge of danger are always sexy—but they're especially sexy when attached to the security of a happy ending. The happy ending allows readers to relax fully into the story and to trust that no matter how badly things are going, events will eventually turn out for the best.

Then there's the theory first explained in detail by Laura Kinsale in "The Androgynous Reader: Point of View in the Romance," collected in *Dangerous Men and Adventurous Women,* which posits that it's not just the heroine whom the reader is interacting with, but the hero as well. It's not a question of gender switching, in which the female reader envisions herself in the hero's masterful, possibly lordly pants. It's more a question of using the hero to embrace the more "masculine" elements of her own personality—the strength, domination, aggression, and power which identify the alpha hero, and which aren't always so welcome in women. The reader can embrace and identify with the hero because she "can experience the sensation of living . . . with masculine power and grace . . . can explore anger and ruthlessness and passion and pride and honor and gentleness and vulnerability."

Kinsale also theorizes that the happy ending is a fictional manifestation of the daily "integration of the inner self" that men and women go through as they reconcile their present lives with what might have been, and confront "turning away from adventure, from autonomy" and "mourn the loss" of that fantasy. She continues, "Romance novels aren't the only manifestations of this fact. Pro football, male-buddy movies, and men's genre fiction all exist for a reason."

Kinsale's essay was penned over ten years ago, and when we asked her if her theory holds up today, she said:

> I'm not a big fan of the alpha terminology. When I wrote the essay, I asked myself why the reader might be so interested in getting inside the hero's experience, and came up with my theory that it's a way for women to explore the elements in themselves that are traditionally called "masculine" in our culture. I certainly believe any woman—and any heroine—can have courage, honor, pride and all those attributes that are typically considered masculine, and I'd like to think most of the heroines I've written exhibit all of them. Romance readers do seem to judge heroines by a more intense standard. But then, often that's the way it is in real life—we see what we want to see regarding the opposite sex when we're in love.

What's truly bodacious about Kinsale's essay is that it identifies outright that for many romance readers, the romance novel itself hinges on the hero. As she says: "The man carries the book." If the heroine is too stupid to live, disappointing, cardboard or otherwise objectionable, a great hero can keep the reader invested in the book.

It's quite a hefty responsibility, really, that whole damn book. Screw Atlas—romance heroes have it hard. Literally.

Jungian analysis of romance novels supports the idea that the hero represents a self of the reader/female heroine—the Jungian shadow archetype, to be precise.* According to Amber Botts, who wrote "Cavewoman Impulses: The Jungian Shadow Archetype in Popular Romantic Fiction" for the anthology *Romantic Conventions,* Jung identified several specific "archetypes . . . common to all people," and states that "for self-actualization, a person must integrate several archetypes, including the anima, the animus, and the shadow . . . [which] represents denied anger, greed, envy and sexual desire." Consider the terminology associated with heroes: darkness, predatory animals, demons, devils, vampires, werewolves—plenty of anger, greed, envy, and sexuality there.

In romance novels, the heroine heals, tames, or conquers the hero. As Botts writes, heroes "represent the shadow impulses which society frowns upon as inappropriate for women . . . [and] the integration of impulses for blatant sexuality, anger/aggression, and danger are represented by the shadow hero's taming." If the hero is the shadow self of the heroine, *and* the reader, then her conquest represents that same integration of selves, and that integration is what makes the hero so crucially important, and also what makes the happy ending so satisfying.

So when we examine all the different types of heroes, and we try to identify and name their influences, we could be examining parts of ourselves. Whether the reader and the heroine alike fantasize about the male hero, or whether the reader partially identifies with him, the romance novel hero is a unique and colorful animal. And when it comes to heroes, two popular categories come up: alpha heroes and beta heroes. These categories are, in some ways, simplistic, because many heroes (especially in romances published

---

* Yes, Jung. Jungian analysis is hawt, and the word "Jung" doubles as a delicious metaphor for man junk.

in the 1990s and onward) display traits from both, and some types of heroes, like the rogue, don't fit into either comfortably. However, divvying up the hero pool into alpha, beta, and rogue* does provide a useful analysis tool for looking at the roles heroes play in romance novels.

The problem with "alpha hero" as a term is that it is strongly associated with the cruel, brutal rapist heroes prevalent in Old Skool romances. At that point, "alpha" and "asshole" are merged and become "alphole." He's not merely strong and confident in his power, he's brutal and cruel in his use of it. So let's be clear—when we discuss "alpha hero," we're talking about strong, dominating, confident men, often isolated, who hold a tortured, tender element within themselves that they rarely let anyone see. We aren't talking about the cruel duke who rapes the heroine because she flirted with him and therefore *clearly* asked for it. Alpha does not mean alphole. Alphole heroes are not even remotely to our tastes, and we'd like to toss pointy objects at their heads.

But one woman's alpha dreamboat is another woman's alphole nightmare. Witness the alphole hero list we've compiled below. If any part of our book is sure to generate copious amounts of hate mail, we're pretty sure this is going to be it, because the heroes named are some of the most beloved figures in romance.

Alphole Heroes We'd Like to Slap Around Some

Clayton Westmoreland, from *Whitney, My Love,* by Judith McNaught

Anthony Welles, from *Devil's Embrace,* by Catherine Coulter

Severin of Langthorne, from *Rosehaven,* by Catherine Coulter

Brandon Birmingham, from *The Flame and the Flower,* by Kathleen E. Woodiwiss

(*continued on next page*)

---

* Also known as the "omega" hero, which we think sounds like a multivitamin.

Jonathan Hale, from *Island Flame* and *Sea Fire,* by Karen
    Robards
Steve Morgan, from *Sweet Savage Love,* by Rosemary Rogers
Rome Matthews, from *Sarah's Child,* by Linda Howard
Rhydon Baines, from *An Independent Wife,* by Linda Howard
Heathcliff, from *Wuthering Heights,* by Emily Brontë (in many
    ways the model of many romance-novel heroes)

Alpha heroes who aren't assholes, or who start out assholes and
reform before it's too late or don't cross into utterly unredeemable
territory, or who are sufficiently explained that we can at least
understand his assholishness:

Devon Crandall, from *The Windflower,* by Laura London
    (Sharon and Tom Curtis)
Sebastian Ballister, from *Lord of Scoundrels,* by Loretta Chase
Derek Craven, from *Dreaming of You,* by Lisa Kleypas
Justin Vallerand, from *Only with Your Love,* by Lisa Kleypas

The evolution of the hero

In contrast with the alpha hero, the beta hero is the buddy hero, the best friend, the kindlier, mellower guy. He's a dude. A nice dude. Witness the pop-culture beta heroes: Chandler Bing from *Friends,* for example—or just about any young, attractive male protagonist from just about any modern sitcom. And every character ever played by Bill Pullman, ever. Let us not forget the number of beta heroes who ultimately have a more alpha secret side—just about every superhero follows this model, including Spider-Man/ Peter Parker and Superman/Clark Kent. The alpha hidden within the beta isn't so much a separate side of his personality as it is the physical manifestation of what makes the beta hero so great: an unshakable core of pure and stalwart good, so constant and abiding it's damn near alpha in its strength.

The problem with beta heroes is that people frequently confuse them with being pussies—or pussy whipped. Concessions of power are often viewed as emasculating. A lack of desire to take power and dominate at every opportunity is also viewed as proof that the wang is neither as heroic or as mighty. Rather tellingly, we've read

online conversations in which readers argued that scenes showing the hero begging for forgiveness after mistreating the heroic were defeating the point of creating a strong hero in the first place. To these readers, never giving up ground is an important indicator of strength and potency. Our view on this is a bit different: it takes real balls to own your mistake, apologize for the shitty behavior, and make amends. A person who refuses to relinquish one iota of power is too brittle and inflexible to wield true control.

And then there are the rogue heroes. They're not commanding and in charge the way the alphas are, and they're not friendly and effortlessly nurturing the way the betas are. Rogues are usually happy to fade into the background, largely because their activities are more than a little shady and too much scrutiny could make things uncomfortable. Because they've had to deal with the darker side of human nature—both theirs and other people's—they're often too cynical and self-centered to make good betas. Rogue heroes, even more often than alphas, require healing and redemption—perhaps with copious quantities of seduced Magic Hoo Hoo. When written well, they're often iconic figures. Han Solo, for example, is a classic rogue, as are many of Anne Stuart's heroes.

Romance heroes embody and combine all the different character archetypes, from the action hero to the swashbuckling pirate hero to the ever-popular rake hero, and each hero evolves from the heroes who came before him.*

Even as that shirt remains unbuttoned but tucked in, the hero, he evolves. We've talked a bit. . . . okay, a *lot,* about Old Skool romance and New Skool romance and the Very Important differences between them, most notably that people who sling the slurs at the romance are usually basing their presumptions upon their knowledge of Old Skool romance. The same is true of the hero: most of the negative dismissals of the hero come from the poor reputation of the alphole heroes, as that reputation has exceeded their actual life span in the genre. Sure you'll meet an alphole every now and

---

* Literally and figuratively.

again, but rarely are there brutally awful heroes such as the early Woodiwiss and Rogers variety.

But in the current definition of romance, especially the newer historicals, paranormals, and contemporary romances of the past ten to fifteen years, the hero, he has his own journey to fulfill. He better get on it, too. Pamela Regis acknowledges the new role of the hero in *A Natural History of the Romance Novel* by examining older courtship-centered romances alongside the romance novels of the modern era. When examining the plot elements that make up the romance, she realized that the twentieth-century romance-novel hero has a much greater role to play because, unlike earlier romance novels, the heroines are already "in command of their lives" and as such the novel does not have to focus on the heroines' journey to maturity:

> When a novel does not have to follow the heroine . . . to trace her assumption of affective individualism, her acquisition of property or of the partner she chooses, the hero can (and does) step to the fore to assume a much larger place in the narrative. . . . The hero is much more in evidence, much more a part of the action.

We take that involvement one step further: whether you agree with the idea of the Jungian shadow self and the integration of selves that is replete with happy endingness, or whether you think that's complete malarkey and like reading about heroes and heroines in stories of courtship and marriage because it makes you as a reader happy, the fact remains that the modern hero has to earn his happy ending as well, and he has to earn it by growing with the heroine, and adapting and sharing her worldview. Ever hear the old joke about how the responsibility of the wedding is on the bride, and all the groom has to do is show up? Used to be that was the hero's role—he'd show up. Either he was a catalyst meant to cause the heroine to achieve the main chemical reaction, or he was the standard to which the heroine had to conform in order to fulfill her own happy ending. Now, the hero must face at the very least some kind of journey and resolution alongside the heroine, and thus demonstrate his own worth. Romance readers expect for the most part a hero who will earn his own happy ending.

So how do heroes earn that happy ending? Taming, or overcoming. Pick one.

The hero to be tamed or humbled—the *Pride and Prejudice* model, if you will—is an enticing storyline that reveals itself in so many romance novels, regardless of subgenre. The vampire who must acknowledge the worth of humanity or his own humanity. The Scottish laird who has never had to listen to anyone question his judgment, who must now compromise, even though saying the word leaves a bitter taste in his mouth. The ruthless businessman who decides to forgo a hostile takeover and instead save the company he was about to swallow whole. As soon as the hero gets over himself and recognizes his own false pride and personal flaws, he can achieve his happy ending. The heroine's role in the taming is often one of strength and self-assurance—"You can try that crap with anyone else, but it is not going to fly with me."

A twist on the taming or humbling is the reformation of the hero. Most often, the hero who is tamed or reformed is a rake who will humperate anything with two tits, a hole, and a heartbeat, and is known throughout the land as a profligate slut. But, alas, he's tormented, the poor rake, by some flaw. Whatever it is that tortures the hero, the heroine is key to his understanding and overcoming that flaw, as he must choose between life as it was, or a chance at a better life with her. Behold, ye, the power of the Magic Hoo Hoo.

Then there's the trauma to be overcome—healing, instead of taming or reforming. It's a subtle but important difference, centered on a situation that is somewhat outside of the hero's control, and for which he doesn't have the tools to appropriately conquer. Sometimes the flaw from which the hero must heal is deadly, such as alcoholism, post-traumatic stress disorder, or a paralyzing fear of bees, heights, disorganization, or death. Other plots involve heroes who must grow up in excruciatingly cruel circumstances to become normal functional adults in whatever time period they happen to inhabit. Laura Kinsale, for example, is a master of that particular plot, most notably in *The Shadow and the Star,* where the hero, who was sold into sexual slavery as a child, grows up and acquires that most valuable of commodities, happiness.

THE HERO'S WANG OF MIGHTY LOVIN'

While this is all very maudlin and important, there's one element that the hero gets right every time. And really, no examination of the hero would be complete without an up-close and personal handshake-and-howdy-doo with the hero's Mighty Mighty Thunderstick. The role of the Heroic Wang of Mighty Lovin' is a crucial one in romance novels. The entire fate of the relationship, the heroine's future as a sexually awakened being, and possibly the future of mankind all hang on the turgid strength of the hero's man root. He may be suffering quietly through any number of personal or physical afflictions, but damned if he can't mount up and ride off in a moment's notice.

In fact, if you had to sum up the magnitude of the hero's Mighty Mighty Wang of Lovin' in one letter, that letter would be "r." Yes: "r."

Penises are important. And heroic romance novel penises, they are *important,* but never are they *impotent.* Do not minimize that "r" of distinction.

Behold the multitude of achievements that can be attributed to judicious applications of the turgid man-staff:

- Heal childhood trauma, one orgasm at a time
- Awaken a woman from a complete absence of sexual knowledge, one orgasm at a time

- Craft the perfect insatiable and instinctively excellent sexual partner, one orgasm at a time
- Elevate sexual intercourse to near heavenly experiences, one orgasm at a time
- Exist in a state of constant hornytoad, alleviated one orgasm at a time.

All this pressure can get to be a bit much for heroes, particularly in the changing plot climate of the romance genre. Witness this series of internal e-mails we uncovered recently from the International Consortium of Heroes (ICH), the body responsible for sourcing the various hero archetypes to romance novels.

From: Lord Hawklencravenbearesfordvilleperegrineton [perryschnookums@icheroes.org]
To: All Heads of Sections
Subject: Problematic new requirements

A certain alarming trend has come to my attention of late, and this is the proverbial straw that has broken the camel's back.

When the hero's worldviews stopped being normative in the late 1980s, forcing our emotional turmoil and growth to equal the heroines', we stepped up to the plate and delivered. When we had to prove ourselves worthy of the heroines, instead of having our status secured by a combination of fiat and our dashing good looks, we worked long and hard hours to ensure satisfaction for all parties. When critics pointed out that we represent the reader or the heroine's Jungian shadow self, we cringed at the indignity of our loss of autonomous identity, but agreed. When told we have to represent and embrace the integration of the reader and heroine's selves, we worked round the clock to train new recruits.

But now I find that bisexual heroes are beginning to gain ground, as erotic romances with ménage scenarios become increasingly popular. I've always conceded without so much as a quiver of my upper lip when new developments appeared on the horizon and new tasks were flung at us; I do balk, however, at having to become acquainted with somebody else's purple-helmed soldier of passion. We have enough pressure placed on our penises as it is, between providing magic orgasms and somehow becoming the symbol of liberation and completion; I'm not sure adding the pressure of another cock on mine is going to be viable. Any thoughts?

Perry
Head of the Rakish Aristocrat Section

"Love will find a way through paths where wolves fear to prey."

—Lord Byron

———————————

From: Captain Sbloodstreuth [surrenderdabooty@icheroes.org]
To: All Heads of Sections
Subject: Re: Problematic new requirements

Am I alone in thinking this sounds kind of fun?

Guys love girl-on-girl. Women love the idea of having two men tending to their every need. I, for one, welcome the additional sex and the idea of splitting duties with somebody else. Those romance heroines can be such a tetchy, high-maintenance lot.

Just sayin'.
Sbloodstreuth
Head of Pirates, Rogues, and Other Scallywags

———————————

From: Vlad McCullough [kiltsandfangs@icheroes.org]
To: All Heads of Sections
Subject: Re: Problematic new requirements

Och, 'tis not more work for me Jimmy Johnson I be worried about. I dinnae ken if you wee heroine can handle two braw laddies like me feeding on her. Also, if there be two in the picture, who gets the transformation credit for turning the lass into a vampire? I need only one mair before I qualify for an all-expense-paid vacation to Bermuda.

Vlad McCullough
Head of the Scottish, Vampire, and Scottish Vampire Section

Poor Perry. He's so misguided, carrying the weight of his own passion around in his breeches, in addition to all that sexual responsibility. Truly, the hero's apple-headed trousersnake has incredibly diverse powers. If it could be packaged as a toy, it would be a top seller and be completely impossible to find come the holidays.* It slices! It dices! It brings women to immense orgasm even if they've never located their own clitoris! And once it springs into action, unless the plot calls for ruination of reputation, the hero and heroine will never get caught. Ever! The mighty wang is its own camouflage. Even if the hero rushes headlong into a fit of murky passion in the middle of an opera box hanging off the balcony in full view of the entire orchestra, the actors, the audience, and the stage hands, they will not get caught. They won't even be noticed. It's a hallmark of romance: once the mighty wang begins its loving assault, the happy couple obfuscates like a seasoned RPG player with an invisibility cloak and no one will ever be the wiser.

But more importantly, the mighty wang offers the Key to True Love. Though he may not expect it, the mighty wang reveals that the heroine is his One and Only. How? He must have the orgasm to end all orgasms, a moment of jizztastic glory that will communicate to his brain from the depths of his man part that This Is the Woman for Him, forever and ever, amen. This moment of realization is usually quite different for the heroine, but for the hero, his happy ending begins and ends in the orgasm. In Old Skool romance, his orgasm of perfection yields anger because she has control over a

---

* Pun intended.

part of him, and as an immensely self-controlled individual, this is intolerable. In New Skool romances, that orgasm of perfection means that she has inspired an intensity that's part obsession, part irritation, and part priapism: he's hard for her, exclusively her, forever. Regardless of the Skool of the romance, she of the Magic Hoo Hoo brings him to monogamous attachment. That is a powerful wang indeed. It identifies the lady love, initiates her into sexual experience, creates a powerful monogamy for the hero, conceals any stray amorous adventures that might possibly get one or both of them ruined, offers the most powerful orgasms ever, and yet is contained in a convenient pocket-size package suitable for travel.

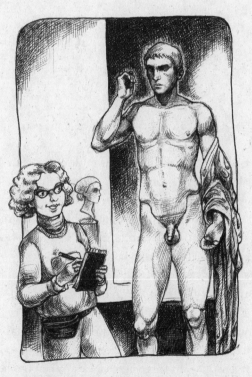

Mavis's doctoral thesis traces the cultural and
sexual history of *Wangus mightus lovinus.*

CREATE THE PERFECT HERO

Now that you have a basic grasp of the hero's mighty cave crusader, and his role and responsibility, let's move on to crafting the perfect hero.

First, if you're writing a historical, you need some colors. Consider the following colors for your hero's eyes:

- Metal
- Slate
- Flint
- Gunmetal
- Steel
- Charcoal
- Granite
- Shale
- Cloud
- Silver
- Stormy
- Partly sunny with a 65 percent chance of showers.

What, twelve shades of gray doesn't do it for you? While your heroine may have jewel-toned eyes of the most priceless variety, heroes, they are usually described in metallic terms, ranging from the ever-popular gunmetal gray to steel blue, cold green, or, in a rare and paranormal exception, amber. Never, however, are the hero's eyes purple. That's indubitably too gay.

Eyes are a simple task, really, and for a while there, most heroes were indistinguishable from the "tall, dark, and handsome" model except by the colors of their eyes. And after the eyes, there's one element you cannot forget: the eyelashes. No hero has stubby, forgettable eyelashes. They're always long, deceptively sooty, and visible from at least two to three acres away. When the heroine gives her survey of the hero, and notes the things about him that she cannot help but stare at, his eyes, and then his eyelashes, are nearly always mentioned. Long eyelashes are that first key that This Is the Hero because somehow eyelashes have become synonymous with some deeper, hidden sensitivity and kindness. No one who has long, sweeping eyelashes is evil, obviously.

Once you've picked the best shade for your hero's flinty, steely gray eyes, consider hair color choices, such as:

- Black
- Brown
- Auburn
- Blond

It can be reasonably simple to physically craft a hero. They have dark hair, most of them, with the occasional blond running about, they wear their hair in such a way that indicates they aren't aware of it in the least—which is just ludicrous when you think about the burgeoning men's hair-care industry and the number of men who obsess about their hair and how much they have of it. Sometimes the hero's hair is a touch longer than is fashionable. Sometimes it's short and effortless. Sometimes it's buzzed off entirely, which is standard operating procedure if your hero is in the military. But whatever style the hero sports, there aren't many scenes of him using mousse, gel, or even a comb and a mirror at the same time. Usually he'll run his fingers through his hair and be done with it—never mind that the average male usually runs his fingers through his hair to wipe something off in the absence of a napkin or a tissue.

Once you've got hair and eye color, you can work out the details of his nose (Roman? Patrician? Straight? Pointed? Slightly crooked from a possible fight in years past? That's always good for a sexy, dangerous touch!) and his lips (Sensitive! Kissable! Full!). The hero's lips can be firm to unyielding, and he can wield them in a punishing manner or press them together in leashed fury. Regardless, the heroine will usually notice them, and come into personal contact with them soon enough.

Now it's time to locate the hero, by which we mean time period. If he's historical, he needs himself a lordly title. Not every hero is a lord, but many of them are. And you know what you need to find the perfect title for your hero?

Us, of course.

Create the Perfect Title for your Lordly Hero! Pick one word from columns A, B, or C to craft the title that conveys both his lordly peerage and his dark, dangerous, sultry, and potentially hilly personality.

Predatory Animal	Geographical Formation	Color or Temperature
Hawk	Crag	Slate
Ram	Cliff(e)	Black
Peregrine	Land	Gray
Eagle	Shire	Cobalt
Lyger	Hollow	Charcoal
Falcon	Rock	Emerald
Lion	Palisade	Cold
Wolf	Ton	Burn
Hound	Swamp	Chill
Fox	Ridge	Fire
Bear	Water	Numb

Note: These titles are not exclusively English. A lordly sort of hero could easily be Scottish, or even from another part of Europe entirely. But most of them are English. As a matter of fact, according to the ICH Facebook status, they're all at Almack's right now, drinking off-temperature lemonade and cursing the lack of brandy and the more lame and obvious titles bestowed upon them.

But suppose your hero is a contemporary sort of fellow. He needs himself a job. He can be any number of color combinations, and he might even have a title, but modern men need jobs, because not only are they jobs, they are identities. This symbiotic linkage of purpose and person is very American, where not a single cocktail hour goes by without someone asking, "What do you do?" and having to give the response, "I'm a _____." Notice the use of "to be." Not "I run a romance review Web site." The shorter, more authoritative answer, at least for us, is, "I'm a Bitch." Marvelous for us, but if you're not so fond of being identified by your occupation, well, in the United States, you're shit out of luck.

And so is the hero. The hero's occupation often forms a shorthand to his character. He's a cop, a SEAL, a security consultant? He has bulging biceps, a tendency toward suspicion, and trusts no one, not even Fox Mulder. He's an artist, or a writer? He's ornery, isolated, somewhat misanthropic, and not at all pleased to see you. He's a diplomat, a CEO, a billionaire CEO diplomat? A tycoon of some unidentified industry? He's ruthless, confident, perhaps even debonair and stylish in an effortlessly authoritative way. See what we mean? Job = identity = shorthand character sketch. So, let us give you a hand: shuffle the deck of romance cliché job options!

Army Ranger	Jewel thief
Art thief	Navy SEAL
Assassin	Police officer
Billionaire	Scrabble champion
CEO, unspecified industry	Secret agent
CIA agent	Security agent
Code breaker	Sheikh
Consultant of unknown specialty	Slayer of evil
Cowboy	Sniper
Detective	Surgeon
Doctor	Tycoon, unspecified industry
FBI agent	Vampire
Former military operative	Weaponry expert
Highland warrior	Werewolf

Heroes are, in some ways, more constrained in their career choices than heroines, because readers want the hero's career to be sexy. Doctors are good—lots of cultural cachet, right? But only sexy doctor jobs are good: the life-saving ones that deal with exotic specialties and bits that aren't too squidgy. Neurosurgeon, cardiovascular surgeon, pediatrician, ER doctor? Ding, ding, ding, ding. Podiatrist, gynecologist, proctologist, urologist, dermatologist specializing in disorders of the sweat glands? Bzzzzt. No.

Jobs that are associated with femininity are also *tref,* unless they involve athleticism or also carry considerable cultural cachet. Hairdresser, dog groomer, and kindergarten teacher are questionable; opera singer, fashion designer, and ballet dancer, on the other hand, are fair game, if somewhat rare.

And furthermore, we want the heroes to have jobs in positions of power, preferably one that's superior to the heroine's. Boss-secretary romances published by Harlequin still sell, if the crop of virgin boardroom mistress titles don't lead us wrong. But one in which the heroine is the boss, and the hero the secretary? Rare. If the heroine has superior rank in some way, it generally has to be balanced by the hero being a complete and utter badass in some other way. Is she the CEO of some Fortune 500 company? Then he's a tough-talking supercop, and he's going to save her very rich, very fine ass from some terrorists.

Pedestrian middle-management jobs are also unsexy and therefore unheroic. You probably won't see a hero who's an accountant, a warranty adjuster, a warehouse manager, or an associate manager of marketing—unless he's embroiled in some sort of massive mess and accidentally becomes an action hero. Danger can make any job sexy.

Except proctology. Dangerous proctology makes all of us want to curl up in a tiny ball and cry.

No matter what your hero's name, color combination, title, or job, there are ten guidelines you need to be aware of in terms of the hunka hot manly man action in a romance. Like the Pirate's Code, these aren't so much rules as they are guidelines. Very powerful, virile, smooth-chested guidelines.

10. Betas are tough—to sell.

Some people adore them, but most romance heroes are alpha males so alpha they erect flagpoles in their front yards so every morning they can take a whizz in the highest possible spot.

The exception to the rule: Candy can go on for about twelve hours about her very favorite aforementioned beta hero, Christy from Patricia Gaffney's *To Love and to Cherish*. The role of forbidden attraction and Christy's marvelously strong character despite not being the typical alpha male are deeeelicious. But usually, alpha males—not alphole males, please!—rule the pages of your nearest romance novel.

9. Heroes are never stupid.

They can be locked within their own bodies following a brain seizure, unable to speak clearly or even communicate at all, but they are never stupid. Stupidity is never heroic. Even in its most twisted, hidden form, so disguised you can't tell it's there, intelligence is always present, like the Duke of Jervaulx in Kinsale's *Flowers from the Storm*. He's a profligate rake, debauched to the very thread of his hemlines, but he's a math genius—so even when he's rendered mute, he's brilliant—and brilliantly angry. When Maddy Timms, a quiet Quaker woman, realizes that he can't talk but can still think, it's a very angst-drenched but powerful romance, among the best written, bar none.

8. Heroes rarely travel in packs, and if they do, they come in those convenient individually packaged single-serving-size packs: in a group, yet completely alone.

With the advent of the werewolf hero, people are right now probably firing up their Gmail accounts to tell us how wrong we are about that one, because their favorite hero, Davien Earlesviscoundukertoffwoffwoff, is totally a werewolf and has a pack of fourteen brothers, each with his own sequel and they are *so good*—yes, yes, we know. But hear us out.

The werewolves travel in packs. The vampires, they're solitary but sometimes show up in covens or dens or mausoleums or what have you. In historicals, men have friends, school chums, or drinking buds from the club—usually who place bets that they'll never get married (silly, silly men) and thus sequels are made. In contemporaries, sometimes the men have partners on the police force or buddies from way back when, but most of the time, they are alone. Heroes may travel in a pack, but within the space of their narratives, they walk alone. Why? Because alphas travel alone. Even in a group, the hero is alone in the crowd. Even running with the pack or streaking through the flying buttresses of your nearest abandoned church, by virtue of being the hero, he is set apart, isolated, and alone. It creates a mystique for the reader, and the heroine, to investigate: the solitary, aloof hero who needs that healing love.

On one hand, that creates a wide and desolate space in the hero's life that needs some shaking up by your friendly neighborhood perky heroine. And on that same hand it means the hero doesn't come equipped with five guy buddies from college or high school or prep school or the gaming hell or the local werebar or blood bank, who will sit around on poker night, drink all the beer, and fart until the living room wallpaper blisters. So that solitude, it's a fantasy for the heroine in more than one way.

7. Heroes are never soft. They are hard. Everywhere.

They may have crisp chest hair, or soft queues of brown wavy hair on their heads (no, the other head), but from the top of that head (still that other one) to the tips of his hairy toes, the hero, he is one muscular dude. He may be described as lean, muscled, shapely, and downright mouthwatering, but there's not a torso tire to be seen on this specimen of manhood. Even in a historical era wherein the titled men took pains to avoid any and all connection to actual physical labor and most likely stuffed their flabby selves into their waistcoats each night, the romance hero, he is a sleek, lithe physique just waiting to be described in minute detail and summarily unwrapped by the heroine. Romance is publishing more books about heroines of size; heroes of size we doubt will ever see their day.

6. Heroes have hair. The covers have mullets.
There is no Rogaine needed.

Honestly, this one mystifies us a bit. We don't know of too many women who give a flying shit whether their husbands or boy-friends have hair. This is something, we think, that men worry about or are told to worry about, so what all that full-headed hero hair is doing in the romance genre, we have no idea. Perhaps it's that same beauty pressure that makes sure the heroines have long legs—hairless even before the invention of the women's razor, of course!—and long, cascading waves of hair, but the heroes all have a full complement of hair on their heads. No romance hero ever has a thinning spot up top. No ripple of sunlight ever bounces off the dome of a hero's head. And the heroic comb-over? Ain't no such thing unless maybe the false hero who is really the villain has a greasy one—and that comb-over is probably the heroine's first clue that he's eeeeeevil.

5. He's an expert. At something.

The romance hero is often isolated by his own brilliance, in addi-tion to being set apart personally and emotionally—or entirely shut off emotionally until the heroine awakens those scary feelings in his loins, followed by a burning sensation in his heart not caused by spicy sausage, unless it's a gay romance, in which case it could be a spicy sausage but that's an entirely different situation. Sorry. Where were we?

Heroes in romance are experts at something. Perhaps he's a mathematician. Astronomer. Scientist. Clever wordsmith. Master horsemen—so many of historical heroes are exceptionally perfect equestrians that it's a wonder how a one of them stand out. The hero could be a marksman, sharpshooter, bomb diffuser, forensic accountant, micro surgeon, flawless Java programmer, possess-ing of the ability to fly or the ability to swim beneath the Atlantic Ocean on a single breath, able to make mental leaps into logic that befuddle mere mortals. . . . Whatever—not only are looks and emotional distance employed to set the hero apart and above, but skill set as well. The hero may have an open advantage or a hidden one, but he employs something with razor-sharp talent and effortless skill, be it swordplay or sword swallowing.

4. Sex with his stick is like sex on a stick.
But in a good way.

The hero, he may be overwhelmed by feelings of love, lust, lusty love, or a syrupy mix thereof, but without a doubt, it is largely his responsibility to bring on the orgasms for the heroine, and in the sexual arena, the hero must prove his ardor and his strength by finding without fail all of the heroine's magic spots. Sex with a romance hero is a form of perfection we mere mortal readers can rarely, if ever, attain.

3. Swinging and gayness: not okay.

There are obvious exceptions to this rule found within erotic romance, and there are marvelous examples of heroes who swing both ways on the sexual spectrum, and of heroes who, with their heroine, engage in a big ring-around-the-rosy-fuck with other couples. But by and large, by which we mean Not Bi and Yes Large, heroes of romance novels in the traditional sense may have had past relationships, but they were with women. And they're over. And likely that woman is a cold, evil nemesis who must be destroyed. Romance heroes are not gay or even remotely possibly gay, nor do they notice other men in any way other than people to move past in the store to get to the manly Cheetos. Not that there's anything wrong with being gay, obviously. Not in our opinion. But unfortunately, even as the market of romance readers clamors for more male/male gay romance, the stereotype of "gay = not manly" still resides in the backwater of Romancelandia, and no hero worth his manly wang has ever used that wang to probe the depths of another man's what-what.

2. Rage, it's in their machine.

Heroes, even the betas, have something that sets them off, just like most people. There's something that pushes their buttons, that turns them into raging hunks of anger. Could be jealousy. Could be crime against the innocent. Could be anything that threatens his teddy bear, Mr. Schrumpkins. But whatever it is, there is no rage like hero rage, and it is a rage that must be tamed by heroine's luuuuurve™ and her Magic Hoo Hoo.

1. Historical anachronisms: they will never die, but they make your hero luscious.

Just as romance writers take heat for historically inaccurate heroines, like the plucky governess in 1813 who just wants to open her own business creating metal cogs for a gentleman named Cogsworth, heroes themselves are also largely historically inaccurate, particularly during the Regency era. As Pamela Regis writes in her examination of the collective novels of Georgette Heyer, "The Regency is renowned for its fops, dandies, reckless 'bucks,' profligate gamblers, and imperious guardians. As A. S. Byatt has noted, it may be the English historical period in which the wealthy were the most secure in their wealth, and the most idle." While those idle men may appear in Regency romances, including but not limited to Heyer's, they are not ever the hero. Idle hands are indeed the devil's work—labor in some form, even oblique, is far more noble and suitable for noble heroes.

Interestingly, Regis argues that the twentieth-century mentality of historical heroes and heroines not only highlights the setting but critiques it through their very presence. Heroes may belong to gambling clubs and frequently bet one or two piles of poundage while at play, drink until their livers cry out for mercy, and perhaps even keep multiple mistresses, but they are still set apart from the profligate wastrelism and are restored in some small way to respectability.

So, how come heroic men can get away with majestically damaging behavior? Suppose you're writing a romance hero, and he's hell-bent on smoking everything that doesn't run away from him, drinking to excess, and perhaps even abusing himself in myriad ways. Therein lies the key. There are some habits a hero does not ever indulge in, because doing so compromises his inner core of turgid, shining, golden, chewy, moral goodness. He can abuse his physical body in all kinds of funny, appalling ways, but he does not mess with the innocence of others, except for, of course, the heroine. To be cavalier with the lives of others is not ever heroic behavior. Irresponsible gambling on the part of a historical hero is a no-no, simply because any hero worth his property is also responsible for the lives—literally—of every tenant on his land. Gambling people's lives is not heroic, and heroes are certainly not going to bet the farm. In the case of a contemporary hero, an attitude of wasteful ignorance about money will dig the happy ending out from under his feet, because what woman wants to spend her Happily Ever After with a man who wastes five dollars?

Of course, the immortal set, such as the vampires and the profoundly long-lived werewolves, they usually have vast Templaresque financial networks setup, because there's no money like old money to guarantee the happiest of endings in the plushest of circumstances.

But essentially, heroism in romance novels comes down to sex. Heroes are fiercely sexual, and sexually fierce. They do not embark on pedophilic affairs, they do not engage in any what-what with horses, sheep, or trained elephant seals, and they do not use their mighty wangs to rape or teabag anyone—except, depending on how Old Skool the romance is, the heroine.

But when the hero does embark upon the discovery of the heroine, whether you see the protagonists as two separate people from yourself as a reader, or the integration of two of your socially influenced personality types, the coming together—and the coming together—of the hero and the heroine are the true crux of romance fiction. Regardless of how or what you see in the hero or heroine, they, and their story, are the major reason we keep coming back for more.

Chapter Secret Cowboy Baby

CRINGE-WORTHY PLOT DEVICES
WE KNOW AND LOVE

You want to know the secret to a really, really good romance plot? Take something utterly familiar, like a fairy tale, or an overexposed cliché so tired it can't even lift its own head, and turn it upside down and shake it until you don't recognize it anymore.

Secret baby? A secret baby plot in the hands of a skilled writer can rock one's socks right to the dryer. Noblemen disguised as pirates? Better yet, disguised noblemen who masquerade as pirates, and who kidnap the absurdly perfect, plucky heroine? Revenge sex? Virginity in absolutely ludicrous situations? Scarred hero healed by the power of love and a dashing good plastic surgeon? Seen it, read it, and while some of them blow windy donkey balls, other romance novels that embrace with both arms the hoary plot cliché work it and work it well.

Nora Roberts refuses to identify her favorite of the goofy cliché plot devices. In fact, she embraces every silly one: "I love them all. Secret babies, amnesia, the letter gone missing for ten years, evil twins, mistaken identity, the feisty runaway heroine disguised as a boy, the thirty-year-old virgin. Hell, I've probably written them all."

But ultimately, Roberts agrees: "It's all about the execution.

One writer's secret baby fiasco is another's heart-wrenching classic, or delightful comedic romp."

If you're reading this book for serious writing advice, don't listen to us. Listen to Nora: "As a rule of thumb, I'd say one cliché per story—and then be damn sure you can make it work. But if you're going to try to write the virginal amnesiac twin disguised as a boy mistaken for the mother (or father depending how well the disguise works) of a secret baby, honey, you better have some serious skills. Or seek therapy."

Each of us has a weakness for the romance plot that is cheeztastic and doofy, but which we cannot resist. One of Sarah's favorites is the attracted antagonists device, which she calls, "I don't wanna love you. I don't wanna like you. I can't stop thinking about your hair, dammit?!" The panicked male overcome by feelings he doesn't like, irritated yet unable to deny his rampant boner whenever she's near? Yes, please! Sarah also loves a plot device that is so tinged by the shades of skeevy that she won't admit it outright, but she still haunts the historical romance aisle looking for more of it. It's so awful, she can't even tell Candy.

Candy's favorite is a bit different: she'll go for anything pirates. Scurvy pirates, noblemen disguised as pirates, kidnapping by pirates—rwor! There's absolutely no reason she should like it, and it's kind of horrifying, but she loves it. If the heroine charms the crew and their pet pig, Candy's all over that shit. You can probably guess which is her very favorite romance of this type.

THE BIG MISUNDERSTANDING

Let's start with the most hoary clichéd conflict of them all: the Big Misunderstanding, or the "Big Mis." The key to satisfying romance, to speak in sweeping generalization, which of course we do with arrogant abandon, is to layer the internal and external conflicts so that they complement and contrast against one another. It's not merely enough that he's a vampire and she's a werewolf; biological incompatibility can easily be resolved by some mysterious parentage or deus ex machina ending. Resolutions that require no effort on the part of the hero and heroine usually result in a slightly less satisfying ending.

The Big Mis is the humdinger of them all because it's an external conflict that causes internal conflict, all balanced on the flimsiest of circumstances. She overhears something incorrect; he sees her kiss her brother and flips out. Whatever the Big Mis is, it could be resolved *so* easily with five minutes of conversation and an arsehair of honesty out of both parties.

The damage of the Big Mis is legion, and the number of plots that have squeaked out an additional two hundred pages based on its flimsy core are too many to count using mere integers. The Big Mis and its continuation cause the reader to doubt the intelligence of the couple and, what's worse, their ability to sustain a happy ending on their own. If the Big Mis is the basis for all the conflict, it's especially damaging.

Now, this is not to say that the Big Mis is a no-no. The great and somewhat frightening thing about romance novels is that just about any hoary, clichéd plot device can be properly devised to add to the plot, provided that plot device is used in a way that adds to the conflict, and is not itself the *only* conflict. Case in point: Jennifer Crusie's *Bet Me* is based on a Big Misunderstanding between the protagonists, but it's resolved relatively quickly, and is used as a device to bring the characters together for additional conflict based on their personalities. Crusie's method of turning that plot device on its head was to have her heroine figure out the misunderstanding, identify it, confront the hero—instead of ruminating on it by herself—and use that misunderstanding to her own advantage.

The upshot is simple: Big Mis leading the Better, Bigger Conflict? WIN! Big Mis is only conflict? Go Thee to the Naughty Corner.

Heather Osborn, editor for Tor, uses this rule of thumb to judge the conflict of a story: "If you ever read a well-written story that you really want to like and yet you feel a little let down when you finish, like you just ate puffed air instead of food, then chances are it was seriously lacking in internal conflict." As far as the Big Mis goes, a heroine or hero who takes the Big Mis at face value and disregards everything they have learned of the other person based on it shows a lack of internal character and intelligence. Such a lack makes them unappealing to the reader. For a Big Mis to work, it needs to be a minor part of the story as a whole, or there needs to be a reasonable and authentic reason for the misunderstanding in the first place. As is oft repeated, if the misunderstanding is one that can be cleared up with a simple conversation, then it is not sufficient conflict. (See if *you* can avoid the relationship pitfalls and reach a happy ending in the Big Misunderstanding game on page 116.)

CRAFT A BRILLIANT ROMANCE AVOIDING THE BIG MIS, AKA EVERY PLOT CLICHÉ, EVER

One of our readers, Nicole Collins, who posts at our site under the moniker "Dr. Strangelove," wrote us after reading what she called the most cliché-ridden romance she'd ever endured. Her e-mail went a little something like this . . . Hit it:

Dear Smart Bitches:
A friend of mine from school picked up an entire bag of romance novels from the university book sale for two dollars and dared me to read them. Seeing as I told her to get only those with the most treated clinch art (you know, waves and wind blowing from every which direction) or with great titles I wasn't expecting much. In an effort to avoid studying for two hours I picked up a Silhouette series book from 1998. It was such a train wreck of every type of romance stereotype I couldn't put it down. You could make a check list of horrible romance clichés.

1. Heroine gets unfrumpified by miraculously losing some pounds and cutting her hair.
2. Hero has guilt complex over death of last wife. He is also hideously scarred along one side of face from accident that killed wife.

3. Hero is millionaire who takes in heroine after fire almost burns down her office. Wants to help her because she reminds him of dead wife (this is really creepy).
4. Heroine has no real education or talents and yet is considered witty and bright, or so the author states every page or so.
5. Heroine is a virgin.
6. Hero can "never love again" (*see* dead wife, self-wallowing).
7. Heroine takes inappropriate live-in job as millionaire bachelor's assistant. Without an education in economics or business, or even an iota of sense really, she manages to kick the ass of every guy on staff at millionaire bachelor's firm.
8. After three weeks of boinking, heroine realizes she should go to doc's and get some birth control. Of course she's already pregnant. She gives some lip service to knowing better but keeps coming back to her being a virgin as an excuse.
9. Heroine has a bizarre bit of backbone-filled dialog that is completely out of character and leaves. Hero then vanishes, as in leaves his company for five months (!) so she can't tell him about the secret baby.
10. Hero gets plastic surgery, offers marriage, and finds out he's going to be a dad.

Seriously, did this little book miss a single stereotype? I don't think so.

PS: As a medical student I'd just like to complain about the heroine's whining about her knee. Jesus, Allah and Buddha, woman, you only had some arthroscopy done. That's an outpatient procedure and not six weeks of lying around because you're too inept to manage crutches.

Unquestionably awesome spontaneous review aside, we don't think Dr. Strangelove's account missed a stereotype of contemporary romance. The big ones are all there:

Heroine experiences life-changing makeover and develops instant self-confidence as a result, like the reverse of instant pudding. It's that fast. Quickly thin = effortlessly self-confident.

Hero has deep personal injury only the heroine can (a) know and (b) heal. It's a health crisis, a bum leg, some random muscle cramp, or a snaggle tooth, but it's manful, whatever it is. And it's among the easiest ways to lend humanity and vulnerability to the hero, hands down: a secret flaw that, on the whole, isn't really a big deal, but to the hero it is everything and then some. And only the heroine can soothe away his shame and anguish.

And of course there's the flip side to this bizarre healing: if the heroine is for some reason infertile (endometriosis, or a completely absent uterus, for example) there's always the miracle of the hero, and his Mighty Wang. Infertility? No problem for the forces of true love. Yeah. Spend five minutes singing that nonsense in the waiting room of your nearest reproductive endocrinologist and see how long before someone knocks you unconscious.

Health problems are always monstrously debilitating, even when in real life it would be no big deal. Yes, a cold could kill you Back in the Day, but a heroine with the sniffles does not necessarily mean she's gonna *diiiie*. And why is it always a cold? One supercontagious congestion could kill thousands Back in the Days of a historical romance, but regardless of time period, one sneeze from the heroine and it's time to summon the doctor and the mortician, because fever and chills are life-threatening. It's almost the flip side to a man cold. You know, when men get a cold and it's the end of the known world because it is *so serious*? For heroines in romance novels, sickness is always dire. It's a straight shot to drama and a dark moment of doom: illness! Their future happiness hinged on the risk of pneumococcal virus strains! Oh, noes!

Then there's the **Secret That Could Destroy Them Both** but probably isn't that big of a deal. It could be a secret identity, a secret baby, a horrible crime that's being covered up. But the secret, it haunts and burns like when you really have to pee and there's only lonesome miles of highway ahead of and behind you, just you and that secret riding shotgun.

Time travel: It's kind of like a metaphor for sex: forward, backward, into and out of parallel dimensions. Someone gets culture shock, but everyone gets nookie.

Another plot that appears in every subgenre: **My Reputation Is Ruined!** Ruination plots deal with the destruction and potential restoration of the heroine and her reputation. Sometimes it's the hero, but since the hero is a dude, he usually suffers little over his reputation. The heroine, particularly in a historical, can be crushed under rumors of her skanky ways. Interestingly, the ruination plot can be found in contemporary novels as well: losing business reputation, enduring humiliation by corporate takeover, or being dumped in public in front of her worst frenemy.

As we mentioned in our examination of the Mighty Wang, and what a lovely exam it was, the strength and frequency of the ruination plot assures romance readers that, unless "ruination" is specified in the plot summary, any and all nookifying is cleared for takeoff. If you're not reading a ruination book, once the hero and heroine start riding the booty train, they will never get caught. The whole world disappears. That in and of itself is another one of our favorite plot clichés—invisible nookie!

And to whom does that fantasy play? Anyone who has ever had to sneak in a sexual interlude, anytime, any place. The assurance that the toddler will not wake up, that the nosy neighbor will not hear, that the parents upstairs will be none the wiser to the bumpus going down in the rumpus room? That's heady stuff indeed.

Combine those with some other masterful clichés, and anyone can create the Most Ultimate Romance Plot Tangle Ever! Looking for ideas? Read on, and see if you can guess in which book (or books) these plot clichés appeared.

- The hero was boinking heroine only because heroine's father inadvertently caused his wife's death. Revenge is sweetest when visited upon innocent, nubile offspring, oh yesss.
- He then blackmails her into fucking him. Because blackmail sex = hottt.

- Heroine hit her head shortly after fucking hero and loses all memory, including the fact that she loathes the hero.
- Hero throws a shit fit when he finds out she's pregnant and accuses her of being a slut because she once smiled at his second cousin.
- Don't forget her virginity shall set her free, due to the Hymen That Proves She's a Lady.
- The hero is unable to control himself and boinks the heroine in all number of inappropriate places, and maybe they get caught and maybe they don't, but it's *her* fault for her irresistibleness, and thus, she's a whore.

Villains are not immune from the dreaded plot cliché, either. Just like in an action movie, in a romance, the villain is almost al-

---

Our Favorites from Moviefone.com's
Worst Action-Movie Clichés

1. *Henchmen Are Lousy Shots*
   Best parody of this ever? *True Lies* when Tom Arnold evades an assassin's shots by hiding his girth behind . . . a 4-inch lamppost. Every shot misses, of course!
2. *The Female Hostage*
   There is always a hostage, and she rarely fights back. Usually, she just whimpers. Lame!
3. *Government Files at Your Fingertips*
   There are always government files accessible with two clicks and a Starbucks wifi connection. Hold on to latte, and for God's sake don't spill on your adorable, Apple-product-placement-appropriate laptop!
4. *Check for a Pulse, Dummy*
   As we all know, there's "dead dead" and "mostly dead." Mostly dead? Slightly alive!
5. *I Think I Love My Ex-Husband*
   He's been wandering around fighting crime and a bad Scotch habit for months, maybe even years. But one widdle cut on his widdle manly forehead, and, oops, she did it again.

ways the one unattractive and not-entirely-saintly person who gets significant screen time. In fact, more than a few movie clichés cross the border into Romancelandia. For example, the wacky sidekick for the heroine is always more slutty, more freewheeling, and more cynical about men than the heroine.

Then there's the symbolic clichés: if you're the hero and you're trying to take over the heroine's company, you're invariably trying to do what's best for the company and represent the March of Progress. If you're the heroine and trying to take over the hero's company, you're invariably attempting to crush the spirit of independent business and represent that Oppression of the Man on Individuality.

And let us not forget: bareback realism. Forgoing condoms means it's true love, baby. Riding the pony sans saddle is another covert nod to virginity, and has been a sex scene cliché since the dawn of the dance as old as time.

Romance Trends We've Known and Loved (and Loved to Hate)

Sometimes, if we romance readers are really lucky, a plot cliché will become a trend, and then, it's just a short hop to becoming a subgenre. All plot clichés want to grow up to be subgenres, and some of them do. And lo, we loved them, or hated them, or both. And we'll start with Candy's favorite.

Trend 1: Pirates!
Real-life pirates were filthy, diseased-ridden rapists, murderers, and thieves. Remove the filth and disease, and hey, presto! You had a perfectly viable romance novel hero. Pirate romances saw their heyday in the 1970s and early '80s, with a minor revival in the late '90s. Back at the peak of pirate romance fever, you couldn't swing a saber without smacking some delicious young ingénue who'd been vilely kidnapped by a harsh-faced yet beautiful seafaring rogue who was really the misunderstood son of a filthy-rich nobleman. The

potential for High Drama on Even Higher Seas was endless. Besides all the exotic locales, there's the skullduggery that attends falling in love with a criminal. She hates him! She loves him! They fight! They make love! They fight! They make love! He killed her brother! But then he also rescued her from being raped by that other pirate—you know, the one who's equally brutal, except he belongs to a different pirate's union, one with less comprehensive benefits, so his teeth are nastier and he has a hunchback. But as the times changed, so did the pirate heroes.

The Best Pirate Romance: The Windflower by Laura London. Possibly one of the best romance novels, ever, and yes, this is Candy's favorite, and a favorite among many romance readers. Charming innocent is kidnapped by mistake by a bored, dissolute aristo-posing-as-a-privateer, big secrets galore, and the heroine charms the entire crew of the ship—including the pet pig. Whose name is Dennis.

Guilty Pleasure Piracy: Suspend your disbelief on a high, high peg, and reach for Gaelen Foley's 1998 debut novel, *The Pirate Prince.* Mediterranean islands, warring families, royals and rebels, and a pirate prince? High Camp on the High Seas, and a reading indulgence like Oreo cookies and milk.

Special Buttpirate Mention: In Darlene Marshall's *Pirate's Price,* the heroine is a cross-dresser, and her pirate ship is staffed entirely by *gay pirates* (plus a gunner with an unhealthy attachment to his pet goose).

Two Great Tastes That Taste Great Together: Nancy Block's *Once Upon a Pirate* combines pirates *and* time-travel. Temporal dislocation + yarrrr = win.

Delicious, Delicious Wrongness: Lisa Kleypas's *Only with Your Love* features a heroine who ends up being involved with a pair of identical twins, and it's the evil twin who ends up being the hero. One of Candy's favorite guilty pleasure novels, the only way this could've gotten any wronger and hotter was if the heroine, Celine, had enjoyed a threesome with the Vallerand brothers.

On Our Wish List: A pirate romance featuring a set of twins, both of whom are pirates. And the evil twin is a time-traveling female pirate. And her first mate is a ninja, and they have kinky sex all up and down the foc's'le. This one hasn't been written yet, but somebody needs to get on it.

Trend 2: The Never-Ending Series Featuring Vaguely Homoerotic Spy Rings, Secret Clubs, and Societies Named After Celestial or Diabolical Elements and/or the Copious Progeny of Some Damn Family or Other; Twee Naming Schemes Mandatory

The 1990s and earlier part of the 2000s saw the rise of the interconnected romances. It's extremely rare for romance novels to have true sequels; the Happily Ever After definitively marks the end of the story arc for the hero and heroine, since the focus of the romance novel is overwhelmingly the discovery and securing of romantic love. As Kay Mussell pointed out in *Fantasy and Reconciliation: Contemporary Formulas of Women's Romance Fiction*, having that arc fucked with and showing the hero and heroine breaking up and getting together with other people would mean the characters had made a mistake the first time around, and we certainly can't have that, can we? There are a few other options, such as killing off one of the original protagonists, but that's the sort of buzzkill no romance author would touch with a ten-foot pole. Or the author can opt for a Series of Unfortunate Misunderstandings (with bonus Long Separation) to milk the conflict for all it's worth, as Rosemary Rogers did for her Sweet Savage Love trilogy, or as Karen Robards did for her Island series, which is a trickier thing to pull now that Old Skool romances have fallen out of favor.

Nowadays, if authors and readers want to revisit old characters and watch them age gracefully, they find themselves some books featuring distinct yet interconnected love stories. Hence, huge numbers of spy organizations, Special Forces groups, and families in Romancelandia suddenly saw all their members being set up in grand old style, often at clockwork intervals. Reunions in later books would usually result in a near-nauseating collection of the most gorgeous, titled, powerful, and progressive-for-their-time couples and their adorable, impeccably behaved children.

Most Humptastic: Stephanie Laurens's Cynster series. It's a wonder that none of the Bar Cynster have dropped dead from heat exhaustion. Their fiddly bits must be made from some sort of titanium-Teflon alloy to withstand the copious amounts of friction. Frankly, we think NASA should look into the composition of their genitalia for spacecraft applications, and perhaps investigate possible uses for overcoming the perpetual motion conundrum.

Most Cracktastic: Probably a tie between Mary Jo Putney's Fallen Angels series and Jo Beverley's Mallorens. The Fallen Angels have two different twee naming schemes going for them (almost all the heroes are named after angels, and the book titles of the original members of the Fallen Angels feature elements of weather), while the Malloren siblings are named after notable Anglo-Saxons. Both series feature court intrigue, spy shenanigans, plenty of high adventure, and cross-dressing protagonists. What's not to love?

Unquestionably Cracktastic: The Black Dagger Brotherhood by J. R. Ward. Ward took the rhyming scheme and khicked it up a nhotch lihke whoa, coupling giant badass vampires with Valley-girl lexicons and a love of luxury and high-end weaponry. Oh, and a life-and-death battle for supremacy with a cloud of powder-smelling weirdos. And hot, hot vampire sex.

Most Adorably Functional Family Ever. Julia Quinn's Bridgertons. Somebody just saint Violet Bridgerton already, eh?

Trend 3: Navy SEALs and Special Forces

A governmental institution with a spotty record of admitting women, and a policy toward gay Americans that we're not supposed to ask or tell about? A job that in current climates guarantees active duty in a military campaign? Training with weapons, strategy, and medicine for athlete's foot? A career that is demanding and often leads to high rates of self-destructive behavior, divorce, and emotional and spiritual fracture, not to mention post-traumatic stress disorder?

Oh, yes, now that is romantic.

The secrecy, the code of honor, the understanding that the moral core of the military protagonist is unshakable and completely dependable—okay, we can see how that can be sexy, especially when housed within a toned, fit, hot, and definitely lethal body. Military romance is a trend that won't dissipate anytime soon, and there are plenty of examples of which Special Forces romances should be . . . okay, between "rear admiral," "saluting soldier," "heat-seeking missile" and all the other possible jokes, our heads just exploded.

Modern Major General of Military Romance: That would be any and all Suzanne Brockmann romances, who took the Navy SEAL and the military hero and dipped him in awesome with a sidecar of Hottie McHot-Hot. From explosive (literally) pairings between protagonists on an elite Special Forces team to a multibook second-ary story that culminated in a much anticipated resolution of the "Will they or won't they" Sam and Alyssa plotline, Brockmann is the military author we salute.

Air Force Colonel: Catherine Mann's Wingmen Warriors series can't be left out of any list involving military heroes and heroines, because many Bitchery members have recommended her books as among the best.

Four Star General: Lindsay McKenna's name is all over just about every military romance list, and her backlist is a big 'un.

Trend 4: Romantic Suspense

Ah, those tough-talking, loose-cannon cops, detectives, private investigators and spies with their big guns and even bigger cocks. Much like the Navy SEALs and Special Forces people, these guys see some of the highest divorce rates of any occupation in real life, with fairly high rates of alcoholism and low life expectancies. No

wonder their counterparts in romance novels are so damn angry—
you'd be, too, if you no longer had your booze.

Romantic suspence gathered steam in the late 1980s and by the
mid-'90s was selling like damn, with authors like Sandra Brown,
Linda Howard, and Anne Stuart upping the dead body and Anti-
hero count in Romancelandia. And then with the dawning of the
twenty-first century (cue theme from *2001: A Space Odyssey*), female
agents came into their own and actually got to kick ass every once
in a while. Many of them were even halfway competent at it, and
some even got to rescue the hero.

*If you like your heroes shouty, with constant, massive hard-ons every time
the heroine walks on the scene:* let Linda Howard and Susan Andersen
be your guide.

Best Antiheroes: Anne Stuart, hands down. Look, *Moonrise* had
a hero who was a cult leader. How awesome is that shit? Stuart's
bad-boy heroes come from some truly dark, grimy places, and they
show it.

Still gives Sarah nightmares: Nora Roberts started introducing suspense elements back when she wrote category, and now her single
title contemporaries often feature a mystery and a romance inter-
twined. Without a doubt, *Blue Smoke* scared the crap out of Sarah,
and she still can't talk about it without making sure the doors and
windows are all locked. And the dog is awake.

Most underrated romantic suspense author, ever: Why wasn't there
more love for Theresa Weir, eh? Why? Whyyyy?

Trend 5: Paranormal and Fantasy Romances

Hard though it may be to imagine, vampires at one point were considered hideous, terrifying creatures. Watch Murnau's *Nosferatu*.
That sort of depiction of vampires was a lot more common for
many, many centuries. And then Bram Stoker came along with his
suave Count, and a century later, getting your blood sucked out by
angst-ridden animated corpses became the hottest thing ever.

Though to be fair, paranormal romances don't just cover angst-ridden bloodsuckers. As we mentioned, the varied cast of characters includes angst-ridden werewolves, angst-ridden shapeshifters of other sorts, angst-ridden witches, angst-ridden aliens, angst-ridden time travelers, angst-ridden psychics, and angst-ridden ghosts. The ones that aren't angst-ridden shoot over to the other side and tend to be flip, lighthearted first-person accounts about what a drag it is to be, say, a demon slayer, or a vampire hunter, or Queen of the Vampires. Paranormals had been on the fringes of Romancelandia almost since its inception but became huge business in the early 2000s. Now, the romance shelves of your nearest bookstore are flush with the undead and hairy.

Best shoe-obsessed vampire queen, ever: That'd be Betsy Taylor of MaryJanice Davidson's *Undead and Unwed.* Read the other Undead books at your peril, however, as they rapidly become a whole lot less substantial and a whole lot more expensive.

Screw Antiheroes, we want some Antiheroines, too: Meljean Brook's Lilith in *Demon Angel* is a lower-echelon changeling demon, and unabashed about it.

Vampires? In Regency England? Strewth!: Karen Harbaugh wrote, as far as we know, the first traditional Regency to feature a vampire viscount, called (drumroll, please) *The Vampire Viscount.* Plus, there's Colleen Gleason's five-part Gardella series, featuring Victoria Gardella, Regency vampire slayer.

We like 'em hairy, but only once a month: Cracktastically awesome Kelley Armstrong's *Bitten* is a paranormal romance with a werewolf hero *and* heroine, and a wonderfully fascinating and functional pack community.

Buttsecks?: Morgan Hawke's *Fallen Star* and Elizabeth Amber's Lords of the Satyr books feature not heroes who have hemipenes. That's right: one dude, two schlongs. Commence acrobatic buttsecks!

Novels with ginormous crossover appeal: People who love books that focus as much on the love story as on the Sci-Fi/Fantasy setting will likely revel in Lois McMaster Bujold's Miles Vorkosigan series (he's not quite five feet tall, angsty as all hell, and somehow a sex god—

don't ask us how Bujold pulls that off, but she so does) and Sharon Shinn's Samaria series (the lives and loves of genetically engineered angels on an alien planet; what's not to love?).

All steamed up: Emma Holly writes some decently entertaining Victorian-era steampunk in her Demon series, which so far includes *The Demon's Daughter* and *Prince of Ice*. And since it's Emma Holly, you know there's going to be humpin'. A *lot* of humpin'. How much? Let's just say they give the Cynsters a run for their money.

The Whole Paranormal Posse: Kresley Cole's *Immortals After Dark*, despite having titles that are difficult to tell apart, feature the entire posse of paranormal creatures, from werewolves and vampires to Valkyrie, demons, and witches, to say nothing of creatures you might not have read about before.

Trend 6: Erotic Romances

This category is a bit of sticky wicket—and we're not just referring to the hero's dude piston. Given that just a couple of decades ago, most romances could barely mention the word "penis" without giving themselves a case of the vapors, the recent proliferation of romances that use words like "cock," "cunt," and "pussy" without batting so much as an eyelid is nothing short of astonishing. It's not just the language; most erotic romances aren't afraid to explore areas previously considered taboo in romance. Anal sex. Bondage fetishes. Sex toys. Bisexuality. Nonmonogamy for both hero *and* heroine. That's right: group sex, and lots of it, please.

Show me your purple-helmeted soldier of love: Bertrice Small wrote Old Skool erotic romances before they were known as erotic romances. Recognize.

Tea for three: Emma Holly has written some fantastic romances in which the heroine ends up with more than one hot man with whom to play hide the salami, most notably *Strange Attractions* and *Ménage*.

Gay Romance: No, not all gay romance is erotic romance, but much of it easily thrusts itself in either subgenre. For a variety of reasons, many women romance readers love romances wherein the protagonists are both men. And the sex scenes are long, in more ways than one.

WE READ BY PLOT AND BY AUTHOR

Behind every plot cliché, and the pirate earls and Navy SEALs and inspired Coast Guard captains and absurdly huge families with populations that overflow their country manor estates, there's a reader who loves that plot. Plots, in fact, are one of the ways romance readers hunt for books. If it's not the work of a favorite author, it's a particular plot—All About Romance has an ongoing database built on reader suggestions that is sorted by plot or character device. Looking for guardian/ward romances, or romances based on marriages of convenience? They have a list for every type, and continue to build new ones by soliciting reader input.

Similarly, on our site, we have a regular column we call "Good Shit vs. Shit to Avoid," in which we offer a scenario or type of character, and ask for recommendations for books that fit that description. When a reader writes in for help finding books that she may like, more often than not her preference is based on plot twist and setting, and not on character. The plot addiction, it is a mighty, mighty buying impulse.

While shopping by plot leaves room for the old "Oh, so they *are* all the same" bullpucky argument, we know better. And there's no time like the present to start knocking down those arguments as to why your reading material is plebian and lame one by dastardly one. So let's get to it, shall we? Yarrr!

The Smart Bitches' Big Mis Game

It's time to head down the happy trail and play with the Smart Bitches Big Mis! No, not *that*. Damn, you're nasty.

The Big Mis is our first-ever interactive board game, where you're the hero, and you head down the Happy Trail (no, we're not going to get tired of saying that) to reach your Happy Ending *(hur hur)* with the heroine. But many, many big misunderstandings stand miserably in your way.

RULES OF PLAY

1. Find yourself some tools.

   Are you one of the few, the proud, the l33t, who have role-playing-game dice in your immediate reach? One of those dies with 45,924 sides? *Cool.* Go get that. Otherwise, grab a deck of cards and prepare to deal yourself random numbers. Face cards are worth 1. Or use your preferred method to generate random integers between 1 and 10.

2. Then, grab a Barbie shoe, a penny, a condom, an M&M, a piece of dry cat food, or whatever is small and nearby, and use that as your game piece.

3. Use a two-out-of-three round of rock, paper, scissors to determine who goes first, only instead of rock, paper, scissors, obviously it's man titty, pimp hand, legs spread—but you totally knew that.

4. Start your game pieces on the picture of our hero, Thorus

Lancelot Magnuscocke III, Duke of Dieppeshitte, and draw a
card or roll your die.

5. Advance the number of squares indicated by the number you
   see. If you land on a blank square, you're continuing
   unimpeded to the promised land of Happy Ending *(hur hur)*.

6. If you land on a Big Mis, read aloud in your most dramatic
   fashion the misunderstanding that befalls your character, then
   go back the indicated number of squares.

7. If you are moving backward due to Big Misunderstandings, and
   you land on *another* Big Misunderstanding, you must move
   backward the number of squares indicated on that square as
   well. Yeah, we know. We did that on purpose. We suck.

8. First player to reach the promised land for the Happy Ending wins!

ADDITIONAL PRIZES, CONTESTS, AND MASS FUCKNUTTY AWESOMENESS

We are holding a contest to celebrate our book's debut—actually,
we're probably holding more than one, but we're definitely holding this one. Send us pictures or video of your game in action to
bigmisgame@smartbitchestrashybooks.com and we'll pick the best
creative use of game pieces, random number generators, and dramatic readings of Big Mis scenes. Winner will receive:

A signed copy of the book compete with Smart Bitch Book Gift
Set:

- a hot pink flask for drinking games
- pink crystal-encrusted game pieces and pink die for Big Mis
  games
- a pink-crystal custom-made T-shirt that reads "Smart Bitches
  Read Romance" in your choice of size

Game ends May 15, 2009. Void where prohibited, and if you live
in a place where you're not allowed to play goofy board games about
Happy Trails and Happy Endings, might we suggest you consider
moving? Because, dude. Lame. You deserve better.

The *Happy* **Ending**

She's in the arms of Slim the ranch hand. She's a whore! But he doesn't see her knee Slim in the nuts and hog tie him for grabbing her breasts and saying "AOOOOGAH!"

-6 spaces

He acts suspicious and mysterious and comes home reeking of perfume each night! He's really a genius scientist developing a perfume in her honor. But she flips out.

-4 spaces

He sees her leave a bar with some sleazy guy . . . but it's her secret twin. She's a whore!

-5 spaces

She hears him say, "I'd never have kids with someone like her," only he's talking about his ex-girlfriend, the town slut. She flips out.

-2 spaces

Happy Trail

He sees her kissing his very hot cousin—who he knows is gay and in a committed relationship—but he still calls her a whore.

-2 spaces

The BIG MISUNDERSTANDING LAND

She's the daughter of his corporate nemesis. A deal goes sour, and he sees her laughing with her dad. Whore!

-3 spaces

The Boardroom

He's in the boardroom with a stiffy. It's because her skirt just rode up a bit, but she assumes he has a sexual preference for the smell of dry erase markers. Perv!

-4 spaces

The Evil Aunt

He meets the Evil Aunt, who schemes to keep them apart. How? She tells him heroine's a whore. Duh.

-3 spaces

She asks him, "Does this outfit make me look fat?" just as his team scores. He says "Yes!" She flips out.

-3 spaces

She's at the copy store . . . with documents she refuses to show him. It's really his surprise party plans, but he thinks it's corporate secrets . . . so she's a spy *and* a whore!

-4 spaces

Her aunt starts calling him by the wrong name. He assumes heroine's ex has been to visit. It's really auntie's early stages of senility and she's actually talking about her late husband, dead more than 10 years. Heroine is a whore!

-5 spaces

His mistress, fearing loss of $$, tells him heroine is having affair with footman. Whore!

-3 spaces

She sees him buying jewelry. She flips out. It's for his grandma.

-3 spaces

His mother doesn't like her. Mama arranges for pool boy to follow her around. He sees. He's pissed. She's a whore!

-2 spaces

Defending the Genre
(No, It's Not Chick Porn. Dammit.)

When we started writing, we called this section a media guide, but it's not the media who question your interest in romance. It's more likely to be friends, family, anyone who sees you reading a romance, or anyone manning the cash register at the bookstore who gives you an arched brow at your eight-book stack of romances. Of course, the thought of your buying eight romances at once fills us with envy, complete with hand-wringing and squeaking, but to most people who don't understand the genre and don't want to, the thought of dropping a cool seventy-five to a hundred dollars on romance induces not envy but indignant, confused spluttering. For some reason, the sight of another person reading a romance gives passersby permission to take complete leave of their manners. Sarah's been approached by total strangers on the New York City subway who snidely comment on her reading material. You'd think people would have more self-preservation than to diss the reading material of an uncaffeinated commuter.

So imagine the opportunity to defend your choice of reading material. You're at a press conference with a dozen microphones, which resemble giant fuzzy electronic phalluses gathered in a bouquet in front of you. You have to field those same old questions about romance novels, and do so in front of thousands on behalf of the millions who read romance. No pressure or anything.

AREN'T ROMANCES ALL THE SAME?

Short answer: *Yes. Also, no. But in asking, you reveal how little you know about the genre.*

Yes, the plots of romance novels are very similar. There are often similar characters (angst-ridden vampire hero anyone?) and the thematic structure is based on a long-established foundation of literary history. But no, romances are not all "the same."

The accusation of sameness emerges from the concept that romances, much like other forms of popular fiction, are based on a "formula." And, as Pamela Regis says, the "connotations of 'formula' are quite negative. The term implies hack-work, subliterature, and imagination reduced to a mechanism for creating 'product.'" The use of the word "product" is key—denigrating romance by saying it's all the same, written according to a formula, implies that writing—and reading—a romance is like manufacturing an item, one of thousands of identical pieces, for sale to consumers who are all looking for the same exact thing. Nothing could be further from the truth.

And if you're bruising for a frosty discussion? We're always down with that. Our advice is to point out the following: all expressions of creativity have a structure at work within them, most particularly those that adhere to a classical form. All romances are the same in the same way that all choreographed ballets are the same. Each ballet is a written sequence of the same steps, but each performance is remarkably different depending on the dancer in the role, the costumes, the dressing of the stage, and the musicians playing the music. All symphonies are the same piece of music each time they are performed, but the nuanced differences of varying musicians and conductors can make a world of difference. For that matter, most music is composed of octave variations of the same twenty-two notes, and we've never heard anyone say that there's no difference between Bach and Copland, or Glass and Brahms.

If ballet and music don't make your argument, try cookies. Aside from the underlying insult to the intellect of both the writer and the reader, which is wide and deep and so very irritating, if we examine the concept of a formula and a product, what we're really talking about is a structure and a result. Consider the Toll House chocolate-chip-cookie recipe. A perfectly functional recipe, it combines the basic dry and wet ingredients, with a wee bit of leavening amid the sugar, salt, eggs, butter, and flour, to create a pretty damn serviceable cookie, suitable for eating while you read a romance novel, and no, you do not have to share your cookies with the people who ask you such nebby, thinly veiled insulting questions.

Now, consider the Toll House recipe in the hands of two different chefs. One, who is Not Sarah, puts nuts in the batter. Sarah thinks nuts in any baked good are a crime against humanity, so instead, she adds nutmeg, some unsweetened cocoa, and a bit of concentrated coffee liquid to her cookies. With three tiny ingredients, she has mocha-chocolate-chip cookies (that are awesome, by the way) while the other chef, who is busy violating the Geneva convention with those walnuts and pecans, has an entirely different cookie coming out of her oven. Both are chocolate chip cookies, but with a marked, and subtle difference.

That's how romance works. There's a structure, a foundation of common elements to each novel, but the variation in how those elements are woven together into a delicious narrative is the art, not the product, of each author. Eighty cooks crafting chocolate-chip cookies are going to produce chocolate-chip cookies, but each and every cookie from each chef is going to be different. And thus romance novels, which share a structure but diverge wildly based on subgenre and the innovation and creativity of each author, are not at all the same. The variations in the space between the narrative elements are the romance.

Those variations create something new in each novel. Nora Roberts, who is called by the actual press time and again to discuss and defend the genre, has said repeatedly (and still they call with the same question): Yes, there is a happy ending. But the book isn't about the happy ending. It's about the journey *to* that happy ending.

Note: Avoid the easy pitfall of violating Smart Bitch Law 1: Thou shalt not diss the reading material of another person merely to elevate one's own. By slapping at someone else's love of true crime novels, thou art not defending romance. Thou art passing the buck, and by doing so, verily thou art being a douche bag.

For example, with a mystery you know that the crime will be solved, the perp brought to justice, and maybe there's some sexxy sexxoring for the protagonists, though often it's behind closed doors, or obliquely referred to with a fade-to-black kissing scene. But in the end, Bad will lose to Good, and the mystery will be solved. Otherwise, it's not really a mystery novel.

Just like romance, there are plenty of mystery novels to choose from, with all manner of settings, protagonists, themes, and deeper significance hidden within. And just like romance, there are plenty of mystery writers. Moreover, just like romance, there are plenty of mystery writers who scare the ever-loving crap out of us, and there are some whom we stopped reading because in our opinion they were too much structure, not enough creative pizzazz.

Of course, mystery novels are socially and culturally acceptable reading material; they are not victim of the "scribbling for silly women" reputation that romances endure. Moreover, because mysteries are often about violence, crime, murder, and bloodshed, they're acceptable. Romances, which feature and focus on sex, emotions, happiness, and love, are not as acceptable, and truly, there's enough wrong with that imbalance of value that it underscores itself. Violence, murder, and crime: okay. Sex, emotions, happiness and relationships: not okay. What, we ask in all serious-ness, the fuck?

But it's not just readers who confront that bizarre imbalance. Authors hear it, too. Nora Roberts told us in an interview, "Once, years back, I did a mass signing with authors from various genres. One of the mystery authors came up to me at some point, patted my hand. I can't remember the entire conversation, but she ended it by saying: 'But you're writing mystery now, dear.' It still amuses me. It was said in the tone you'd use to someone who'd recovered from a long illness, or had recently been paroled. She meant well, but in her mind I was now legitimate."

Lisa Kleypas says, regarding the idea that those pesky romances, they're all the same, that "everyone knows the basic plot or for-mula, and then a lot of writers, including me, have discussed how to write 'outside the box.' But after twenty-two years of being pub-lished, I've come to realize that what makes a romance novel suc-cessful, not only in financial terms but also in a creative sense, is to think inside the box. The constraints, the limits, the structure of the romance novel is what allows a good writer to soar creatively."

It's not the structure that counts. It's the structure in the hands of a talented, creative, and enthusiastic author. What's more, some authors have had considerable success creating for themselves an additional narrative structure within the existing romance.

Some readers love the series of a specific author, partially be-cause a specific series may take place in a world with very clear and identified rules. There are several authors who have developed a structure of their own so unique it becomes their trademark of sorts within the structure of the genre. Usually at that moment, the marketing department of their publishing house gets down and does a booty-shakin' happy dance because authors with strong se-ries can sell to a thirsty, eager audience.

And that can be when "formula" becomes the best word to de-scribe the structure-within-a-structure, because that repeated structure can become boring, trite, repetitive, and banal. And

TIME FOR SWEEPING GENERALIZATIONS WITH YOUR HOSTS,
THE SMART BITCHES
Match the author to their "formula," in convenient haiku style:

1. Femme M.E. cooks stuff.   A. Janet Evanovich
   Enter: third-party villain   B. Jude Deveraux
   in last third of book.   C. James Patterson

2. You see in color?   D. Mary Higgins Clark
   Dude. You're toast, in the   E. J. R. Ward
   luurrrrrve™ sense.   F. Patricia Cornwall
   Bring it doggy-style!   G. Christine Feehan

3. Victimized female
   Fumbles into danger. Then,
   Surprise! Finds the perp.

4. She tells you apart?
   From your identical twin?
   Lather. Rinse. Repeat.

5. I have so much ahnghst.
   The cure. Wuss Woman. Her name?
   Carve it in my back.

6. Two-to-three-page chapters.
   Shitloads of white space. Plus some
   Real sick violence.

7. Torn between two men
   Between sexing, I wreck cars.
   And somehow solve crime.

1.F 2.G 3.D 4.B 5.E 6.C 7.A

that's when we, as readers, get really pissed off, because there is no journey between the narrative elements. There's just more repetition of the same from the last book, from the book before, and the book before that. Those, unfortunately, are the books that can easily give romance—and any other genre that operates on a solid, historically grounded narrative structure—a tawdry reputation.

Well, that and the man titty.

So Why Is Romance So Often and So Frequently Denigrated?

Good question. Why do mysteries, thrillers, spy novels, military-intrigue stories, and the rest hold a slightly more elevated position in the social ranking of "Other People's Opinions of Your Reading Material" than romance?

Are you a woman? Look in your pants. That could be why.

As Nora Roberts says, "Romance is the hat trick of easy targets: emotions, relationships, and sex." Add to that hat trick the instant handicap of being a genre written mostly by women, mostly for women, and the stereotypical images that surround both the readers *and* the writers, and it's a one-stop express to Highly Denigrated Genre land.

It's not easy being green any more than it is easy being a romance reader, or a romance writer. Consider the plight of the writer: for example, come Valentine's Day, reporters appear out of nowhere asking for quotes on sex tips, bedroom decor, love advice, and romantic date ideas—merely because, as the author of a romance novel, clearly the writer knows more about this stuff than the rest of us mere mortals. We won't even discuss the number of times romance writers have been asked by leering reporters how they research their sex scenes.

But romance readers, let's go back to our press conference. We are on the receiving end of snide comments for reading it, and we suffer under the presumption that we're undersexed housewives in puffy-paint sweatshirts who are eager for any and all escapist fantasy drivel, and we're too dim to notice that it's "all the same."

Ultimately, your choice to defend romance will likely lead to the ultimate in condescending question, *"But you're so smart! Why do you read those books?"*

We sighed deeply with discouragement just typing that.

"I read these books because I *am* so smart."

That's the bottom-line frustration that we have, and it's why we founded our Web site and named it Smart Bitches Who Love Trashy Books. We love romance novels. We're smart women with sharp intellects and a love of discussion and debate. And one does not cancel out the other. Romance novels do not make you stupid, we promise.

Many smart women love romance. We can personally verify by our own marvelous existence and the community on our site. Romance novels attract an erudite, intelligent, and unspeakably educated readership. That same readership is also a lucrative audience, as romance novels sell in the billions. And yet, romance is about the only thing marketed to us as romance readers. The only tie-in product that links romance fans and advertising is Fabio shilling for I Can't Believe It's Not Butter, and that seems more a play on his celebrity than an attempt to reach the limitless pot of money that is the romance-buying public.

But bottom line? We're smart, and we have money.

The RWA commissions two studies to examine the industry and the readership of romance. The readership survey is always a bucket full of fun when it comes to the results. Why? Because there's so damn many of us romance readers, it's amazing we put up with any of this crap. Let's throw around some statistical numbers with gleeful abandon, shall we?

According to the RWA, 64.6 million Americans read at least one romance in the past year. That's a lot of fucking people. You know what happens with 64.6 million people do the same thing? Taylor Hicks wins *American Idol.* Wait, that may not really strengthen our argument.

Anyway, of those readers, 42 percent of us have bachelor's degrees, with an additional 15 percent having acquired postgraduate education as well. And how much are we educated romance readers spending?

$1.37 billion dollars on romance.

Seriously. Educated people with financial buying power are spending a freaking shit ton of money. So you're not alone. And if someone hands you the "Why do you read *those* books" question, a handy short answer may be, "Because I enjoy them. And so do 64 million other really smart women who, incidentally, won't like that question, either."

So Why Do Smart Women Love Romance?
We know that:

- Romance is better than folks believe it is.
- Anything written for an audience of mostly women by a community of mostly women is subversive, reflective of the current sexual, emotional, and political status, and actively embraces and undermines that status simultaneously.
- Happiness is good. Emo may be chic. Angst is undoubtedly chic. Happiness is definitely not chic. But happiness is *good.*

And therein lies the crux of the matter: We smart readers of romance know that romance is Not All Bad.

The problem?

It's Not All Good either. It's like any other genre, with vacillations in quality, but because it gets dismissed as universally and unilaterally bad by those who don't read it, there is a remarkable tendency to defend romance as if it were infallible.

So what's the best defense against anyone who sneers at your reading material, who asks why a smart person could read romance, wasting brain cells with wanton, thoughtless abandon? Ignoring them works for us much of the time, and really, is there a ruder thing to do than put someone down based on what she reads? It's a classist, obnoxious, and utterly grotesque use of energy. Feel free to go ahead and tell the person he or she is being a classist jackwad, but that doesn't always work, either.

If you're really, really hoping to slam-dunk someone for dissing your books, we've got your back. So do romance authors—so we asked some for their best defenses of the genre. Of all the types of romance, category probably takes the most heat because there are so many assumptions made about readers of category romance. Among the top assumptions made about category lines: "The lines are marketed by how much sex is in them, and therefore the women who read them are in for a low-reading-level, titillating minibreak of porntastic cheese."

Or, how about, "They're about the same size as a Sweet Valley High novel, so they don't require much stamina in the reading, plus they reinforce the idea that women are stupid and can deal with sexuality only in the most lush and nonthreatening of packages."

Let's be real—titles like *The Sheikh's Virgin Mistress* do not help anyone who wants to defend romance, but neither do any of the clinch-laden historical covers, or the high-heeled cartoon legs of impossible thinness that so often adorn contemporary romances, either. But the posse of people inside the genre—the ones who write it and the ones who know how much you love it—they know how good it is.

What's Your Best Tip for a Romance Reader Who Is Consistently Given the Snarky, Derisive Treatment for Her Love of Romance?

RUTH RYAN LANGAN: "I'm always surprised that a reader would feel the need to defend what she reads. . . . I guess I'd have no defense for it. I simply love romance. And have always been drawn to it, from *Romeo and Juliet* to *Pride and Prejudice*. I do believe we've moved beyond the need to mount a defense of our love for romance. Both readers and writers have contributed to the public's acceptance that this genre has become the backbone of the industry. Without romance, many of our major publishers would be facing even more economic chaos than they currently claim during these challenging economic times. I say Long Live Romance. I read it, I write it, and I love it."

JULIE LETO: "Stop it. Stop defending it. Cut. It. Out. Learn a few key phrases to repeat to yourself that include naughty expletives. Seriously, embrace your love for romance and take it to the next level. If people laugh, laugh with them and read what you want anyway. Life's too short to have people influence what you read . . . or anything else for that matter . . . For every jerk who makes a stupid comment, there are hundreds if not thousands of readers who love what we do. Concentrate on them!

KATHLEEN O'REILLY: "I think it's a miserable commentary on our society that people cannot discern between romance and sex. Yes, they are linked, but they are not the same, and I worry about my daughter growing up in a world where people don't know what true romance is.

"Honestly, there are no witty comebacks that can grow the size of a small mind. My best advice to . . . romance readers is be smug and superior in your own self-knowledge, and to pity the unenlightened reader who doesn't understand the myriad choices available to them. I know there are people who rag on the quality of category, but look at the people who started in category: Linda Howard, Nora Roberts, Suzanne Brockmann, J. R. Ward, Jenny Crusie. My favorite Nora Roberts book is *The Heart of Devin*

Mackade (a category novel). My favorite Jenny Crusie is
Manhunting (another category). The classic Linda Howard is
Mackenzie's Mountain (a category). 'Nuff said."

Romance = Subversive

Suppose, however, that you're in the midst of a very intellectual
crowd, one that cannot reconcile your intelligence and your love of
romance. Hit 'em with a few choice examples of how romance is
subversive, powerful, political, and lucrative when your goal is to
save lives. This, to be sure, is not a genre written by, or written for,
wussy, wimpy, wallflower women.

Example the first: repeat after us. "Littattafan Soyayya." What
now? That would be Hausa, a northern Nigerian language spoken
by the religious Islamic community, and it means "Books of Love."
Soyayya novels are little paper booklets sold in high-foot-traffic
areas in northern Nigeria, and according to an AP article published
May 1, 2008, they are sought by women readers and set on fire by
male religious leaders.

Why? Because the books, written in the local Hausa language,
"extoll the values of true love based on feelings, rather than family
or other social pressures." In a conservative community in which
most marriages are arranged and may involve multiple wives and
forced obedience or seclusion, Soyayya novels explore themes of
marital choice and female education through tiny paper-bound romance narratives. They're part fiction and part instructional assistance for uneducated women on navigating conservative culture.

And did you know that romance novels helped liberate Jewish
victims of the Holocaust? No, seriously.

Mary Burchell published over 130 novels for Harlequin/Mills &
Boon in a career spanning more than fifty years. Burchell was the
pen name of Ida Cook, one half of an opera-mad pair of sisters who
made it their life's purpose to scrimp and save every farthing so that
they could travel Europe to see their favorite sopranos. When the
Cook sisters learned of the effect of Hitler's rule in Germany from

a Jewish friend, Ida Cook began devoting the profits of her novels, which were considerable, toward their travel, which, under the guise of opera tourism, was in reality a mission to interview families hoping for passage to England, and to smuggle the possessions of Jewish families in portable form. In Ida Cook's obituary after her death in 1986, Francesca Segal wrote, "The mild-mannered spinsters became expert smugglers, regaling border guards with tales of the previous night's performance, switching labels in fur coats, and wearing real diamonds with outfits so dowdy that customs officers would presume the jewels were paste." Ida and her sister Louise saved the lives of at least 29 people, and were named Righteous Among the Gentiles by Yad Veshem in Israel.

And let us not forget the increasing numbers of fully licensed Ph.D.-carrying badass intellectuals who are turning the power of their brains on to the romance genre. From Pamela Regis's *A Natural History of the Romance Novel* to the Professors Brilliant at Teach Me Tonight, a blog devoted to scholarly examination of the genre, there are some big, big brains examining the power of the romance, and the power hidden within it. The political, social, and, yes, feminist implications of the genre are examined with full brain powers on. The continual play of female-centered and male-dominated characterization is part of what makes romance so fascinating for those who love to pick apart narratives with scholarly scalpels. That play is also why it's not so easy to dismiss romance as patriarchal pap, reinforcement of the dominant male paradigm, or merely rape and adverbs.

And speaking of rape, let's turn to another common question asked of romance readers that reveals the insult and the assumption: *It's all pornography for women, isn't it?*

Option 1: Utter silence. A few seconds of shocked awe may make the person asking rethink, or rephrase, the question.
Option 2: Sarcasm. *"Oh, my goodness. Women? Having sexual pleasure?! Ought to be avoided at all costs."*

Option 3: Full-frontal assault. "What's wrong with sex?" Or, flash
him and see if he looks, while saying, "I got your porn *right here*."

The problem with the "chick porn" assumption, and the question, is that ultimately you argue about what pornography *is*, and
whether romance novels fit into that definition. One person may
say no, while the other says yes, Yes, *YES*, oooh yessssss, it is. Porn
lies in the eyes of the beholder and the hands of the masturbator.
And for some people, anything containing descriptions of sexual
acts qualifies as porn. As Candy says, "I know that when I was a kid
and burningly curious about sex, I'd systematically flip through my
sister's romance-novel collection, looking for all the naughty bits,
prurient curiosity redlining all the way."

But are romances porn? Sorry to give you the cagey answer, but
there it is: maybe, or maybe not. With a self-important blowhard, or
anyone who tosses the romance = porn accusation without looking
both ways first, you can try to debate what is and isn't pornography,
and whether romances really ought to be classified in that category.
If he says yes, and you say no, you're both right, because we sure as
shit don't think it's up to one single person to define what is and
what isn't pornography since just about anything can be used porno-
graphically. Name an act, *any* act, no matter how disgusting or odd
or innocuous, and we can guarantee you somebody, somewhere, is
jacking off while thinking of somebody doing that very thing. There
are fetishes centered around people sneezing, and bald men in hats,
and people brushing their teeth in their pajamas. (Why, yes, we do
spend an awful lot of time on the Internet. Why do you ask?)

So in that context, written explorations of sexual autonomy
and self-actualization for women and establishment of equal sexual
status with a willing and satisfying partner within the confines of
mutual commitment seem really fucking tame. Yet, because it's
descriptions of sexual intercourse, that's porn. And because some
readers get off on it, it's porn.

And therein lies the other spear hidden in that ignorant question: regardless of whether you agree or disagree with the idea that romance is pornography for women, Bonehead McAsshat is still implying by asking in the first place that women ought to feel ashamed about sexual pleasure, especially self-pleasure. Such a castigation doesn't exist for men. Sarah regularly gave subscriptions to *Playboy* to two of her husband's friends as a holiday gift, and they kept multiple back issues on their coffee table for guests to read. No shame, there. Cue the standard jovial humor about reading it "for the articles." And, hell yeah, there's some great writing in *Playboy*, but c'mon. There's also a good portion of the readership who look at *Playboy* for the models who aren't wearing much in the way of "articles" of clothing.

But vehicles for women's sexual pleasure, on the other hand, are not so eagerly displayed on the coffee table, or tolerated by visitors. Women's sexual pleasure and the education of women on the means to that end are simply not accepted or even celebrated. Then here come romance novels, potentially including sex scenes of various levels of explicitness.

Do we think romance novels are porn? Nope. Do they turn us on? Sometimes. It depends. Candy won't pick up the phone after finishing an Emma Holly erotic romance, if that answers your question.

We recently had a lovely discussion to break down the question of "Romance = chick porn" and came up with short, one-line defenses to the "chick porn" question. Test drive at your leisure:

SARAH: "Mmm. Porn."
"There's nothing wrong with porn."
"Monogamy and a plot—so common to porn, yes?"
"You know a lot about porn, don't you, dear?

CANDY: "If romance novels are chick porn, then Tom Clancy and Stephen King are dude porn."
"Have you ever read actual porn?"
"If romance novels are porn, where's my twincest anal sex scene, goddammit?"

SARAH: *Twincest?! HA!*

> "If they're chick porn, the sound track must be very throbby.
> What music do you like?" (Minefield of music taste
> question, ahoy! Commence debate!)
> "Romance is not at all chick porn. There is not nearly
> enough anal to qualify."

So what's the very best way in our opinion to fend off the "Aren't
they just chick porn?" question? Even if you disagree that romance
is pornography, the person asking the question isn't going to sit still
long enough to listen to an informed monologue about the variations within the genre such that some books contain no sex at all
while others focus on sex as the primary driving point (har har) of
the relationship. Your best defense is an offense that takes offense at
the question:

"I don't think they are, though some people obviously do. And
even if they were, what's wrong with that?"

The sad truth is that anyone who presumes that romances are all
dumb, and that the readers thereof are as well, will never appreciate the genre unless they read one. They most likely will never do
so, or won't recognize the romance for what it is because it's not
wrapped up in a more attractive and socially acceptable cover. If a
romance is marketed outside the romance bookshelf, then that
book "transcends the genre" and doesn't count anyway. So those
people will go on putting down your reading material because
smart women don't read romance in their worldview.

So you know what? Fuck 'em. Fuck 'em hard. They can read
whatever they want, and so can you. We lovers of the romance
genre can celebrate the good parts and the parts that make the baby
Ganesh weep with the badness. Because only real fans of romance
can appreciate the best—and the worst—of the genre.

Chapter Bad Sex

RAPE IN ROMANCE

Birds do it. Beetles do it. Even asshole alpha heroes do it. Let's do it—let's rape the girl!*

If there's a legacy that has lasted much longer in the popular conception of romance than its actual continued presence, it'd be the existence of rapist heroes in romance. Whenever a certain school of feminist thought attempts to argue how romance novels are yet another example of the Man keeping us down, the rape scenes are the first thing trotted out. Whenever a commentator of the genre attempts to point to the more ludicrous aspects of Romancelandia, he generally goes to the rape scenes—right after the covers, of course. And rape scenes have scarred many an unsuspecting reader who pick up classic bestsellers like Kathleen Woodiwiss's *The Flame and*

---

* By the way, we're not kidding about the birds and beetles, leaving aside the rather problematic usage of the term "rape" to describe animal behavior. Ducks are known to engage in coercive sexual behavior, up to and including necrophiliac homosexual rape, as documented by an enterprising Dutch researcher in a paper entitled, appropriately enough, "The First Case of Homosexual Necrophilia in the Mallard *Anas platyrhynchos*"; the males of several different species of diving beetle systematically hunt down and submerge the females underwater to weaken their resistance and prevent them from mating with other males. Mother Nature: more fucked-up than a Rosemary Rogers hero!

the Flower, expecting sappy boy-loves-girl stuff, only to find boy-stuffs-girl-without-her-consent-while-she-weeps scenes.

The truth of the matter is, although rape scenes have largely disappeared from romance novels published from the early 1990s onward, they were ubiquitous in romance novels from the early '70s to the mid-'80s. Hell, if the heroine only got raped by the hero in a romance novel, she was lucky. Rosemary Rogers and Catherine Coulter, among others, wrote infamous gang-rape scenes, in which the heroine is completely and utterly brutalized.

But there's some contention as to whether rapist heroes do, in fact, exist. Jayne Ann Krentz, for one, argues in "Trying to Tame the Romance: Critics and Correctness" in *Dangerous Men, Adventurous Women* that there's no such thing as rape by a hero in romance—that what people have labeled "rape" is, in fact, an unusually aggressive seduction that is "intense and unrelentingly sensual." She goes so far as to compare the rape of the heroines to the seduction of private eyes in hard-boiled mysteries and of the heroes of thrillers by dangerous dames. According to Krentz, these heroes are passive and rarely initiate the seduction, and their resistance is token at best. If these aggressive seductions by women who present real threats to the heroes (they're often the prime suspects) aren't labeled rapes, then doing the same for romance novels is hardly fair.

This dismissal by Krentz, which heavily implies that the rape accusations are due to sexual double standards, is downright puzzling, because some rape scenes in romance novels aren't quite as she describes. There's no passivity on the part of the heroine, and no seduction on the part of the hero. The heroine often explicitly says no, and in the vast majority of instances, they're not feeling ambivalent about allowing the hero to seduce them—they're actively fighting him off. Some of the heroes, such as Anthony Welles of Catherine Coulter's *Devil's Embrace,* actually tie the heroine down as she weeps and struggles. During the act, the heroines feel considerable pain; screaming and crying from distress is not uncommon. If they do feel pleasure, they loathe themselves for responding sexually to the hero.

All this may still be subject to interpretation, since the line between forced seduction and outright rape is fuzzy at best, except for this fact: The hero and heroine often agree that the heroine has been raped. When both the characters agree that the hero's turgid battle ram of love has slammed into the heroine's postern of passion without her consent, it makes it more difficult to deny that rape has, in fact, occurred.

Ultimately, Krentz's comparison using private eyes would be analogous to the typical rape scenario in romance novels only if the dangerous dame had tied the hero up as he'd kicked and screamed and struggled, then donned a strap-on and showed him a good deal of what-what in the butt, all while the private eye wept and felt humiliated because he'd had a hard-on. Then, in the aftermath, the hero questioned his sexuality, full of loathing for himself and vowing to hate the heroine forever. It's okay, though, because by the end of the story, the private eye falls in love and ends up marrying the dangerous dame. She's right: he'd come to enjoy the penetration with time.

Labeling romance-novel rape as not-rape and calling it a day is too easy a route. Whether or not the hero's violations constitute rape according to the standards of the books when they were written, and whether or not some readers and authors are able to accept them as rapes, the majority of romance readers today and almost all outsiders interpret the actions as rape. The romance community—authors, readers, commentators—need to accept rapist heroes as part of the genre's history and take a good, long, hard, look at the workings of rape in romance. It's an ugly part of romance's past. We must look at it.

Nonconsensual Sex: It's Historically Accurate; Therefore, It Must Be Okay!

"It's historical accuracy!" is one of the more popular banners waved around by readers on discussion boards and Amazon.com reviews when the issue of romance-novel rape is brought up. Women were nothing more than chattel back then, goes the logic, and men had more freedom to rape—they didn't even necessarily know what they were doing was wrong. This argument does a disservice both to males and to history. While marrying for love was not the norm (blame the Victorians for that particular idea), rape has almost always been decried as socially unacceptable—more than socially unacceptable, actually: it's one of the most consistently recognized criminal acts, with deliciously gruesome punishments ranging from death by stoning to castration. Just about any code you can think of—from the Torah to Augustus Caesar's *Lex Iulia* to modern-day statutes governing sexual assault—recognizes rape as a serious crime.

Why? Because even at the nadir of women's rights, women were still acknowledged as being valuable commodities, and rape damaged the goods—especially if the woman was valuable politically or economically, and was a virgin. Rape, if nothing else, was an infringement on the possessory rights of the husband or father over the body of the woman, and held a high potential to muddle paternity.

The definition of rape has changed in tandem with the conceptions of a woman's personhood. The focus wasn't always on consent and the violation of that consent, as it is now; the focus used to be on women as property and how the rape would affect their market value. Marital rape wasn't recognized until a few decades ago, for example; ditto the rape of sexually experienced unmarried women.

Evidence of violent assault on the part of the rapist and resistance on the part of the victim were often important parts of the definition. For example, Deuteronomy 22:23–24 exacted capital punishment on the victim as well as the rapist if the act took place in a city and the victim didn't cry out loud enough to be heard; in contrast, 22:25–27 exempted the victim if the same act was committed in the country. The idea that insufficient resistance by the

victim invalidates rape because the lack of consent was not unequiv-
ocal has remained in the popular conception of rape to this day,
even if it no longer has a place in our laws.

By the time the nineteenth century rolled around, however,
the violation of the woman's will became an integral part of the
common-law definition of rape, but notions of female identity and
sexual purity meant that actions like marital rape or the rape of sexually promiscuous women were considered impossible—paradoxical,
even.

However, the vast majority of the rapes in romance novels don't
fall into these narrow exceptions. Almost all of the heroines raped
are young virgins of good birth, and the heroes, while almost without exception notorious rakes and scoundrels, are typically great
lovers who avoid virgins because they're more trouble than they're
worth.

Some of the rapes occur because of a genuine misunderstanding
about the heroine's sexual experience, but the message is muddled
because when the heroine's virginity is revealed, the rapes don't
always stop. The first rape in *The Flame and the Flower,* for example, occurs because the hero assumes the heroine is a prostitute,
but subsequent rapes occur even after he finds out she's actually
a gently bred virgin girl, though the hero assures the heroine that
she'll come to enjoy it if she'd stop struggling. Oftentimes, the
rapes occur despite the knowledge of, or specifically because of,
the heroine's virginity; for example, in *Devil's Embrace* by Catherine
Coulter, the hero deliberately rapes the heroine to prevent her from
holding on to any hope that she can return and marry her then-
fiancé with honor.

Rape in Romance as Permission to Write About Sex

Another popular argument—and one that holds up better under
analysis—is that the rape scenes gave the heroines permission to
explore their sexuality without appearing to be a slut (the wages of

which are either death or ridicule—sexually promiscuous women are either villainesses or comic sidekicks, neither of which tend to fare particularly well in romance). Sexual autonomy and expressing honest desire just Wasn't Done by Nice Girls worthy of a true Happily Ever After; by having their control taken away, the heroines were also exonerated of all moral blame for ultimately becoming sexually active and for enjoying her sexuality.

There's still an underlying tension, however. Even if the heroine is excused from the taint of sexual promiscuity, she is still culpable for the hero's sexual brutality. Whether it's because she's completely sexually irresistible, or whether it's because he's punishing her for some wrongdoing, whether real or imagined, the focus is often on the heroine and the effect her physicality or behavior has on the hero. The centrality of the heroine is crucial in romance novels, especially Old Skool romances written primarily from the heroine's point of view, but it also reinforces ideas that women are inherently sexually dangerous. The act is not the man's fault because the heroine somehow made him do it, either by tempting or goading him beyond bearing.

And pleasure, schmeasure: during the rape, especially the first several times it occurs, the heroine rarely feels pleasure. The rape is, in fact, accompanied by pain—the physical tearing of the hymen is presented as excruciating, while shame and disgust predominate the emotional landscape.

And in the few instances in which the heroine does feel pleasure during the rape, it's often accompanied by a generous serving of self-loathing. She feels that her body has betrayed her, eerily echoing how actual rape victims feel when they feel sexual pleasure during their assault. However, these portrayals of aggressive male sexuality tend to grate modern sensibilities more because of how differently rape is viewed today, thanks to the No Means No movement and a better understanding of how rape affects its victims. Older conceptions of what actually constituted a rape controlled the depictions of romance-novel rape in Old Skool romances, so the scenes often substitute other things for consent, such as pleasure (if she feels pleasure, it's not rape), or gentleness and lack of injury (if she's not torn and bloody, it's not rape). To a resistant reader, all these factors are irrelevant, because the heroine does not consent; the hero's reassurances that she'll eventually enjoy it, or that her struggles will only make it hurt more, actually make the rape more egregious, not less. However, for the less resistant reader, any pleasure the heroine may feel against her will and the loss of control by the hero is proof of his passion for her; it underlines how the sexual interactions between hero and heroine will eventually lead to the happy ending.

The fantasy of a heroine being forced to relinquish her autonomy—and to feel pleasure against her will in the process—may be deeply appealing to some readers by explicitly allowing them to vicariously abdicate control, providing an escape from the control they need to maintain in their real lives. Conflicts in the reading emerge when the heroine clearly isn't deriving any pleasure from the abdication of control, but this assumes that the reader identifies strictly with the heroine. Some of the tension goes away if you accept that many readers often engage in a process that is simultaneously masochistic and sadistic. It's masochistic because they enjoy experiencing the suffering of the heroine—it's cathartic, after all, and it's a safe way to exorcise insecurities and demons. It's also sadistic because they also enjoy watching a heroine—who's often quite deliberately grating and annoying—receive her comeuppance, either by taking a more detached outsider viewpoint or by identifying with the hero.

The security offered by the Happily Ever After is nothing to sniff at, either. Because the readers are guaranteed a happy ending, they are able to assure themselves that no matter how brutal the hero may be to the heroine, or how much she declares her hatred for him, all will work out for the best, and the hero's assurances that the heroine will come to enjoy the sexual interactions in the future will come to fruition. The readers occupy a superior position; they know that the heroine is wrong, and that happiness and orgasms will burst forth like veritable Care Bear Stares, except with more jiggly bits, by the end of the book. The Happily Ever After, while often decried as one of the most limiting aspects of a romance novel, provides a secure anchor to the reader and allows a romance author considerable leeway in the sorts of conflict she can present, as long as she doesn't cross a reader's personal line in the sand, beyond which no happy ending can be possible. Rape is that line in the sand for many readers today; it wasn't for most of the readers in the past.

THE IRRESISTIBLE WOMAN'S MAGIC HOO HOO TAMES THE UNTAMABLE MIGHTY WANG

Romance-novel rape in Old Skool romances, like popular conceptions of rape at the time, depend in many ways on the myth of the irresistible woman and the then-prevalent view that sexual violation stemmed from sexual desire, as opposed to a sexualized way to exercise anger and power. The focus was on the woman's sexuality and the uncontrolled responses it elicited, instead of on the responsibility the perpetrator had in securing consent and restraining his behavior.

In some ways, the myth of the irresistible women is appealing: even though it exonerates the man of the responsibility (He couldn't help himself! Her blazing beauty addled him! Her Magic Hoo Hoo could not be resisted!), having the ability to drive men mad with desire gives the heroine considerable power, even if it's not a power that can ultimately be wielded for her own ends.* Significantly, the Old Skool hero is unfailingly portrayed as being completely in control of all his responses—jaded and cynical, in fact—*except* when it comes to the heroine, which in turn infuriates him. After all, he's

---

* The women who do wield their sexuality for their own ends are villainesses in much of fiction, not merely romance novels.

the premier cocksman in all the land, and here comes this insignificant little chit who's making him spooge prematurely, even though all she does is move her body with shy, clumsy inexperience during the dance as old as time. Even worse, after getting a sample of the heroine, he finds that no other hoo hoo in the land will do, because lo, she is in sole possession of the Magic Hoo Hoo. Women he formerly found luscious are now overblown and undesirable. This leads to more anger and even more highly charged interactions, until he's forced to acknowledge his feelings for the heroine and eventually gentles his treatment of her. The heroine, in being raped and having her will overborne, gains power because the hero himself is no longer in full control of his actions. The fact that the hero Loses His Shit every time he's around the heroine is an indicator of True Lurve instead of a True Need for a Restraining Order.

And because the rape is portrayed either as the heroine resisting destiny or the hero's inability to control his desire for the heroine, two other aspects of romance-novel rape make it more palatable.

First, the rape is rendered more palatable as long as the violator is somebody the reader would find attractive. Therefore, the rape is okay as long as the rapist is sexy, beautiful, and has pots of money—not as okay if the violator is old, ugly, or (and this is harped on as being synonymous with moral turpitude in older romance novels) fat.

Second, the fictional rapist, unlike a real-life rapist, is completely reformed by the lovesauce emanating from the heroine's Magic Hoo Hoo, which is the fount of all healing, happiness, and contentment. Whether or not he ever actually apologizes or acknowledges the wrongness of his acts during the course of the book, the ending holds the promise of future behavior that, while not completely bereft of shitmonkey moments, is at least a reasonable approximation of what a decent human being should act like. As Jayne Ann Krentz notes in "Trying to Tame the Romance," the outcome is much more satisfying when the heroine successfully tames a truly dangerous creature instead of a milquetoast fop. The eventual taming of a sexually dangerous and aggressive hero thus allowed women a safe space to explore—and invert—the power relationships in a rape. Romance-novel rape ultimately placed women in control.

AWAKENING SLEEPING BEAUTY

Romance-novel rape also serves as an awakening for the heroines, who are often repressed about or completely unaware of their sexuality. Sleeping Beauty needs to be awakened, but not with a mere kiss. The hero's violation is a way of waking the heroine up to the inevitability of her conquest and the rightness of their love, a way of forcing her to see that will she, nil she, the hero is the right one for her. The literal rape and violation of the heroine's will is translated into a metaphorical ripping aside of her doubts and reservations, forcing the heroine to acknowledge the fact that she's a sexual creature, except romance novels starkly contrast with previous literary traditions because the heroine's sexuality is portrayed as a good thing, not a force to be feared and punished—as long as she expresses it exclusively with the hero.

The rape then becomes not-rape because he *is* the hero, and his worldview is the normative view. The hero is generally right about everything, from the dire consequences should the heroine attempt a foolish stunt to the fact she'll eventually beg for his hot, hot mansauce. If the heroine is infatuated with somebody else, the other man is usually portrayed as too weak or too stodgy for her feisty ways; the hero assures her she would've run roughshod over the rival, consequently become bored, and lose respect for him. The sexual aggression becomes a way of contrasting the hero with the less sexually effective rival. The idea implicit in most Old Skool romances seems to be that an aggressive, lively woman needs an even more aggressive, lively man to "tame" her, a term that shows up with regularity in Old Skool romance novels; like much of the fiction of that time, lack of aggressiveness in males is often presented as emasculating.

THE MARTYR THEORY

Romance-novel rape, because of the way it's framed, may appeal to readers for its martyr fantasy value. This is especially true in which the hero feels great remorse for his acts and grovels for forgiveness by the end of the book. Oftentimes, the heroine is the only one who knows she's virtuous and doing the right thing, despite horrible misconceptions by the hero. The readers, however, are privy to her virtue, thus making them complicit in her virtue and martyrdom. In the hero-normative world of the Old Skool romance, the hero finding out he was wrong about the heroine's sexual purity was pretty much the only victory allowed the heroine, and this victory, because of its incredibly limited nature, is disproportionately satisfying. The catharsis and vindication when the hero apologizes by the end of the book are especially delicious as a consequence.

RAPE OF THE PAST; RAPE OF THE FUTURE

Romance-novel rape mostly disappeared from historical and contemporary novels around the late 1980s; perhaps not coincidentally, this came shortly after the prevalence of date rape was recognized and legal standards switched the focus from the victim's behavior and sexual history (Did she somehow sexually tempt the man? Was she sexually promiscuous?) to the perpetrator's failure to secure consent. Romance-novel rape, however, still exists and can be found in paranormal and erotic romance; the shift to these subgenres suggests the rape elements are even more explicitly presented as fantasy.

However, the direct descendant of the romance-novel rape may not merely have changed genre, but changed form. The involuntary change, in which the heroine is transformed into a vampire or superpowered being or three-toed weresloth, usually with copious amounts of blood, trauma, and sex, uses much of the same language and framework as rape in Old Skool romances. There is often unwillingness and pain, followed rapidly by confusion and shame over her changed status. Resignation, then acceptance set in, but always, the heroine blossoms into her new role and finds that her new powers open completely new avenues to her.

That seizing of new power and the acquisition of self-reliance and autonomy are much more prevalent themes in romance literature, particularly as pertains to sex. Sex in romance is not all bad. In fact, in a number of very special, sparkly ways, sex is good.

Chapter Love Grotto

GOOD SEX, PLEASE!

When, oh, when does the good sexxoring start? It starts right here, baby. Let it never be said that we view romance as a set of paint-by-numbers elements meant to be strung repeatedly into a redundant order, or that writing romance is as easy as finding the necessary pieces and snapping them into place, substituting Lord Bonerhead for Angst the Vampire or Kurt Schlong-Hardass, P.I. But there are some elements that are consistent features of most, if not all, romance novels. Obviously, the protagonist pair have to meet, there's some attraction, and they ultimately acknowledge or act on that attraction. Then, maybe there's some sweet sexual action.

If you flipped through this book looking for the naughty parts, pick any page. If you're looking for the nookie in a romance, where do you look? Good question. Many Old Skool romances follow a very particular formula: sex will occur relatively early in the book, usually within the first sixty or so pages—but it will be *horrible*. We once picked up five famous Old Skool romances at random—strictly for research purposes, of course—published between 1972 and 1982, and that was the schedule for Every. Damn. Book. The heroine is raped before page 70. The hero ejaculates prematurely. There's crying and weeping and bleeding and sometimes cream.

And then the rest of the sex scenes focus on the heroine eventually allowing herself to be pleasured by the hero. Notice that there's no question of the hero learning to pleasure the heroine, because of course he can—he has the Heroic Wang, and that thing couldn't hold back the pleasure if it tried. But there's only so much the Heroic Wang can do when the Magic Hoo Hoo won't cooperate; it's only when the heroine finally gives herself up to the carekeeping of the hero, whether or not she consciously admits to it, that she experiences true pleasure.

In the less rapey romances from the late 1970s and through the '80s, particularly historicals, the sex shows up just after halfway point. It was a dependable location—if you wanted to find the sex scene, start flipping pages somewhere after the midpoint of the book. These were thoughtfully marked by Zebra and Dorchester Back in the Day, as the midpoint of the book had a cardboard insert with a postage-paid card inviting you to subscribe to their book clubs. Just after, before, or straddling the cardboard there was some nookie action. You could count on it.

That was the sequence of the storylines then: just after the midway point of the narrative, it was Time for Nookie. You can dig through the older offerings to test this out, but according to our impeccable research, there was an introduction, much conflict and drama, much attraction, much denial of and resistance to the attraction, and finally the protagonists (or maybe just the hero) succumb to the power of that attraction and look-out-virgin alert, it's business time.

In contrast, newer releases of romance in all subgenres locate the nookie in the larger context of the storyline, and really, the sex moves around quite a bit.* It either comes† as part of the emotional climax or it exists separately from the emotional climax and commitment. The sex might be in the beginning or the middle or the end, or all three—it's kind of like the Jewish High Holidays, which

* No pun intended.
† Pun totally intended.

always move around and are never, if you ask any Jewish folks, on time.

If the sex comes in early in the story, there're usually postsex ramifications that become part of that story. She might feel guilty or self-flagellate that she gave it up too easily, or she might find herself unaccountably attracted to the hero and not sure how to address that. He might feel equally conflicted, but for other reasons.

Early Sex in the Plot

More than a few romances feature the sex right from the first few pages. If you're really impatient, or if you want to see how the story holds up when the nookie opens the narrative, here are a notable few:

Midsummer Moon, Laura Kinsale. It's a rather tame scene by any standard, but it sets up the conflict between hero and heroine beautifully. Beware of the salt, is all we're saying.

Strange Attractions, Emma Holly. Actually, most Emma Holly novels feature mucho rumpy-pumpiness right off the bat, and it's a testament to her skills that she makes them such a seamless part of the story. And unlike the scene by Kinsale, these will probably leave burn marks on your fingertips.

Passion, Lisa Valdez. You open the book, and bam: sex. In public. Well, behind a palm, if you want to be technical. At the Crystal Palace, with a stranger, and from behind.

And never miss the opportunity to check out the opening pages of Virginia Henley's *Dream Lover,* or *The Pirate and the Pagan.* You know, if you like cocks and wet salty heads.

I Gotta Bang That Girl Right Outta My Head

So often in a story in which the sex is *not* part of an emotional climax of admission and commitment between the protagonists, and in which the sex comes *before* that emotional climax, the hero follows the "get it out of my system" thought process. He's met the heroine, and she gets under his skin for one reason or another. He's obsessed with her and wants to boink her like madness, but figures if he does so and, you guessed it, "gets it out of his system," he'll be able to move on and forget her, no longer plagued by thoughts of this infuriating woman.

Enter Her Magic Hoo Hoo. Magic Hoo Hoos are like Pringles: once he's popped, he can't stop. She may be an itch he has to scratch before they engage in coitus most awesomeus, but afterward, he has that itch for the rest of his life. Even if he has done the horizontal tango with every woman in town, he'll never successfully "get her out of his system" because their sex, and their relationship, was Meant to Be and cannot be resisted. He's spoiled for every other woman and is hers and hers alone—oh, the power of that Magic Hoo Hoo.

Sometimes the sex is late in the sequence of the overall narrative. Sometimes there's so much sexus interrupts you wonder why none of the secondary characters holler at the two dueling fools to get on with it already. The protagonists might come close dozens of times, but they never actually do the deed—and therefore sustain a great deal of sexual tension for a few pages more.

Usually, in this circumstance, their sexual climax is also the climax of their emotional admission of feelings for each other: *I love you! I want you! We are finally alone! Commence nookie action!* Pairing sexual climax with emotional climax is a very heady combination.* One or both protagonists cannot help themselves and must obey their insistent instincts, and the conflation of sexual intimacy and emotional intimacy is explosive.

When the first sexual encounter between the protagonists is separate from the emotional climax, it can be less satisfying, unless the emotional climax is equal to the sexual climaxes that lead up to it.

If we take stock of the books we've read, we find that the books we enjoy more feature the combined element of sexual and emo-

* We'll let you decide if we meant that pun.

tional consummation—when the booty call has a subtext that makes it meaningful for both characters, even if neither of them is willing to admit the depth of that significance. Intimacy (sex) begetting intimacy (emotional or personal connection) is a tried-and-true method, but regardless of how the author wields the emotional thunder rod, we tend to find a sexual scene memorable when going down the love canal means going down the love canal, and thus she's not just any old port in his storm.

WHO TELLS OF THE GREAT SEXING: SEXUAL POV

Any fiction-writing instruction book worth its $12.95 (more in Canada) will tell you that point of view, or POV, is a most important consideration. It's particularly crucial when describing the view of his pointed man-spear as it heads toward the valley, also known as the Sex Scene. In the early days of Old Skool romance the scenes were mostly written from the female point of view, but nowadays, unless it's a first-person narrator, odds are you'll get a mix of both male and female perspectives as the protagonists indulge in a little of the old in-out, in-out.

In Sarah's reading experience, 90 percent of the sex scenes in romances are from the female POV, told in and through the female's experience, with the notable exception of erotic romance, wherein the reader can reside in the hero's head(s) for quite a while. Candy's reading experience is different: the 90 percent figure is true for Old Skool romances, but in romances of all genres in which both points of view receive equal time, sex scenes were described from either perspective in about equal proportion, except for the Great Defloration. Why is that? Theories abound! And of course, they are irresponsibly researched theories.

In Old Skool romances, you only rarely experience the sweet, sweet love through the hero, but that's largely because the Old Skool romances were mostly told from the heroine's perspective in the first place. In novels in which both POVs are given equal weight, most authors dedicate roughly equal real estate to both sexes for the POV of the nookenatin'.

The male point of view is present in most recently published romances not only because the hero's journey now has close to equal weight with the heroine's, but because the added POV adds greater dramatic impact—at least, it does right now, simply because, like seeing a live penis on a major network at 8:00 p.m., it's more unexpected. Hell, penises in general are unexpected. So it is with the male perspective during sex.

The thrust of the dramatic impact is usually in the emotional revelation smack dab in the middle of coitus, to wit: *"Oh, shit, this sex is meaningful and I can't control my—AAGGHHHHHHHH!"* The rake is undone and bound to one woman, the lothario is shackled for good, the gay hero is cured of that pesky preference for men (just kidding)—the Power of her Magic Hoo Hoo is almost as great as that of the Heroic Wang of Mighty Lovin'—the She-Ra to his He-Man, if you will. (Except without the implied incest, what with She-Ra being He-Man's twin and all.)

In a nutshell, the male point of view is used to reveal that it's not just another boning in the mist. The male's coital or post-coital thought process can follow any number of patterns, but at its essence, the male has a great "Oh shit!" moment at the same time he has an "Oh, God!" moment, which communicates to his head and his loins that this is not his father's Oldsmobile. To coin a bad pirate joke, male sex point of view can be summed up in eight magic words: "Ahoy, there! Mating? This sex is meaningful! ARRRRGH!"

The realization can take any number of forms, from "Sex was never this good before—what is it about this woman?" to "This was supposed to be rote and meaningless, an experience to cleanse her from my system, and now I cannot get enough. I must have more!" But at the root of the rumination: her Golden Passage is the path to monogamy, redemption, and really, really hot boot-knockin' for-ever and ever, amen. Marriage and monogamy are never a bad choice when the sex is *that good,* and of course the hero must choose the heroine, and her Miraculous Magical Mystery Tour Bus Tunnel, forever and ever. Nobody says no to perfect sex.

Sexual explorations aside, romance capitalizes on the idea that both men *and* women need emotional connections to truly enjoy sex, and thus it's extra-more-better if the male realizes as well that in the math of scrumpin', *sex + feeeeeelings woo woo feeeeeeelings* = Really Good Sex!

HER VIRGINITY, HER POV

The heroine's great deflowering is told almost exclusively from the heroine's perspective. One notable exception: Anne Stuart's *Shadow Dance* features two concurrent love stories, and the mighty rending of the hymen for one of them is told from the perspective of the male. Why? While we'd love to say it's because that particular hero had spent the vast majority of the book in skirts (crossdressing romances are such a guilty pleasure), really, it's because that portion of the love story focused mostly on the hero and his struggles over his love for the heroine since as far she knows, he's a freakin' woman, so it made sense to view the first sex scene from his POV. And that, right there, is a good rule of thumb for determining which POV we'll see the inaugural rumpy-pumpy: Where goeth the angst over the loss of virginity? There goeth the POV it's told from.

Perspective is everything, and at those most intimate and possibly acrobatic moments of coital wonderment, whose head is describing the action of that other head can make for a great scene in the hands of a skilled writer. But damn near every time, the first sex scene will be in the point of view of the woman, the prose can easily delve into the purple, and both parties will have orgasms of rainbow brilliance—but not the gay kind of rainbow, unless it's a gay romance, of course.

Create Your Own Deflowering Scene!

Someone losing her virginity? Hooray and excellent! Let us help you with the vocabulary. Rearrange the following words and craft your own homage to deflowering your favorite virgin heroine. Or play along at home and see if you own a book wherein any of the following appear. (Hint: It's an easy game. Just close your eyes. Point at your keeper shelf. Open your eyes. You win!)

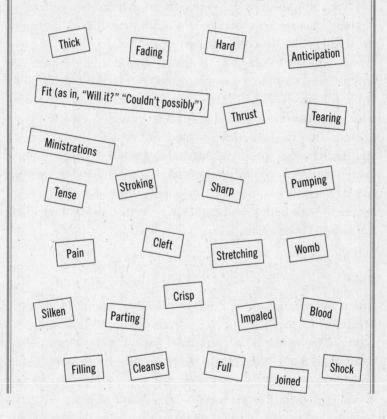

Thick · Fading · Hard · Anticipation · Fit (as in, "Will it?" "Couldn't possibly") · Thrust · Tearing · Ministrations · Tense · Stroking · Sharp · Pumping · Pain · Cleft · Stretching · Womb · Crisp · Silken · Parting · Impaled · Blood · Filling · Cleanse · Full · Joined · Shock

So What's with All the Conquering Imagery in Romance Sex?

Well, that conquering works both ways. While the heroine and her pesky virginity (if she has one) can be conquered through all sorts of political machinations or accidental trip-and-fall situations, the hero, he's conquered as well. It's not a "tie him down with apron strings and spank him till he cries" type of emasculating conquering. Heroines are not usually after the hero's balls, unless they want to play with them in a friendly kind of way—with the exception of BDSM play, which comes with a whole other set of rules and turns the idea of conquering upside down on its ball gag.

If you think about sexual intercourse as an intimate combination of consummation, connection, and commitment, both parties in the actual nookie dance have to participate in all levels for the three elements to work cohesively. If one of them is a virgin, then not only is there virginity to overcome but then sexual education to enjoy. If both are sexually experienced, there's the joy of learning what turns the other on, and what secret crannies in the body are express lanes to the nonstop nookie. But despite the number of rape-and-conquer scenes that littered Old Skool romance like discarded petticoats on the floor of the nearest pirate ship, current romance creates not so much a conquering through sex as it does a cohesion, with both sides equal players in the sexual, emotional, and physical boom-shaka-laka.

SEXUAL EDUCATION, ROMANCE STYLE

Laura Vivanco, one of the Professors Brilliant who write at Teach Me Tonight, examined the role of romance novels in sexual education of the reader in an entry from August 2006. Her analysis, that romance novels are one of the few genres that focus not only on women's sexuality but on *instruction* of women's sexuality and sexual enjoyment, reveals romance as a source of both the sexual teaching and the sexual healing.* Romance novels, she says, "play a role in educating people about their bodies" and, more important, are responsible for "shaping attitudes towards sexuality":

* Cue Marvin Gaye, please. Perfect musical sound track to this chapter.

In general, romances may give some basic information about the mechanics of reproduction, and though the incidence of contraceptive failure seems extremely high if one looks at romances as a group, as do the numbers of secret babies produced as a result, the depiction of the use of contraceptives during sex scenes, particularly of condoms, suggests to readers that condom-use is not incompatible with passion and enjoyment. . . .

For many of the Smart Bitches readers, romance novels were their first introduction to sex. Long before they had any actual sex, they read about it in various configurations and in various historical time periods. Candy, for example, learned about oral sex from Anne Stuart.*

Being an enterprising and bright little girl, she had reasoned out, by the time she was nine or ten years old, that if people kissed each other on all sorts of places other than the mouth, then conceivably they would want to kiss each other *down there*. She immediately discounted that idea as disgusting and hilarious.

And then, one glorious day in 1992, she read *Special Gifts* by Anne Stuart. And lo, she saw that it was good. Seriously: horizons were opened forever, and naughty bits were suddenly made sexy in whole new ways.

Sex education, beyond the mere mechanics, within a romance also embraces the idea of sexual appetite for women, and embraces that idea with both arms *and* both legs. Jennifer Crusie, in one of her essays for the Romance Writers of America's *Romance Writers Report,* examines why that multilimbed embrace of sexuality and sexual education is revolutionary:

Women shouldn't experience a lot of sexual encounters, conventional wisdom ran, because that would soil them, and it's not in

---

* Candy still dreams of the day when she can shake Stuart's hand while telling her that—hopefully, without Stuart asking for some sort of restraining order.

their nature anyway. Men who had a lot of sex and enjoyed it were studs; women who did the same were unnatural sluts. In truth, it was rarely the sex patriarchy objected to—men have usually been intrigued not threatened by lesbianism—it was the sexual knowledge gained from other men: God forbid a woman should know more about sex than a man. Romance fiction not only says women want that knowledge and have a right to it, it often gives it to them explicitly on the page, telling them it's not wrong to want a full sexual life and showing them how to get one.

Consider the one-two-three kick-punch-knee-to-the-groin given to traditional standards of sexuality by the average romance novel:

I. **Women can enjoy sex.** Once sexually and emotionally awakened to the masterful fizznuckin', romance-novel heroines enjoy sex. A Lot.

II. **Women can ask for and initiate sexual congress.** Once they've started enjoying the nookie, as sexually empowered creatures they can be eager for the action without compunction. In fact, it's better if the heroine enjoys and pounces on her partner: it makes for clever sex scenes on the stairs.

III. **If she likes it and enjoys it, it's perfectly acceptable, whatever it is.** Women can experiment and explore different sexual options, because no matter what it is, from reverse cowgirl to anal to BDSM to being the cream filling in a man sandwich, if she's happy, then more power to her, and to the reader.

Seriously, consider how revolutionary that trifecta of sex bombs is for not only women in the 1970s and '80s, but women of the current era who are bombarded with hypersexual imagery that capitalizes repeatedly on virgin/whore dichotomy. Romance says, screw that—whatever it is, if the woman enjoys it, and it's not pushing her into moral ambivalence, it's perfectly and marvelously okay.

And speaking of sexual imagery, consider the rape scenes in light of the sexual education in romance. Vivanco examines how romance's tolerance for rape in the early days sends a completely different message about rape victims and women who are sexually experienced. Whereas outside of the romance genre, women who were knowingly involved in prostitution, or who were raped, were considered "damaged goods"; in a romance novel, particularly some stunningly good ones, such women deserve and earn happy endings:

> Whereas novels such as *Tess of the d'Urbervilles* tell a woman that, if she's raped, she's degraded, the modern romance genre, even with its rather high number of virgin heroines, does, on the whole, assert that a woman who has been raped or otherwise had sex outside marriage is still attractive, is still valuable as a person. Rather than condemning her, it celebrates her as a person.

Romances are not about sex. They include sex, often, and sometimes frequently. But the sex within a romance makes both elements better. Most important, in a romance, ignorance is *not* bliss. Sexual experience and enjoyment are bliss. More of it, more bliss, all the better for the heroine and the reader.

What's Your Erotica Pen Name?

What, you don't necessarily want your mother, your grandfather, and you neighbors to recognize your name on that Poserific cover of two men and a lady doing the what-what in a rushing mountain stream?* Fearful of your work colleagues finding out that you are really the prolific and creative genius behind the hit series saga of the corkscrew penis werebird who has multiple forced partners . . . in space? Well, sure as yogurt shootin', honey, you need a pen name.

(*continued on next page*)

*Ew. Germs.

While romance is flush with women who write under pseudonyms, erotica is a whole new level of pen name. For some reason, the pseudonyms of erotica writers seem to have a lot of vowels. Their first names are extra more vowel-y for that extra-more-special feminine touch, and their last names can evoke images of WASPy yacht clubs, British houses with hedges, or a verbal combination of staid convention with over-the-top exuberance—which, come to think of it, pretty much sums up the role of erotic romance in the whole genre right there.

Never one to leave you hanging, the Smart Bitches have your guide to creating your own Erotica Pen Name:

1. Take your name:	Sarah
2. Add 2 e's, 1 a, and an I, or four vowels of your choosing	Saeirah
3. Pair with last name that could conceivably appear on the back of a yacht or on a pastry ingredient brand name, or is simply the plural of a common surname	Parker, Toll, House, Pillsbury, Arthur, Doyle, Clay, Stephens, Jameses, Claytons, Smiths, Anals.*
4. Bonus: a middle name, and the choice is obvious. The name of the street where you grew up.	Hey, why not?

Sarah thus becomes: Saeirah Reynolds Clay. Now that's hot.

* If your name is Anal and you write erotic romance, you are automatically full of win.

Anal Is the New Oral: Sexual Trends and Adventures in Romance

There's more to erotic romance than "Yar! Here be buttsecks!" Kind of. Because pushing people's boundaries sexually means pushing the boundary in the narrative sense as well. Erotic romance has also helped challenge some of the heteronormative assumptions about romance in general. Bottom line,* erotica pushes boundaries. Literally and figuratively.

With the increasing power of erotic romance and its ability to educate the masses, sexual techniques that used to be entirely taboo are now a possible part of even historical romance fiction. Specifically? Buttsecks. What used to qualify as extremely impossibly hot, too hot for network TV and publishing, is making headway into publishing with each new release. Raelene Gorlinsky at Ellora's Cave told us that "at a writer conference about two years ago, the editor panel was discussing this topic. One of the New York editors said 'Anal is the new oral.' That's an example of how readers have become 'acclimatized' to the sex due to the popularity of erotic romances. Oral sex in a romance novel was uncommon and titillating five or six years ago, [and] now it is standard and very vanilla. In fact, anal has been common in e-pubbed erotic romance for quite a while now and is becoming more so in New York print erotic romance; it is no longer at all shocking or considered excessively hot."

But anal isn't the only action that's crashing the romance sex party: consider these other group-friendly techniques, which Raelene was kind enough to give us details on as she explained how erotic romance has begun to influence the rest of the romance genre. Somewhere, a licentious rake hero at the ICH just passed out from the excitement and anticipation.

Ménage à trois: The M/F/M tango of body parts is a hot, hot market, and as Raelene Gorlinsky told us, the flood of ménage stories began sometime after 2004. Now readers grab them with both hands, and authors incorporate ménage into their narratives. While a ménage scene in a historical romance or a contemporary line that's not known for adventurous sexuality might raise more than a few eyebrows, especially among those readers devoted to

* Pun intended.

monogamy between the protagonist pair, no one blinks at the three-person tango in erotic romance.

Bondage: Consider the possibilities that have already risen within mainstream romance, both historical and contemporary. It was never a big deal to tie a partner to the bedposts; Sarah remembers scenes like that in the early 1990s. Yet now, a heroine might deliberately stock a few toys for such playtime activities that involve some light whipping, teasing, or submission. Raelene Gorlinsky says, "A little playful submission or tying-to-the-bedposts is common in erotic romance now. The heavier 'lifestyle' BDSM with strong Master/Slave elements is for many readers considered pushing the envelope of what they feel comfortable with." We're not saying that the next historical romance will feature strap-ons and the Regency version of *Bend Over Boyfriend*, but on both sides of the bed, we expect to see more tying up and tying down. All in the name of good, sexual fun and happy orgasms, of course.

SPEAKING OF SEX: AN INTERVIEW WITH EMMA HOLLY

Emma Holly, one of the most recognizable names in erotic romance, has written some books so hot Sarah's face turned so red while reading one that a fellow commuter asked if she were feeling ill.* One of the auto-buys for fans of the genre, Holly's books have won a ton of awards from both readers and professional organizations. What's even cooler about Holly is that her Web site not only discusses her own writing and offers excerpts, but it gives online guides to writing sensual sex scenes with skill and legitimacy so that the most outrageous sexual adventures will ring true.

Holly's books embrace sexual activities that some people may not have even imagined, and her plots may allow for happy endings that include more than two people. *Strange Attractions,* for example, published by Berkley in 2005, follows dropout Charity Wills, who agrees to travel to a reclusive scientist's home in exchange for an

---

* Sarah: "No, no, not ill. Not ill at all."

opportunity to attend college, all expenses paid. Once she's at Mr. Reclusive's mansion, however, there's multiple partners, bondage play, sexual games, and a whole mess of sex. And hot men. And a lot of fanning yourself.

So when we started working on a discussion of sex in the romance novels, we had to ask her some burning (in a good way) questions.

SMART BITCHES: To what do you attribute the growth of erotic romance?

EMMA HOLLY: I have a theory—which may be entirely bogus—that Republican administrations are good for the popularity of steamy stuff. Rightly or wrongly, citizens expect to have their wilder side infringed upon. Buying erotic romance could be considered the average Josephine's quiet rebellion.

If that seems too ridiculous, perhaps the trend has simply gathered sufficient momentum to keep going.

SMART BITCHES: Did you ever encounter any opposition to the sexual content you wrote?

HOLLY: I wouldn't say anyone's reaction has risen to the level of opposition. Occasionally people are uncomfortable with what I write. I'm sure some authors would be happier if the erotic branch of the romance tree could simply be lopped off. I understand their fears. They think the explicit nature of what authors like myself write lessens their chance of getting the respect they crave from the world at large. The problem is, the only respect that ever matters is the kind you give yourself. The moment you give anyone else the right to say whether what you do is worthy, you're up the creek.

SMART BITCHES: Does being an erotic romance author in our culture mean that you are doubly protective of your private life? Romance authors face all sorts of doofy questions about research; do even more prurient assumptions ever plague you?

HOLLY: I'm naturally a very reserved person, so I suspect I'd be protective of my private life no matter what I wrote.

Sometimes readers seem to assume I'm living a life of constant sexual adventure—which is flattering, I suppose. More often, they offer a little TMI about their own sex lives, as if—given what I write—I couldn't possibly be shocked by them!

SMART BITCHES: Do you ever feel that what you write is subversive and powerful?

HOLLY: There was a sense that the writers who were helping to mainstream both erotica and erotic romance were pioneers. To depict sex as a positive activity, especially a positive activity for women, felt new. Naturally, we were standing on the shoulders of authors who'd plowed the ground before us, but at the time, I was excited to be even a little part of the succeeding wave. Today, I feel as if what I write is powerful for more reasons than its sexual content.

BUT WHAT ABOUT . . . ?

Yeah, all that sex ed, it's not all roses and deep-stamened lilies. There's some sexual what-the-fuck awash in Romancelandia, and it's time to knock down a few tried-and-true sexual myths routinely populating and propagating in romance.

We've already discussed the hymen, and where it is, and where it is *not*. But consider the sexual mythology on the whole that is contained within the romance novel. Yes, the sex is usually consensual, and often within the boundaries of a committed relationship. That is awesome, but it doesn't mean that the following sexual myths need to be dipped in gold and held as the perfect standard of sexual intercourse.

1. The Simultaneous Orgasm

COME ON NOW and WE MEAN IT. This has to stop. It's a rare thing, people! All these authors who presume that sex means both parties come together and then come together? Puh. Leez. They crest together, they fly together, they shatter together, they walk into the gates of paradise together, they do the sweaty tango and dip into the twist of orgasm together. At every moment, their sexual congress is like one of those sweaters that covers the man and woman like they're conjoined twins, with two neck holes, one sleeve for each person, and ample cotton weave between them for all sorts of second-base action underneath.

There are not that many simultaneous orgasms in the sexual universe, and to have each and every romance couple embarking on conjoined shattering orgasmic bliss each and every time in each and every book is patently ridiculous.

Sexually speaking, women are wired differently than men, and that's a hormonal and biological fact. Many women don't orgasm without direct clitoral stimulation, and find penetration to be a distant second in preference to actual strumming of the nubbin flower.

Which leads us to the second sexual romance myth. Many a romance sex scene will feature the hero reaching down to stroke her in a most sensitive spot in the midst of missionary position coitus:

2. Human Males Do Not Have Impossibly Flexible Arms

So the hero and heroine are going at it like a roof on a hot-tin pussy, and he's breached the velvet boundaries of her deep cinnabar cave. To put it bluntly, they're fuckin' away. And somehow he reaches between their sliding, pounding bodies to find and stroke her clitoris in just the perfect amount of deft pressure that BAM she flies into a shattering, mind-numbing moon-swallowing orgasm with one flick of his finger.

WHO ARE YOU KIDDING!? For one thing, who can reach like that with their arms without encountering massive rotator-cuff injury or at the least a good amount of shoulder strain? And for another thing, how does he curl his fingers around to stroke the magic button? It would seem to require his elbow be pressed against his rib cage but his arm held straight down without bending, plus full mobility to his fingers in an area that's a bit crowded at present, *all while they are humping away in perfectly toned ecstasy.* Apparently all heroes are double jointed in their fingers, shoulders, and elbows, and no heroine would even think to be startled by a muscular arm nudging its way down to her cavern of happiness.

3. Penetration Does Not Yield Instant Orgasm

This is marginally related to the first and the second, but as we said, women often like clitoral action as a path to orgasm. The number of romances that feature the heroine mounted on this manly manpole and two seconds later finding the golden fields of orgasm is a disservice to anyone who has had sex with a man who couldn't find a clitoris if it introduced itself.

4. Loss of Virginity Doesn't Always Involve Pain or Copious Bleeding

Yes, there are stories of women with incredibly forthright and blood-rich hymens who, upon losing their virginity, really did bleed all over the bloody place. And there are certainly women for whom their first sexual experience was painful, though not necessarily because of the hymen of impassable fortress-strength steel. It might have been because first sex can be nervous sex and nervous sex is not well lubricated sex and thus can be chafing sex.

But for most women, the savage shrieking of pain at the loss of her hymen? Never happens. It might sting or stretch a little, but come on. The pounding on his back? The screaming and kicking? The tears and the sobbing? Not the most normal first experience for most people. Maybe she hits her knee on the gear shift and it throbs a bit, but the tearing, horrible pain? And the stains everywhere that proclaim Avast! Virginity, It Hath Been Lost?

Doesn't happen. Quit scaring the virgins, all you romance authors.

5. Give Mortal Men a Moment to Rest. But Not Romance Heroes!

The ICH particularly hates this one, as all these superhuman romance heroes are a disservice to the men of the world. The mullets, the muscles, the manhoods, they arch over the heroines, they groan out their orgasms, they collapse in sweaty, panting heaps on top of the heroines.

And in 5 . . . 4 . . . 3 . . . 2 . . . 1 . . .

They're hard and randy and ready to go one more time! Faster than an Olympic gold medalist sprinter can haul ass down a hundred meters, the romance hero is hard and eager for more action. What the almighty freaking shit is that about?! Unless the man is seventeen years old, THIS DOES NOT HAPPEN. There is a concept of recovery time that never really affects the romance hero, and thus casts mortal men with normal turgid boners in a shameful light, because immediately after having a great orgasm, real men need at least a half hour before they can think about going another round.

And of course, she is, too. No chafing, no sensitivity, no sense of, "Dude, are you kidding me?" Oh no, it's boners and natural lube bringing another set of simultaneous orgasms to the reader's eager eyes. There is some weight and validity to the accusations that romance novels are really overblown sexual fantasies. This particular sexual myth is nothing but overblown fantasy. Real men wish they could achieve sexual reboot in such record time.

But fantasy, mythology, or reality, romance novels are one of the very few genres that examine sex for its own sake, and explain it often in marvelously precise detail. So while some readers embrace the sexual education inherent in romance novels, and others decry it as perversity, or sexual miseducation, the root of the turgid truth is simple: romances are about intimacy. Intimacy often includes sex.

There is absolutely nothing wrong with that.

Chapter Phallus

The Covers,

and the Reasons to Snark Them

One of the most popular features of our site is the Cover Snark. Who'd have thought that a weekly gallery of the worst of the worst romance-novel covers would attract such a giddy audience eager for snark and deplorable art? Then again, the Internet exists for three reasons, and the third is to make fun of anything that's not nailed down (the first two being porn and pictures of cats or dogs, captions optional). Even though the Web and print differ greatly in terms of what we can do with illustrations we didn't draw, we can't miss the opportunity to talk covers, and Cover Snark.

Paperback romance covers are the gift wrapping on the erect package that is your average romance novel, and that gift is really meant for the people who see you reading the book in the first place. Romance-novel covers are likely 65.9 percent of the reason romance novels take the mockage from the rest of the known world so damn hard. The cover images leave ample room for it. It's not hard to abjectly dismiss a genre when much of it is adorned with mullet-sporting heroes grasping at buxom, open-mouthed heroines, both of whom appear to be caught in a wind storm. Sometimes the couple featured on the cover look as if they're in pain more than any degree of passion, and can appear as if they have some voraciously hungry skin disease, or, in the case of Poser art, as if they are deceased as of many moons ago. It's frankly difficult sometimes to defend a love of romance novels when those novels are wrapped up in the visual assault that is some cover art.

What Is Poser and Why Do You Hate It?

Poser is a 3D drawing and animation software program that is used for—wait for it—posing human figures. A computer version of the old wooden posing model used for sketch artists, Poser has spawned several niche communities—developers who craft Poser models, and artists who use those models for computer-generated art. Some of this art will knock your eyeballs out in wonderment and awe.

Some of it, like those featured on more than a few romance-novel covers, will make you wish your eyeballs could check out on vacation for a while, at least until the memory fades.

Where do these covers come from? The humid depths of Satan's asscrack. No, we kid. That's just bad Poser covers. No, the cover, specifically the clinch cover, has its roots, according to the oral history of romance, in the male gaze, but what good sexual image doesn't? Here's the funny thing about romance covers: the cover art originally was not about reaching the romance reader. Really, we're not kidding. The sexy, clinch-laden covers with peri-orgasmic women with giant breasts, giant hair, and dresses that were one quick tug away from total nudity? Never meant to entice you as a reader. So why do the O-faced couples continue to haunt you as you shop for romance?

According to Kate Duffy, Kensington editor, the clinch cover art became a self-fulfilling prophecy because of how and why it sold. It sold because it was clinch cover art, and it was clinch cover art because it sold. Chicken, egg, meet clinch cover. "As little as eight years ago there were over seven hundred different wholesalers and distributors," Duffy says. "And your safest option in developing a romance cover was the clinch. It was never a discussion of what the consumer wanted, it was 'What signal can we send to the distributor to get the book in front of the consumer?'" So the books themselves weren't necessarily designed to attract, say, Sarah and her ten-dollar allowance, which was earmarked for nothing but romance. The cover designs, at least back then, according to Duffy, were created to catch the eye of the distributor and the wholesaler, who placed the orders ultimately to get the book to the consumer.

These wholesalers and distributors? At the time, they were men. They liked the clinch cover, and that was what was ordered for and thus sold in bookstores. Hence: self-fulfilling prophecy. Duffy mentioned that there were variations, but always revolving around the clinch. For example, there were the years of Jude Deveraux's covers wherein the heroine had impossibly long hair. The book buyers thought long hair was romantic, they bought more copies, and it boosted her sales. So the cover art is—or was—undeniably a factor in boosting a book's sales, but the sales target was not the reader. The target was the person buying the book to put it on the shelf in front of the reader.

Many a grocery store today still features a bookshelf laden with about-to-be-undressed women lined up like half-dressed Rockettes, and they sell. Even now, as book-cover designs have tried to shift away from the clinch, there's still many a cover on the shelf nearest you featuring grasping, gasping women, and firm, equally buxom men. They sell like hotcakes made of gangbusters because the clinch cover has become an iconic image that's shorthand for romance. If you see a beefy man with incredible pectoral muscles grabbing a flouncy tart,* it's a romance. Most historical romances feature a clinch image somewhere, be it on the front cover, the back cover, or in a stepback, which is when the cover has a cardstock overlay that lifts to reveal a full-color piece of clinchtastic illustration beneath. Stepbacks are expensive, but lovely for hiding the half-naked sexing that may embarrass you as you read on the subway. Nothing

---

*Female, not pastry.

says "This book has descriptive sex in it" like a cover featuring illustrations of people in Kama Sutra–worthy sexual positions.

Ask a romance reader on the Internet for her opinion of clinch covers, and you'll get an earful. Some women hate, hate, *HAAATE* them, find them offensive, and go to great creative lengths to cover their romance novels with fabric, brown paper bags, or a magazine.

Some women are inured to them—Sarah falls into this camp—and are so accustomed to the art of passionate cover embrace that they don't even see it anymore and look to the cover copy or the first fifteen pages to determine if the book is worth purchasing. Oddly, these are the readers who are so used to them that they use the images as the visual shorthand mentioned earlier: in a sea of paperbacks on a jumbo-jet-size bookshelf, the romances are easily spotted at thirty paces because of the colorful, nearly orgasmic, partially dressed uglibumpin' going down on the cover.

There are some readers who like the clinch covers, and who appreciate the art skill required to render the illustration in the first place. One artist, Pino, has painted illustrations for well over three thousand books, according to his personal Web site, and his style is so unique Sarah once identified a Pino painting for sale from across the rolling ballroom of a cruise ship on rough seas. His art, it is identifiable at fifty seasick paces. Fans of his art host image galleries online, some of which are so decorated with animated Java applications that they crash the nearest Web browser faster than you can say, "chest pillows."

Laura Kinsale's *The Prince of Midnight* was one of the very first romance novels featuring only the hero on the cover. Of course, it was Fabio who graced the cover of her novel in 1990, but her book was the first diversion from the "clinch" cover, as she puts it, and the first image that neglected to position an "overendowed" female on the cover:

> The persistence of the clinch cover goes beyond market identification and the subconscious appeal of pornographic illustrations of

females to male wholesale book buyers. . . . Everyone—publishers, art directors, and book buyers included—has been convinced that readers are identifying with the heroine; therefore the illustrated heroine should be gorgeous and well-endowed, because that is what all women wish to be, right?

Wrong.

At first, like everyone else, I attributed the enormous popularity of *The Prince of Midnight*'s hero-only cover to the fact that romance readers are sick and tired of illustrations that focus so heavily on something in which they have no interest whatsoever—big-breasted, lust-crazed women—and are ready and waiting for a cover that emphasizes something in which they are highly interested: a hunk.

Since Fabio's appearance on *The Prince of Midnight,* though, the hero-centered cover has grown to be nearly mainstream, as books by authors such as Marjorie M. Liu, Kresley Cole, Christine Feehan, Kalen Hughes, and others feature the man front, shirtless, and center. And the male models, they enjoy quite the eager following.

Game Time! It's Time for the Anatomy of a Truly Excellent Romance Cover (and by Excellent We Mean Eye-Searingly Bizarre or, Better Yet, Just Plain Awful) Treasure Hunt!

Hie thee to thy nearest used bookstore, complete with musty book smell (almost as good as the bread-baking-at-Subway smell), and locate the romance-novel shelf. It's time to play Find the Worst Possible Cover. If you find a cover with a high point score, please, send a scanned image or a link to that cover to covers@smartbitchestrashybooks.com—we need to know about it!

- Does the overall illustration appear as if there is Vaseline smeared on the book cover, on your eyeballs, or both? 2 pts
- Is the hero's head bent at an impossible angle, suggesting a broken vertebrae or two? 1 pt

- Do the following colors appear on the cover?

  fuchsia: 1 pt   lemon yellow: 2 pts

  lime green: 2 pts   pink: 2 pts

  lavender: 1 pt   more fuchsia: 1 pt

  sky blue: 1 pt   pastel pink: 2 pts

  burgundy: 1 pt   neon yellow: 3 pts

  All of the above: 10 pts

- Is the heroine grabbing her own bare leg like she's in a Nair commercial? 2 pts
- Is the heroine posed in a bent position that seems at the least uncomfortable and at the most anatomically impossible? 3 pts
- Is the heroine's neck bent back at an angle such that you suspect she is no longer alive? 3 pts
- Mullet? 5 pts
- Mullet on the heroine? 10 pts
- Multiple depictions of the mullet from various angles? 9 pts
- Is the couple outside in the grass and flowers, rolling around on some sweeping hillside? 2 pts
- Is the couple inside? 5 pts
- Are they in bed? 2 pts
- Is the heroine's hair contained in a cap, hat, or crown/coronet? 4 pts
- Is the heroine's hair so enormously out of control in its volume and curl that you think you and she could both use it as a blanket? 4 pts
- Is the heroine's eye shadow a color you've never before witnessed on a human? 4 pts
- Does the book take place in a time before it was socially acceptable for women to wear cosmetics? 5 pts
- Is the heroine blond? 1 pt
- Is the heroine a redhead? 1 pt
- Is the heroine's hair a deep, solid black? 1 pt

(continued on next page)

- Is the heroine a (gasp) brunette? 5 pts
- Is the heroine (holy shit) wearing glasses? 10 pts
- Do the amorous couple appear to be on fire? 3 pts
- Do they appear to be glowing? 2 pts
- Do they appear to have a possibly contagious skin disease? 3 pts
- Does the hero have his shirt off? 3 pts
- Does the hero have his shirt unbuttoned but still tucked in? 1 pt
- Is the hero wearing a wide, wide belt, similar to the belts weight lifters wear to keep their kidneys from flying out their backs? 4 pts
- Is it possible that you might see a hint of cameltoe in the hero's pants? 6 pts
- Is the hero completely naked? 3 pts
- Is the hero holding a sword or elongated weapon at such an angle that it seems to represent something, perhaps something large, turgid, throbbing, and phallic? 4 pts
- Is the heroine smoking a cigarette? 10 pts
- Does the hero have a big porny mustache? 4 pts
- Does he have his mouth open? 5 pts
- Does she have her mouth open? 0 pts*
- Is his man titty bigger than yours? 5 pts
- Are her bosoms bigger than yours? 6 pts
- Are her bosoms bigger than his? 4 pts
- Is there a rearing horse? 3 pts
- Does the rearing horse appear to emerge from someone's ass? 5 pts
- Is there a swan? 3 pts
- Does the swan appear to be having some sort of conniption? 2 pts
- Is there another animal freaking the fuck out in the background? 3 pts

---

*Heroines all have their mouths open. It's called "O-face."

- Is it a recognizable species that you can visually identify? 4 pts
- Is the couple facing each other? 5 pts
- Is the heroine facing away from the hero, in a position we call "Invisible Buttsecks"? 10 pts
- Is there no possible way coitus could occur in the position they're depicted in? 4 pts
- Does their position possibly indicate actual coitus? 8 pts
- Is there actual coitus that you can see? 100 pts

THE ELEMENTS OF ROMANCE COVERS

If you're not choosing to partake in our Hunt for the Worst Cover Ever, or you're not sure what we're talking about, have a look in your nearest used-book store. The pastel and screaming neon color schemes, the purple sunsets and orange flowers, the big hair and the peri-orgasmic faces: the classic Old Skool clinch is a sight to behold.

The two never-fail elements that seem to populate way too many romance covers, however, are the shirt and the hair. The hero's shirt is almost always unbuttoned, but still tucked into his belt. Also, if you're truly fortunate, that shirt will have wide, puffy sleeves, the likes of which no male of your acquaintance would ever wear unless he was heading right to the Ren Faire already in costume.

The hair, however, is a two-pronged beast. The hero, unfortunately, for a long, long time, was pictured in that most unfortunate of hairstyles, the mullet. We've never actually read a romance wherein the hero was *described* as having a mullet, but four out of five dentists agree that four out of five romance covers feature a man with a mighty, majestic mullet. We do not know why, either.

The heroine, on the other hand, has hair. Lots and lots of long, wavy, incredibly huge hair. Sometimes it's spilling down her back, and sometimes it's blowing in the stiff breeze (a breeze, by the way, that might be going in the opposite direction from the hero's hair) but the heroine will have stunningly opulent lengths of hair, because long hair, instead of being something that paralyzes the woman when the hero rolls over on top of it, is effortlessly sexy. It's never tangled, or in the way, or in their mouths.

The clinch cover is still in use today—and we are so very grateful, for so many reasons—but that doesn't mean it's the only type of romance cover you'll see. As the neon and pastel humptastic clinch gradually moved out of favor, and readers saw less of big hair, bigger boob, and biggest man titty, the Drippy Landscape and still-life art moved in. Around about the mid-1990s, most of the big names, from Julie Garwood to Jude Deveraux to Nora Roberts, had covers that depicted a still-life item, like a mask or a feather, a brooch on a ribbon, or a landscape captured in soft-focus pastels. Castles in the distance? Cottages in fervently green hills? Art that makes you think Thomas Kinkade, the Painter of Light$^{TM©®}$? All in your bookstore now. Go have a look.

The rainy-focus landscapes are still in use, echoing the style of Monet and other Impressionist painters. You'll see the Impressionist romance art influence on several of the newest cover types, particularly Loretta Chase's latest novels, which feature a close-up of a woman's back, with ethereal and Impressionist flowers in the background.

And speaking of close-ups, that's the other trend of note—one that is almost as tired and irritating as the pastels-and-neon clinch of O-face boobage: the Back and the Headless. The Back is just that—a woman's back. The women were shown from behind, either close up or full length—Jane Feather's covers, particularly *The Widow's Kiss*, were among the first to show the silhouette of a woman from behind, with no facial features. Very attractive—Sarah picked up *The Widow's Kiss* at least four times before remembering that it hadn't passed her thirty-page test—i.e., Sarah's interest wasn't captured in the first thirty pages.

The Headless is pretty self-explanatory, too. Headless men and headless women have appeared in various formats, at about the same time as covers featuring extraneous body parts, as if a model

**Everything I Know About Biology and Physics,
I Learned from Romance-Novel Covers**

1. Wind direction: Winds must be generated directly under or facing individual model, with another source directly under skirts and shirts. Think, "The grass is exhaling. Forcefully."

2. Flexibility of human backs. The human vertebrae can bend in marvelously flexible directions to the point where three heroine spines can be braided with minimal effort.

3. Freaked-out horses and other animals enhance any sexual experience, especially if they are within twenty-five feet of a booty call.

4. Sex in a swamp = good for your health.

5. Lurid sky = a sign of true love, not impending hurricane.

6. Hairlessness everywhere except the top of one's head is a sign of true feminine beauty and not of selective breeding.

7. Plenitude of hair on head on a male is a sign of masculine strength. More specifically, mullets = sign of virility.

were hacked to pieces and sold off for parts. For a time there were arms holding swords, or male backsides wrapped in plaids or bum-hugging breeches.

Then came the glut of headless heroes (Loretta Chase's *Mr. Impossible,* for example) and the headless heroines, such as those featured on Susan Elizabeth Phillips's hardcover releases, which depict not only headless women but dancing, frolicking headless women. We can only presume the headless chop was designed to allow the reader to imagine whatever face and head they wanted on top of a very virile or buxom body, but it was still an alarming trend. Nothing said romance like "Extreme close-up—headless edition."

And then what happened? Same thing that happened with the clinch cover: oversaturation. Like an overplayed popular song, something that once caught your eye and looked unique became tired and, well, overplayed, once the trend caught on. From the clinch cover to the nondescript, plain-yogurt landscape, overuse leads only to the overuse of the next big trend. And in one big circle of life, trends repeatedly become shorthand for subgenres.

Witness the urban-fantasy tramp-stamp heroine. A tramp stamp is a tattoo on the sacrum, or the lower back, right at the hips. Take a look-see at the crop of urban-fantasy romances featuring one of our favorite new creations, the Kick-Ass Heroine, and you'll see a bunch of ladies, illustrated from behind, wearing low-slung pants and cropped tops. Sometimes there's a tattoo, or maybe a weapon of some kind, and sometimes there's endless skin with the sultry promise of middle-aged muffin top in ten or so years, but the back of a woman's midriff, weapon optional, has become shorthand for "Ass-Kicking Heroine in Urban Fantasy, ahoy!"

The danger in shorthand is that once every publisher has piled on the bandwagon, readers can't tell any of the books apart. Author Gennita Low explained on her Web site the danger of oversaturation of cover image perfectly: "I'd look at the cover and try to remember whether I've seen it or bought it, and then put the book back on the shelf because I wasn't sure. And of course, when I'm home, I'd forget to check. Repeat vicious cycle."

MAN ON TOP: THE MALE MODEL IN ROMANCE ART

A curious facet of romance-cover art is that the male models are much more famous than the women. Consider the number of famous romance cover models who are male: Fabio. John DeSalvo. The late Rob Ashton. Nathan Kamp. Even people who are completely unfamiliar and uninterested in romance novels know who Fabio is, mostly because he built his career on a foundation of romance-cover modeling, before he went on to embrace charitable work, parody, and whether margarine is, or is not, butter. Fansites for male cover models fill the Internet with man titty and spinning, blinking animated gifs, the visual embodiment of the rabid fangirl squee.

Contrast that with the number of female cover models whose

names you know. Think of one. No, we'll wait. Still tapping your chin and frowning? So are we. It's a fascinating reverse of the traditional model culture: for every one male supermodel in the fashion and print advertisement world, there are at least five known females. But in romance-cover land? It's the men who get all the attention. The women are much less famous as cover models, unless the female model in question is already a celebrity, such as with Julia Quinn's *The Lost Duke of Wyndham,* which featured Ewa Da Cruz, a soap opera actress with a considerable fanbase of her own.

The fact that the male cover models are infinitely more famous than the female cover models says something about the community of romance readers. On one hand, it says, "We like lookin' at men," apparently. Which, hey, why not? Nothing wrong with admiring the muscular male form, especially when that male form is riding a horse bareback and possibly sliding off the horse's back end as the animal rears up to paw at the moon against a purple sunset. Males with that level of horsemanship cannot avoid the fame.

To explore the odd celebrity surrounding male cover models, Sarah chased down John DeSalvo and was on her very best behavior for an interview with him. Sarah will tell you personally: "He's polite. And truly striking visually in person. And polite. Which is worth way more points with me than any set of cheekbones, and his are quite stunning." Both DeSalvo and Fabio are subject to a good bit of lusty and somewhat pinchy attention from fans, and a good bit of dismissal as showboat boner ponies from elsewhere. We decided it was time to meet the men behind the mullets, the man titty, and the mythology of romance covers, and ask how being romance-cover models has changed their lives.

SMART BITCHES: In my experience romance-novel covers are one of the few areas of visual media where the men have enjoyed more fame than the women. Why do you think romance-cover models are so famous, while the female models are barely known? Is it the fantasy of "being" the romance hero come to life?

DESALVO: Well, romance novels are mostly written by women for
     women. . . . The females play a big role within the story, but I
     would imagine that the readers fantasize themselves in that role
     with the male hero. So I could understand why the male hero is
     really the focus of the fantasy and why the male models are much
     more popular.

SMART BITCHES: Speaking of that fantasy: Are there expectations
     that you have encountered which come with being a male
     romance-cover model, in that readers expect you to act a certain
     way, or embody some of every hero you've represented? Is the
     pressure ever overwhelming?

DESALVO: I think it's just one of those things where people are
     curious what I look like in person. Do I have the presence in
     person as the hero I portray on the cover? It's nice when I can just
     mingle into a crowd. . . . I'm always a gentleman and I'm polite
     to everyone. Understandingly, and it's bound to happen,
     sometimes I find myself in an awkward position if an individual
     expects too much.

SMART BITCHES: When you first started doing the cover work, did
     you think to yourself, This might make me famous? Did you ever
     expect the attention and fame, or was it a surprise?

DESALVO: I'd be lying if I told you I didn't think it might make me famous. After being on so many covers and winning the Mr. Romance competition in 1994, which happened to be a big media event that year, I knew I would be getting some attention. But what would surprise me was whether I was walking the street or out somewhere, strangers would call me by my first or last name. I would think for a second, How do I know you? and then realize how they knew me.

My eleven-year-old nephew recently said innocently to me; "Uncle John, you are kind of famous, you know." And he's right in the sense where I'm a celebrity and famous in a certain industry. Other than that, I would say I'm just a little popular.

SMART BITCHES: Obviously, being a romance-cover model created the foundation for your career in film and television and opened a lot of opportunities for you. But lately covers have moved into stock-image photography, computer-animated images, and art that is in the public domain, and publishers aren't using as much original artwork as they did when you were posing. Are you still working within the romance cover-image world? Can other men looking to create modeling careers hope to emulate your path, or has that route mostly dried up?

DESALVO: Every once in a while I work with a couple of the studios. When I first started in the early to mid-'90s, the artists were still illustrating covers by hand . . . they were classic, beautiful, and had their own unique style. I felt honored to be painted, especially when it came to being solo on the cover.

Then in the late '90s the transition to digital evolved, and some of the artists made the change, some moved on. After the transition, some of the covers were still colorful but more photographic. Although sometimes change can be good, I can't say that I appreciate those computer-generated ones. I was very fortunate to be a mainstay through the peak of an era, which I believe will never be the same again!

SMART BITCHES: Your image portfolio is, in a word, huge. Is there a photographer or artist you enjoyed working with most of all? Is there a cover that's your personal favorite?

DESALVO: Arlene and Bob Osonitsch were the veteran photographers in the industry. Bob was the best . . . nobody knew how to consistently light and capture an image like he did! When I came along they took me in like a son and I worked with them more than any other photographer, for over ten years. Even if they needed just a shot of a torso, an arm, or a back, they called me. . . . I miss them!

I've worked with many great artists over the years. In the beginning there was Pino (an extremely talented artist), who was old-fashioned and illustrated everything by hand. He alone must have at least a hundred portraits of me.

John Ennis, a very colorful and detailed artist, illustrated *Jackson Rule,* which is one of my favorite pieces. For several years he pretty much worked with me exclusively, and I

remember him catching flack from a group of women for it. He
went on to tell them in an interview: "You might think that we
[cover artists] have a lot to choose from, but in fact, it is very
hard to find someone who is good-looking, muscular, and
extremely talented, and John is all three. He appears on many of
my covers because the alternative is to use a model who is lacking
in at least one of those three qualities." I'll always remember that
. . . thanks, John!

Jon Paul Ferrara is another incredible artist who became a
good friend of mine and has done many great works of art with
me. One in particular that he recently did is a portrait of me as a
boxer, for *Beyond the Glory,* which is a screenplay I've written. It's
really an astonishing work of art.

SMART BITCHES: I know you're not in control of the props and
fashions of the old cover shots, but do you have any thoughts
about the Romance Hero Wardrobe of a shirt unbuttoned but
still tucked in?

DESALVO: Looking back at them now, YEAH, they do look kind of
funny. SOMEBODY CALL THE FASHION POLICE!! Well,
mostly they want the body showing, and I believe that it's more
of a technical issue, to where I guess that it looks better uniform
than if a shirt was just hanging out and considered sloppy looking.
. . . A lot of shirts (especially the old-fashioned ones) really could
hang as low as past midthigh.

I would also imagine that some see it as the very first step to a
sexual encounter. Thank heavens that some styles do change.

At this point, our investigation of Cover Art and How It Got to
Be That Way turned into an investigation of how these covers are
made, which led Sarah to Jon Paul, whose art you've seen, even if
you didn't know it at the time. Jon Paul, who along with Pino and
John Ennis form the trifecta of romance-cover art, is among the
most prolific romance-cover artists currently working in the field
today. And he was gracious enough to tell us all about the behind-
the-scenes details that go into crafting the cover art.

Painting a cover, according to Paul, is a multistep process, one of which the artist himself is largely in control. After being hired by the art director at a publishing house, the artist chooses the models, develops the poses, hires the photographers, arranges the costumes, and then, using the basic photograph, creates the full-color illustration.

"People would ask me who did the makeup. I did the makeup. The model wasn't wearing any. I painted it in the illustration," Paul said. Part of the challenge is working with models in an environment that is drastically different from their normal assignments: "I . . . have to tell them that it's about the story, not about them. Usually models are used to working fashion assignments, where they are part of the job. This is about the story."

Cover art, it seems, is as personal an experience for the readers as the book plots themselves, and readers respond personally in kind to the artists as much as they would the writer. Paul says he does get fan mail, which for a time befuddled him because he hadn't signed his own cover art in years. Most of it, he says, is thanks and appreciation for the art, which is a unique experience for him as a book illustrator: "With book covers, before the Internet, there was no contact. I wouldn't hear anything until the book came out three, four months later. But the Internet opened up contact between the readers and me as the artist that I'd never had before as a cover illustrator." Paul says the feedback is almost always good—which is reassuring to him because the industry, he has noticed, is changing drastically. Fewer publishers use artists to illustrate their covers, and more houses, he says, are producing their art in-house, which leads to something we Bitches have noticed: the rise of the repeated stock image.

Don't get us wrong: there's nothing wrong with stock photography. Some of it is pretty damn evocative. But there's a shortage of images that work for romance covers, and while there are some talented designers working in publishing houses, there's not enough stock art to go around, and thus the repeat cover is born. Whether it's a pair of legs in a flippy pink skirt* or a corset being unlaced from the back, seeing the same art over and over is just irritating. It reinforces the idea "These books are interchangeable! They're all the same!" and underscores how much the publications from very disparate houses will end up resembling one another in their sales attempts.

Nowadays,† the pressure to be new and different is enormous, because everything has to be constantly updated in the search for the Next Image Trend that will sell romance, even as the industry continues to rely on the tried-and-true methods. This could mean death to the Smart Bitch Cover Snark, but ultimately, we hold on to our faith that so long as artists fire up the Poser, we'll never go hungry for cover images that make us want to break out the eyewash station.

So what sells? Men sell. Naked guys sell. And then there's preferences by editor. Some editors and art directors like the kick-ass female. Nathan Kamp, judging by how ubiquitous his image has become over the past two years, sells well, as do torsos, even when the hero described within the book isn't brawny in the least, such as with Joanna Bourne's *The Spymaster's Lady*. There's still an abundance of covers featuring couples in acrobatic clinches, with heroines displaying an abundance of cleavage—which Duffy calls the "nursing mother covers": nowhere "except on nursing women do you see breasts that big on women that small." Even though the wholesalers have combined and there's very few of them now, clinch covers sell. And, as Kate Duffy said, "Covers matter." Damn right they do.

The Ultimate Romance Cover
as per the Smart Bitches

The purpose of the classic clinch cover is to portray turmoil. Sex turmoil, love turmoil, anger turmoil, weather turmoil, animals-

---

* Which we've seen on four covers in various Photoshopped forms, and on an ad for a New Jersey leg vein specialist.
† As opposed to the Days of Yore.

freaking-the-fuck-out turmoil: the more kinds of turmoil you can throw onto the cover, the better. Excitement and conflict sell, and the harder the covers can teabag the consumers on the forehead with how the book is Full! Of! Passionate! Love! And! Storm! Filled! Sagas! (and by "sagas," we mean "Oh lawdy, the fuckin' "), the better it'll be. Doesn't matter whether it's a rapefest full of Big Misunderstandings, screaming fights, and long separations, or a story about star-crossed lovers quietly struggling to make their love happen. The covers want to catch the eye of the consumer any way they can, and anything that makes the potential reader do a double take and pick up the book is a good thing—even if she's doing it out of revulsion. It certainly worked with Candy for Loretta Chase's vastly underrated *The Lion's Daughter*; Candy picked it up only because the male model's greasy Jheri-curled mullet startled her with its awfulness.

Let's take a look at the cover we've carefully cultivated in our Smart Bitch labs, shall we?

1. **Hair:** Hair is key. The heroine's locks must be lush and tumbling; the hero's mullet should be every bit as fierce— the manly counterpart to her wavy tresses. Hair is culturally associated with fertility and sensuality, and when portrayed flying every which way, the hair becomes a visual indicator of the forces that bring the couple together and tear them apart. See how the hero's hair is blowing off to the right? That signifies how the winds of Big Misunderstanding are leading him to believe the heroine is a money-hungry whore, when she's actually a virginal heiress who rescues kittens and starving orphans in her spare time. See how the heroine's hair is strangely still? That signifies her unawakened sensuality, the depths of which await a vigorous plumbing. Yet, of course, note how her hair is long, lush, utterly free of snarls and perfectly obedient? So is she, some of the time. Her personality is as limp and lustrous as her hair. Her ribbons floating eerily to the left? That's the little signal that despite her reservations and her

distaste for his high-handed ways, she's ready to be led to true
passion by his fleshy divining rod of love.

2. **Turbulent weather or other natural catastrophes in
the background:** If the sky doesn't look like it's about to
dump five different kinds of nasty precipitation at once on the
our erstwhile lovers, then there has to be something else to
compensate in the background. A tastefully exploding volcano?
Crashing waves that would make Charybdis writhe in envy?
The turbulence in the background has to mirror the
(supposed) turbulence promised in the pages of the book.
Here, the volcano not only indicates the passions and tempers
that run hot, but its explosion promises a fiery culmination to
our protagonists' desires. Few things in nature are as subtly
porny as an exploding volcano.

3. **Animal freaking the fuck out:** If it's not a stallion, it's a
swan. If it's not a swan, it's a kangaroo. If it's not a kangaroo,
it's a pack of enraged dolphins. (Fun fact: "dolphin rape" will
yield thousands of search results on Google.) There's no
passion like animal passion, but there's also no squick like
bestiality squick, so the animals aren't ruttin', they're runnin'.
Witness the impassioned flappings on the swan on this cover.
Its beak hisses "No!" but the way it flaps its wings is pure "Yes!
Yes! Yes!"

4. **Phallic monument or object:** Cover artists aren't allowed
to advertise the hero's masculine attributes in the most obvious
way possible, so they go for the second-most obvious way
possible: a large sword. An obelisk. A sword-shaped obelisk.
Shooting white fire out of its tip. Oh, fine, that sort of phallic
hyperbole is usually reserved for bad fantasy or science-fiction
covers. Still, when it comes to alarmingly unsubtle
representations of wangery, romance novels are a close second.
Hence our manly hero has a sword that's nearly as long as his
mullet, and our heroine, she's no dummy—she's pushing
that turgid steel lovestick way the hell away from her tender
sheath.

5. **Location Clusterfuck:** Many an Old Skool romance flitted from setting to setting as if Regency misses and their rakish heroes could charter a private plane at a moment's notice. London! Paris! Greece! Some random desert! Maybe Egypt! Whatever the locales visited within the novel, at least a few of them will appear on the cover as part of some amalgamated geographic WTF, such as the Parthenon alongside a volcano. It works, if you think about it: explosive passion and erect columns do seem to go together in a lusty kind of way.

6. **Chests, Chests, Chests:** The hero sports the Required Hero Uniform of a shirt unbuttoned but still tucked in (because really, who doesn't undress like that?). The heroine, she is about to bust out of her bodice faster than you can say "Rip 'er? I don't have to—that bodice is ripping itself."

7. **Hairlessness:** Oh, the odd and restrictive standards of twentieth-century beauty that impress themselves in razor-sharp, waxy, Nair-like fashion on heroes and heroines. They might have acres of hair on their heads, but nowhere else is there a hint of stubble. His chest is hairless, which puts him oddly in the company of professional swimmers, professional bodybuilders, and men who wax themselves bald in all places. And no romance cover would be complete without the heroine lifting her skirt to show off her oddly hairless and utterly smooth legs. No stockings needed, no, no. If this book is a time travel, her next stop is Rockette auditions.

8. **Overblown flowers poppin' out of fuckin' nowhere:** And what better to balance the testosterone-drenched sword imagery than the girly fecundity of flowers? And not just any sort of flowers—big, fragrant flowers, blooming with manic intensity? Petals, dare we say, embracing the idea of "deflowering" themselves? Georgia O'Keeffe, eat your heart out.

Controversies, Scandals,
and Not Being Nice

While the romance genre dances merrily with its happy endings in both meanings of the phrase, within the genre there are some kerfuffles that pop up now and again, some small, some large, some ongoing and without seeming resolution. We'd be remiss if we didn't mention a few of them, so have a look at our dirty laundry: minorities and gays in romance, plagiarism, and the pressure of the Be Nice culture in Romancelandia.

MINORITIES IN ROMANCE: YOU MEAN IT'S NOT JUST WHITE ENGLISH PEOPLE?

One of the complaints that most often faces historical romance is that it's very white, very British, and very classist.

Yup. It sure can be. A vast majority of the romances taking place in the historical period known as Days of Yore feature white protagonists and some assurance of financial security, plus a really spiffy title. We Bitches love spiffy titles.

The segregation isn't unique to romance, but we must be honest. The face of romance is overwhelmingly white. That's also a problem with much of American media in general. The default face in popular culture in American is white—and this means pop culture in many places of the world is also default white, because America's biggest export, arguably, consists of cultural products. Movies. TV shows. Books. Video games. Fashion. And the accompanying advertising. Internettage.

But since the prospect of writing something that would adequately address all of that makes us reach for the smelling salts and some paint thinner, we're looking specifically at the issue of minorities in romance. And when the marketing and shelving affect romance authors' bottom lines, there's plenty of opinions to go around.

Romance is pretty homogenous. Historicals are usually about white characters, though there are notable exceptions, and notable exceptions of great quality in terms of writing. Contemporaries are a touch more diverse in terms of the overall number that feature minority characters, as is erotica; and mercy, paranormals feature a rainbow hue of protagonists—literally, in some cases.

Currently on the market are several lines specifically targeted toward minority readers—a systematic marketing of "otherness" that makes many an author and reader of romance see red. There are lines of romance for Latina readers, in English and in Spanish; for African American readers; and even some niche lines in e-pubs for those looking for erotic combinations of many different ethnicities, in many different positions. (It is erotica, after all.)

The debate of racism in romance is a large one, and it's unresolved. Why? Because it's all in the marketing and the shelving. It's not what you write but what color you are when you write it; what color the folks are on the cover; and what marker appears on the spine of the book, which may determine its shelving. If the marker says "African American" or "African American Romance," that book will most likely be shelved in the "African American" books section of the store—which for Sarah and her local Barnes & Noble means, "Way the fuck yonder clear on the other side of the store from the romance, nestled between psychology and Asian literature."

To segregate or not to segregate, that is the question.

Yeah, we're serious. No, we're not kidding. And we're as be-fuddled as you.

Presently, when a romance by a black author approaches the phase of publication that determines marketing, any number of divisions and decisions could be made to market that book as black romance by a black author, potentially to be sold in the African American fiction section of the store. And those sales, marketing, and artistic decisions are based on what, according to publishers, the readers want.

One African American romance reader said to us directly, "Black people like to read about other black people. And I look for romance about black women in the black section of the bookstore." One bookseller, who asked to remain anonymous, told us that when it fell under her responsibilities to shelve the black romance, if she put the new releases from authors like Brenda Jackson, Noire, or Michelle Monkou in among the romance, apart from the African American books, readers who wanted those books would go hunting for them and then complain that they were incorrectly shelved. They didn't belong in the romance section, according to those readers. There was a vocal preference among the customers who came to browse the African American authors section that African American romances be shelved separately for easier browsing. Our anonymous bookseller's solution was to create an end cap—the display area on the narrow end of a bookshelf—that featured all the newest black romance, so that it was in the romance section proper, but collected in a special section.

Ultimately, what we're talking about here is segregation and separation in terms of marketing and shelf space. Black romance is marketed toward the black reading community and, as such, usually features dark-skinned individuals on the covers; these titles are most often published in specific lines within mainstream publishers, like Harlequin's Kimani, or New Spirit, or Kensington's line of Arabesque romances.

But let us be blunt: you know what happens when a section of romance is shelved away from the money-spending romance-hunting book-buying fans of romance? Those books have a lesser chance of being purchased, and those authors lose out on sales to romance readers who shop only in the romance section and who take chances on authors they may not have read before. There's a certain number of sales that are made to readers who follow a particular author, and no matter where the book is shelved, they'll find it, buy it, and possibly complain if it's not where they think the book ought to be. But if the black romance isn't on the romance shelf, the readers who browse and shop without a list won't see that title and buy it, and they probably won't think to leave the romance section to look for romance in another part of the store. So by shelving black romances and black romance authors separately, sales are possibly lost.

That's a big fucking deal to some authors who hate being shelved separately. Do publishers market romance based on the cultural or racial identity of the person writing them, or the persons who appear in them? Both. Does the image on the cover affect where a book is shelved and in what part of the United States a book is sold? According to romance author Monica Jackson, who is vocal in her dislike of the segregation of romance, there is no doubt. She believes that the lack of what publishers call an "urban market" means that her books may not reach shelves in parts of the country.

Despite all that, the black romance authors we spoke with were firm on one point universally. Whether they agreed with the separate shelving or wanted to be included in the Great Stack of Romance in the local bookstore, each and every one said they were writing love stories, with passion, attraction, and sexual tension, and the racial makeup of the protagonists shouldn't, and doesn't, matter.

Ultimately, the publishers and the bookstores are trying to predict what readers want, because fulfilling what readers want translates into readers buying books, and that would be the goal of both publishers and booksellers. And because every reader has a different opinion on the issue of segregated publishing and shelving, there's no way to satisfy everyone. Shelve all the romances together? Create separate shelves to highlight the black romance, the Latina romance, the gay erotica, the Jewish inspirationals? File the romance fiction published by black authors among the other black authors? Behold: a smaller yet powerful facet to the Rise of Online Booksellers and the even bigger rise of the e-pubs and the erotica market. No worries about who to shelve near whom. They're all in one database, and they're linked by topic, plot, author name, or historical period. There's no "black romance only" section at Amazon. com unless a user creates a list specifically designed for the topic.

The issue of marketing and ultimately shelving is a very hot one in online discussions of romance. Author Millenia Black sued her publisher, Penguin, on grounds of racial discrimination after they restyled the cover of her previously self-published novel *The Great Pretender*. Black's lawsuit alleged that upon discovering that she was a black author, despite there being no racial identification within the narrative, Penguin marketed the book as African American fiction, using cover images and marketing classification guidelines. The suit was settled out of court in 2008, and as part of the settlement, Black had to purge all mention of the suit from her personal site and refrain from discussing it ever again. Except for other blogs and Web sites that discussed the suit, there are few available documents about it, but without a doubt, it was the first time to our knowledge a black author has tried to fight the classification and potential shelving segregation by taking the issue to court.

Black authors are not the only ones who find the "African American" classification a frightening damper on sales. Paula Chase Hyman, who wrote the successful Del Rio Bay Clique series of young adult novels, found one of her books mislabeled as AA instead YA, for young adult. While one bookstore adjusted the shelving despite the labeling on the book, another major chain did not, and not even the publishing house telling the book chain directly that it was mislabeled could correct the problem.

So if classifying black romance as African American fiction results in a segregation that decreases potential sales, what's the solution? Some editors and authors don't disclose the racial identity of an author deliberately so that they won't be marketed in an exclusive fashion. But authors and readers who discussed the topic at length on our site say that part of the solution lies with people like us, and people like you. If readers become aware of black romance authors and go find them and buy them—online or in stores— that's one thing. But there's no reason for the romance community to treat the black romances as if they are separate and "other" just because the bookstores and the classification system presently in place insist on doing so, or because a vocal number of readers insist that it remain that way. Ultimately, the only thing that will change the way sales are made is the sales themselves. Much of romance, from the cover art to the shelving designation, is a self-fulfilling prophecy.

THE GHEYS: LESBIANS, GAY MEN, AND THE STRAIGHT FOLKS WHO WRITE THEM

We talk a lot in terms of "hero" and "heroine," and while that is sexist language that defines and assigns gender stereotypes (boy howdy, does it ever), we are not excluding gay romance. Like a metaphor that's gone on too long, constantly saying "hero or heroine" each time we refer to one of the protagonists would be cumbersome. And implying that heterosexual romance is easily substituted with gay romance is slightly insulting to the GLBT romances we love. Moreover, the standards and stereotypes that apply to heterosexual characters in romance novels do not equally apply to hero/hero romances, or heroine/heroine romances. To put it another way: the love may be the same, but the heterosexist archetypes that often display it are not, and it's unfair and inaccurate to assume that the same tropes in heterosexual romance apply to gay romances.

Like the thighs of a really horny erotic romance heroine, erotica itself is open to all manner of kinky, interesting plot developments and characters. Raelene Gorlinsky from Ellora's Cave noted that the erotic romance genre is more open* to plots and protagonist combinations that might otherwise be considered risky: "The readers of erotic romance are already in the riskier end of the romance spectrum, so they are more likely to be readers who will take chances, want something different, who desire over-the-line excitement." Therein lies an interesting rub: one of the steaming hot elements of the erotic romance market is gay erotic romance, that is, erotic romance between two men. And much of it is penned by straight women. Gorlinsky says, "The current hot fad of male/male romance is for the female fans in the erotic romance market. Most of the authors are heterosexual women. Just as the vast bulk of readers are heterosexual women. There is a separate—and not necessarily overlapping—market segment of gay men or women who write more realistic stories for gay male readers.

The flexibility and friendliness of e-publishers to gay erotic romance is no secret. Author Selah March told us that "small presses in general, and e-presses in particular, can afford to have a much more 'throw everything at the wall and see what sticks/sells' attitude. For example, I write for the Heat and Allure imprints of Amber Quill Press. A year ago, Amber Quill discovered male/male erotic romances were outselling "hetero" romances in their erotic Heat line, so it opened the Allure line just for m/m and f/f. Sales have more than doubled over the past year."

So where is all that gay romance? Most of it is online from e-publishers, but folks who go searching for it in the bookstore may have a difficult time of it. Just as with the African American romance, the issue comes back to shelving and marketing. As March tells us, "Some e-publishers who also produce m/m romance in . . . trade paperback are finding it tough to reach their readership because of shelving issues in the big-box stores. In my local Borders,

---

*Insert "more open" joke here . . . insert joke about "insert" here . . . oh, never mind.

all gay romance is shelved with 'LGBT studies,' no matter who published it or whether it might sell better snugged up against all the other trade paperback erotica in the romance section. Chicks who dig erotic romance [are] buying this stuff by the butt-load, so to speak, but I don't know how many would think to go looking for it in next to nonfiction books about the Stonewall riots and how to draft a will that doesn't leave your life partner out on the street. . . ."

Yet again, even as folks whine that e-marketers like Amazon drive individual stores out of business, the allure of the online bookstore when it comes to finding and purchasing books with a minimum of effort cannot be understated. But the real controversy over gay romance is the number of people who insist it doesn't belong in romance at all, and the shrill responses some fans deliver at the growing strength of the gay-romance trend. It sounds, not surprisingly, much like the shrill response to any advances into mainstream America made by gay individuals. Whatever the negative response, whether it be removing gay-romance promotional material at conventions or not creating a gay-romance category for romance novel awards despite the number of gay romances published each year, gay romance isn't going anywhere any more than romance readers themselves are giving up their reading material. So we'll all have to learn to get along. And exchange tips on proper buttsecks techniques.

Be Nice

One of the most peculiar aspects to the romance community, online and off, is how that community reacts to criticism from within itself. Romance readers, writers, authors, and fans take all manner of multicolored shit for our involvement in romance, and each one of us has a story whereupon a diss was laid against our reading material. But that mess pales in comparison with the slapping that goes on within that community. It is, for lack of a better word, bugfuck.

Never in your life have you seen a more dysfunctional community than when the evil demon of Not Nice rears her critical tongue about the romance genre.

We fully admit, we knew we were wading into vague waters when we started our site. We found that most reviews of romance novels online were unfailingly too nice. Not nearly critical enough, and in our opinion likely to recommend highly books we both loathed. Our grading curve, we knew, was harsher than most.

But romance novels, we thought, deserved the harsh eye simply because we loved them as much as we loved the literary canon at which we were encouraged to level the power of our sexy, sexy literary analysis abilities. Criticism is good in a literary context. Criticism is Not Nice in a romance community context.

We also admit with grins and nodding that we aren't by any means nice. We don't sugar coat, but when we harsh on a book, we can guarantee that we back up any points we don't like with a full explanation. The genre gets nowhere when criticism amounts to "I didn't like it, because it sucked." Sure, maybe it did suck, but why it sucked is of crucial importance.

But then, describing in detail why you think something sucked? Not Nice.

Author Marta Acosta probably put it best when she asked in utter fucking bewilderment, what is it with the romance community that it acts like a minority, even though it's a majority? As we've stated, romance = biggest genre with biggest profits, biggest man titty and biggest market share of fiction sold in the United States. With the billions bought and billions sold, one would think romance would get a swelled head.* But no, our egos and our manhoods are flaccid like green balloons on March 18. We behave as a much-persecuted minority. Persecuted, sure, but minority? Come on, now. What Acosta means by "majority behaving like a minority" and what we mean by "wrapped inside a crunchy taco shell of bugfuck" is the panic and censure that erupts whenever anyone for

* No, not that head, the other one.

whatever reason dares criticize any element of romance. It's as if any criticism within the romance community cannot be tolerated lest it give additional ammunition to those who attack us from the outside of that community. We can't criticize each other when we're being criticized by our detractors, the frail logic goes.

But without criticism, there is no growth. And when a genre is crapped upon and denigrated as much as romance is, the only people we think are qualified to criticize it are those who read it and love it. So we brought in the noise, the funk, the snark, and the "Oh, hell, no." And in doing so, we proclaimed ourselves Bitches, because we knew the whole package probably wouldn't go over well.

The general backlash against criticism in romance roots itself in the idea that to criticize someone else means to admit there's something wrong with you as well. To admit flaws in another's book is to denounce your own work. And we'll admit: authors have it pretty tough when it comes to promoting one another. It's next to impossible to give any public criticism of a fellow author without damaging your own public image. Few authors bash one another in any genre; when they do, it's rather startling.

That said, it blows us away how often some authors in romance act as if they're members of a social club rather than as individual small business owners operating a monetary enterprise. Nowhere is this more evident than with the rise and fall of some e-publishers. Rumors began popping up months before a few e-publishers like Triskelion, Lady Aibell, and Mardi Gras went out of business, with authors telling of bounced checks, ignored e-mail, and delays on publication of books. When rumors began to appear on blogs like ours and Dear Author, well, imagine a giant kiddie pool filled with pink sand. Then imagine authors shoving their heads in it, saying, "I love my publisher! My publisher is the best! They are so great and I get paid and I don't know what you're talking about! Nyah, nyah, I can't hear you!" In any other industry, rumors of financial instability would usually mean people pay attention, or at least ask questions. But in Romancelandia, it means falling on one's sword as

quickly as possible, in dramatic fashion. Public loyalty means everything, especially if an e-pub makes decisions on who gets published
and who gets published in paper based on author participation in
e-mail loops and whether an author has defended the publisher in
public on message boards and blogs.*

But that kiddie pool of pink sand got a whole lot bigger in January 2008. In December 2007, a friend of Candy's, a classics student
by the name of Kate, asked her for a sample selection of romance
novels so she could try out the genre. Candy gave her three: one
that represented what Candy thought was the best of romance, a
Loretta Chase novel; one that represented the most popular, a J. R.
Ward novel; and one that represented what Candy thought was
among the worst, a Cassie Edwards novel, *Shadow Bear.* While reading *Shadow Bear,* Kate noticed a major shift in didactic tone when, in
a postnookie scene, two characters remark upon the behavior of the
black-footed ferret. Kate discovered, through the magic of Google,
that *Shadow Bear* was riddled with passages lifted directly from historical textbooks, memoirs, and in the biggest what-the-fuck moment a *Defenders of Wildlife* article about black-footed ferrets by
journalist Paul Tolmé.

Initially our posts on the similarities attracted a little attention
from people who couldn't believe it was true, people who made
jokes about the relative quality of Edwards's novels in the first place,
and people who said we were sick and had no lives and justified
beating up an old lady who had millions of fans just because we
thought it would be funny. The most we had to worry about in
terms of Web traffic was a few trolls, and a few hours of lost sleep
as we googled anything suspicious from a random selection of
Edwards's novels.

Then Signet, Edwards's publisher, released a statement that indicated she'd "done nothing wrong." That would be when the excre-
ment hit the air-circulating device. Signet's statement placed the

* Wait, you mean that isn't how all business decisions are made?

entire debate on ethical grounds—grounds that didn't leave Signet or Edwards much earth to stand on. If they'd said she did nothing illegal, well, we wouldn't have had much to say. Neither of us is an attorney, and many of the works that were identical to passages in her novels were already in the public domain.

On Wednesday, January 9, the Associated Press published an article about our findings and Signet's response. The article also contained a statement from Edwards, who said she had no idea she was supposed to credit her sources. The most startling part for us, aside from the idea that the AP would cover the story, was that they published our URL. At that moment, our server curled up in a fetal position and began to weep for its own bandwidth. The story was picked up from the original AP article and posted on the *USA Today* Web site, various entertainment Web sites, and the front page of Yahoo:News. That weekend, an article appeared in the *New York Times* about the allegations surrounding Cassie Edwards.* Paul Tolmé wrote a marvelously pointed article for *Newsweek* online in which he expressed his bemusement at seeing his magazine article quoted in a romance novel—as postcoital pillow talk, no less. Then NPR's *Wait Wait . . . Don't Tell Me!* used that story as part of its Bluff the Listener segment, which asks listeners to guess which of three outrageous and weird news stories is real and which are fake.

Our readers responded by going to the library with their own copies of Cassie Edwards's novels, which supports Sarah's theory that Edwards's backlist is so ubiquitous that everyone probably owns at least one, to find additional sources used verbatim without attribution within the narrative prose. We received many e-mail messages from people simply saying, "Thank you." Librarians,

---

* By that time, our Web host, Esosoft, Inc., had moved our site from one server, where we shared space with about eight or nine other Web sites, to a dedicated span of ten servers, each sharing the load for our site, and barely managing to keep it online.

teachers, college professors, and writers e-mailed us privately to express their thanks that we'd taken the time to research and publish what we'd found.

But, oh, the backlash.

The reaction from some in the romance community online, at least the comments that we read and heard, were as disillusioning as when the heroine wakes up from the bliss of amnesia and realizes that she's not a princess and has to do the dishes. As fans and followers of romance, seeing the depths to which some authors would refuse to See the Point was beyond disappointing, and moved clear on into frightening and infuriating.

Part of the drama and nasty came from the fact that some authors and commentators focused on the name of our Web site instead of the issue at hand. By calling ourselves "Smart Bitches" and calling the romance genre "trashy," many accused us of doing the genre a great deal of damage because we opened it up to public scrutiny and ridicule. If you ask us, Edwards levered open the can of humiliation when she used unattributed source materials in *Shadow Bear*. A scientific discussion of ferrets following connubial bliss is hilarity on its own. We didn't open the genre to ridicule and mockery. Cassie Edwards's decision to plagiarize did.

**"You guys never liked her anyway.
You're just being mean."
"You just have a vendetta against her."
"You're nothing but nasty bitches!"
"You're just in it for the hits to your site
and for the publicity."**

We'll see you on the first six words, but we take issue with the rest. Indeed, we have never been fans of Cassie Edwards's novels. And while we defend the right of any reader to enjoy the literature of his or her choice—come on, we've been crapped on liberally for our taste in romance novels—we also reserve the right to state our opinion on our Web site. And in our opinion, Edwards's novels use a poor choice of words to refer to Native Americans* and capitalize on the racist, antiquated mythology of the "noble savage." We don't like her novels. We've said as much. And because Edwards is shorthand for romance in that her books are shelved and available in many, many locations where there's two feet of space reserved for romance, not just in bookstores but grocery stores, drugstores, and interstate gas stations, we referred to her novels as shorthand for "really, horribly bad romance novels that represent the worst, most offensive selections of the genre." Candy also recommends referring to the unedited self-published Dara Joy novels as similar shorthand reference for "romance that is not of the best quality, if you don't mind our saying so."

Value judgments of good and bad quality notwithstanding, our point in revealing the evidence we found was not to make the point yet again, "Wow, we think her novels suck."

Our point was simple:

"Wow. That's plagiarism. That really fucking sucks."

The issue is not whether we like Cassie Edwards's novels. We don't. Never have. She is our standard by which any book approaching an F grade is measured—the Cassie Edwards asymptote is a line which few books manage to approach, much less cross, but once they do, it's a pantheon of craptastic writing.

The issue is ethics. There's no expiration date on addressing unethical behavior, no matter when it's discovered. Plagiarism, using another person's words for profit without attribution or compensation, is unethical. Frankly, our discovery was not even newsworthy in the least until Signet released their first statement regarding the matter that said, in part, "Cassie Edwards has done nothing wrong."

* "Savage"?!

Again, "right and wrong" are value judgments, and apply to ethical debate, not legal debate. There are plenty of acts that can get you failed in English class that won't get you arrested.

And speaking of ethics, once the story became public, we saw the truly nasty and appalling side of many, many people, including writers whose books we admired.

If you took a stroll around the Web the first two weeks of January 2008, there was plenty of Bitch bashing going on. Normally we don't pay attention; any frankly stated opinion is going to attract negative attention. When it came to an issue that affects the public perception of romance, a genre that's already scrutinized and dismissed as meaningless pornography for women, it was beyond disappointing to see attacks on our morality, and worse, silence altogether. We never took the opportunity to discuss our reaction to the reaction until now.

If an author's work is her business, not in the privacy sense but in the income-generating incorporated-business sense, then wouldn't someone else's unethical practices be a reason to defend her own business? Wouldn't speaking out against plagiarism, and defending her own research practices be a no-brainer?

Not that it is exactly the same, but when one toy manufacturer was revealed to have lead paint on their product, we saw plenty of press releases from other toy manufacturers saying, "We do not import our toys from China and we test our paint for lead." There were plenty of "Our toys are safe!" newsletters in the in-box. Those manufacturers wanted to make sure folks pointed their wallets toward them when the safety and integrity of another line of toys was called into question.

When dog food from several product lines was recalled for toxins, we had plenty of pet food alerts in the in-box saying that the pet foods manufactured by a host of other brands did not contain the toxic ingredient, that they were safe and were not affected by the recall—and gee, wouldn't they love to have us as customers? It's damage control, pure and simple. Protecting your product seems normal in a business setting when another product of similar ilk is called into question.

But that's not the case with many romance authors and these accusations of plagiarism—because as usual, it would look better if they said nothing. Somehow, it's better to remain friendly with other authors than to stand up against an ethical issue that should be pretty clear.

That absence of damage control in favor of silence or niceness was one thing. But the anti–Smart Bitches commentary was just breathtaking. Some authors and fans of the genre wrote on message boards and began their posts with the absolutely jaw-dropping words, "Plagiarism aside."

There's another issue besides plagiarism?

Silly Bitches. Of course there is: nasty women like us who weren't being nice, and mean authors like Nora Roberts who publicly stated that they thought what Edwards did was wrong. Some authors posted vitriolic screeds against Roberts and against us, asking why she was being praised for slapping at an author who "did nothing wrong." Roberts's actions of "slamming another author" took more heat than Edwards's thirty-year profit from use of unattributed source material written by people who couldn't give permission because they were dead.

We stand by what we did, what we wrote, and how we presented it, and we'd do it again without compunction. Moreover, we know and recognize that for every one author who decided we were the first cousins of Satan, many, many other authors backed us up, because they felt as we did—that plagiarism in the romance genre demeans every writer and every reader. Learning that there's an author whose work we don't like? Not really that horrifying. Learning that a thirty-plus-year career was based partially on the plagiarism and unethical use of other people's words made us feel rather sick. *That* is what makes the genre look bad. Not calling yourself a Bitch and loving romance.

While some folks, particularly Nora Roberts, came out and

said, point-blank, "That's plagiarism, and that isn't right," the silence spoke volumes. And we are impatient Bitches, so it was difficult for us to accept that it would take some time for the effect to be visible.

But visible it was. At the Romantic Times BookLovers Convention, three grand dames of romance, Bertrice Small, Jennifer Blake, and Roberta Gellis, led a session about incorporating historical research into fiction by using the same encyclopedia entry to draft three different pieces of sample fiction. It was like watching Celine Dion, Barbra Streisand, and Madonna showing people how to audition—effortlessly professional, and a very solid response to the entire controversy.

Nora Roberts, who herself was the victim of plagiarism and copyright infringement in 1997 when Janet Dailey used in her own books several lengthy passages from Roberts's novels, was by far the most outspoken about the issue, and she was among the first people contacted by the AP for comment on the original story. She was the person in the article who called what we found "clear evidence of plagiarism," and she took a lot of heat for it.

Roberts also put her money where her mouth is, challenging our readers to raise money for Defenders of Wildlife and their efforts to revive the communities of black-footed ferrets in the upper Midwest. In under forty-eight hours, our site raised over five thousand dollars, which was matched by the Nora Roberts Foundation. That ten-thousand-dollar donation was created from small donations from hundreds of readers of our site around the world, most between five and ten dollars.

And to our great surprise, on April 18, 2008, Signet released a statement that after a review of her books, they have parted ways with Cassie Edwards citing "irreconcilable editorial differences." Her books are no longer published by Signet. Her backlist continues to be published by Dorchester and Kensington.

The long-term benefits of exposing plagiarism on the part of a historical romance author remain to be seen. But as Sarah wrote in a guest article for *Affaire d'Coeur* magazine, the essential conclusions we've drawn from the experience have not changed. Plagiarism is wrong. It's an insult to every writer, ourselves included. And if we had the chance to do it again, we would. Twice. A dozen times without compunction, because if you missed it the first time, we'll say it again. We don't care if you like us or you like what we say. It should not matter who says it at all: plagiarism is wrong.

Choose Your Own Man Titty

People accuse romance novels of being impossible to differentiate from each other, and nobody knows the untruthiness of this more acutely than we Smart Bitches. If nothing else, just look at the mind-boggling variety of heroes who inhabit Romancelandia. You have your choice of tall, dark, alpha billionaires; tall, dark, alpha police detectives; tall, dark, alpha dukes, tall, dark, alpha pirates; tall, dark, alpha (and angsty, so very, very angsty) vampires; tall, dark, alpha werewolves . . .

Okay, so we kid. There are the occasional tall, blond, alpha males.

With such a mind-boggling variety of heroes to suit your palate, how do you choose which one is right for you?

By shamelessly stealing an idea from our geeky childhoods, of course. We here at Smart Bitches are proud to present: Choose Your Own Man Titty. That's right: using only the finest diagramming technology available (also known as "a pencil, a piece of paper, and a whole lot of erasing"), we provide you herein with an invaluable service that allows you to match the perfect hero to the type of heroine you are, thus allowing you to cohabitate forever and ever in amazing nookerific (if fictional) bliss, amen. Just follow along with these tantalizing scenarios, make your choice, and turn to the appropriate numbered sections.

The Adventure Begins!

You wake up in the morning, the sun bright in your eyes. You stretch and sigh, anticipating the start of a new day, and sit up. The mirror across the room catches your eye. What do you look like?

- You're unremarkable-looking, in your opinion. A perfectly ordinary, perfectly pleasant face with regular features; people oftentimes think it is a face that has been untouched by the mark of passion. *Turn to Option 1 (below).*
- Glorious tumbling tresses fall down your back and frame a heart-shaped face with winged brows and a mouth just a touch too wide. *Turn to Option 15 (page 227).*
- You have a ritual tattoo of a snake swallowing its own tail encircling your left eye socket, and your hand is wrapped around the *katana* you always keep within arm's reach. *Turn to Option 24 (page 244).*

Option 1

You're just barely getting started on your first cup of coffee when the cell phone rings. It's your surly boss, and he wants you to come in early. What does your boss look like?

- He's swarthy and chiseled and a captain of enterprise. His mistress is blond and icy, and her manicures are more immaculate than a pregnant Jewish virgin. He occasionally grabs you and shouts a lot. *Turn to Option 2 (page 210).*
- He's short, chubby, intensely hairy, and kind of repulsive, and he's the head of the newspaper you work for. *Turn to Option 7 (page 214).*

Option 2

The boss is in fine mood today. His mistress is storming out of his office just as you get in, and she shoots you an especially poisonous look from beneath her perfectly groomed brows, making you feel like even more of a mouse than you usually do. The boss comes out of his office shortly thereafter, barking that he wants you to do an impossible task before lunch and pick up an order from an exclusive and prohibitively expensive lingerie store during your break.

Do you:

- Do as you're told? *Turn to Option 3 (below).*
- Quit, because nobody needs this shit? *Turn to Option 4 (page 211).*

Option 3

You complete the impossible task perfectly, despite its impossibility, all the while daydreaming in excruciating, redundant detail about your boss's brooding masculine presence and feeling a writhing mass of emotions roil through you every time you contemplate picking up the order from the lingerie store: a strange amalgam of jealousy, resentment and . . . something else. Something you can't quite put your finger on.

Just then, Travis, the flirty but extremely gay coworker drops by your desk and starts talking with you. He leans down to give you a big hug after taking a look at your haggard face and offers to take you out to lunch. Just as he makes the offer and rubs your back comfortingly, Boss Man walks in and sees the two of you, and you suddenly realize that it must seem like he has just interrupted a romantic interlude. Your heart sinks as his face darkens with anger, and he icily tells Travis to go back to his cubicle, and then summons you to his office.

In the office, he closes the door. "Sit," he says, voice curt. His black scowl and the way he moves with leashed fury back to his desk make you think of a very large, very angry panther, and your heart speeds up with fear and . . . something else. Something you can't quite put your finger on. When he gets back to his desk, he doesn't take a seat; instead, he leans his hip against the corner of his desk and looks at you, making you squirm just a little in your chair.

"The office isn't a dating service," he finally growls out. "I expect impeccable behavior from all my employees, but especially from my personal assistant. Your behavior reflects directly on me, and I'd appreciate it if you'd tell your swarm of Lotharios to bother you after work hours. This is a professional setting, and I will not tolerate unprofessional behavior from anybody under my supervision. Do you understand me?"

Do you:

- Quit, because nobody needs this shit? *Turn to Option 4 (below).*
- Feel indignant and attempt to defend yourself? *Turn to Option 5 (page 212).*

Option 4

This is the last straw. You look your boss calmly in the eye and say "Consider my resignation tendered, sir." As you pack up your desk, you feel both relief and terror. You double-majored in economics and math at the University of Chicago, and it's kind of ridiculous that you're stuck in a dead-end job as this short-fused schmuck's personal assistant. The pay is good, and God knows he's a hot piece of ass (which, to be honest, is part of the reason you've put up with so much), but the shouting and grabbing are really starting to get out of hand. Speaking of which: you realize you owe it to yourself to file sexual-harassment charges. Even if you don't win, at least there will be something on record for the next poor sap who gets your job. *Suck it, Trebek,* you think.

You go out for drinks afterward with Travis, your office friend, to celebrate getting out of the company. You've always assumed he was gay because he's slim, wears fitted shirts in jewel tones, and talks with his hands. The two of you proceed to get thoroughly smashed, and you find out that Travis actually really, really, really likes girls. He has, in fact, harbored an intense *tendre* for you for the last couple of years. Later, he demonstrates this to you—and it turns out he can do a whole lot more with his hands than talk with them. The two of you fall madly in love, and with the settlement from the harassment suit, you decide to start a consulting business. It becomes a thriving concern, and you live Happily Ever After with Travis in a beautiful little condo in the heart of the city.

Option 5

You toss your head in defiance. How *dare* he? You and Travis have a perfectly innocent friendship! "I don't understand why you're so angry!" you finally shoot back at him during a pause in his tirade. "Travis is a good friend, and he's also—" But before you can say the word "gay," your boss interrupts you by grabbing your arms in a brutal grip and dragging you out of your chair.

"You little fool!" he grinds out between clenched teeth. "If you are so desperate for attention, I suppose you should have some, then." He claims your lips in a punishing kiss, his mouth moving over yours with ruthless skill.

Do you:

- Struggle briefly, escape from his grasp and then quit, because really, *nobody* needs this shit? *Turn to Option 4 (page 211)*,
- Struggle briefly, and then melt into the wonder of his firm lips caressing yours? *Turn to Option 6 (below)*.

Option 6

You struggle briefly in his grasp, hating him with every fiber of your being. But just as you gasp in pain, his lips magically gentle and start caressing yours with infinite skill, and his tongue traces the seam of your lips. You gasp in surprised pleasure.

As the kiss continues and becomes even more passionate, filling your innocent body with wild urges you barely understand, you are dimly aware of the door opening behind you, but you are so lost in the wonder of his kiss that the significance doesn't register until you hear the voice of his mistress, her clipped French accent rending your sensual fog asunder: "Sorry to interrupt such a tender tryst. I'll come back when you're done with your whore, Demetrios. You know where to find me."

Your boss releases your lips, but does not let you go; instead, he cradles you protectively against his chest. "It's over, Amandine," he said. "I told you this morning I'm in love with someone else."

Her gray eyes sweep over him with contempt. "You are stupid, indeed, if you think she can satisfy a man like you, *mon chèr*." She shrugs her shoulders and turns to go. As she leaves the office, she turns around and says, her voice dripping with disdain, "You will want me back soon enough, and I will take great pleasure in denying you."

The slam of the door echoes off the walls.

Your heart sinks within as you begin to unravel all the implications of what she has just said. *He's in love with somebody.* So intensely that he's quite literally shown his mistress the door. Ordinary creature that you are, what chance do you have at winning his heart?

For you have now realized that you *do* want to win his heart, for he has won yours. How could you have been so blind for all this time? The anger, the frustration, the intense jealousy you felt toward his mistress—all were indicators of your love. The realization burns through the core of your soul, and you burst into tears.

Your boss seems startled and holds you close as you sob against him. As your tears show no sign of abating, he whispers in an aching voice, "What is the matter, dear heart?"

"You . . . you shouldn't hold me like this!"

"Why ever not?" he asks, a note of amusement creeping into his voice.

It's unbearable! Your heart is breaking, and the brute is laughing at you. "You're in love with another woman!" you cry out, and beat him in the chest with a futile fist. "I shouldn't be here in your arms. She should be."

A look of puzzlement crosses his harsh, dark features, and then it suddenly clears. "Oh," he says, voice suddenly husky. "But she already is." And he bends down to kiss you again.

Even as you drown in the sensation his lips evoke in you, your mind reels in confusion. It almost sounds as if he's saying . . . but it cannot be! When he at last releases your lips, you gaze at him with disbelief. "I don't understand," you say faintly. "You can't possibly be saying what I think you're saying."

"Oh, but I am," he assures you.

"But your . . . that is, Amandine was so beautiful. . . ."

Your boss makes a dismissive sound. "She was cold, cold to the core. I need somebody to warm me up; that was when I realized the person I want most has been under my nose the whole time. Why do you think I call you in to work early all the time? When I saw you talking to Travis, I was so afraid I had waited too long that I lost control. And you, my darling, are infinitely more beautiful than she is."

"Really?" You look up at him in doubt, but the adoration in his eyes is clear enough even for you to see.

"Yes, really," he says, and his lips descend to claim yours once again, you surrender your heart fully into his keeping, for you have become . . . *The Boss's Virgin Boardroom Mistress*.

Option 7

Hearing your boss's voice over the phone gives you chills that you attempt to suppress. For weeks, you've dreamed about him almost nightly. In your dreams, his face is twisted with hate and glee, his hands darkly wet; when he's done, he dumps the children's bodies near a landfill outside the city.

What fills you most with foreboding is the fact that you have a history of having Dreams That Come True, but this time, it's patently obvious your dreams are ridiculous. There's no way you can be working for a murderer; sure, your boss is fat, hunchbacked, obnoxious, and smells like sweaty feet, and sure, you've seen him kick at puppies when he thinks nobody is watching, but he's not a killer. You've been working on a big feature piece about a recent rash of child disappearances, and looking at all those pictures and talking to all the grieving parents and teachers must be affecting you more than you think.

You arrive at the office and discover everybody in an uproar. Early this morning, the body of one of the children has been found by the big landfill just outside the city; no other details are available, and everybody is scrambling to find more information. You ignore the uneasy lurch of your stomach and decide to call Detective Nick Hawking, a renegade with a reputation for getting the job done by any means necessary, and infamous for the massive size of his . . . guns.

"What the hell do you want?" Hawking drawls into the phone. His gravelly voice is a slap to your face. "The shit has hit the fan, and I have better things to do than talk."

You gulp down the fury you feel; Hawking is difficult to work with, but the history between the two of you can make it just about impossible. Being the hotshot homicide detective's journalist ex-girlfriend can be a real bitch.

"I just heard that you found the body of the Northrup child by the McFadden landfill," you say, keeping the tone of your voice even, "and I wanted to see if you had anything you wanted to say, strictly off the record, before the press conference begins."

There's a silence over the phone, and when he speaks, his trademark insolence is gone; his voice is now deadly serious. "We haven't released the identity of the body. We had a positive identification only a couple of minutes ago. Right now, maybe five people know just who we've found, and I know for damn sure nobody has talked. Tell me: how did you know?"

What do you say in response?

- Tell Hawking the truth: that you had a dream about the boy the night before. *Turn to Option 8 (below).*
- In your panic, experience a blackout. *Turn to Option 9 (below).*

Option 8

"Hawk, this is going to sound crazy, but—"

"Oh, try me," he says, the sardonic edge in his voice hard enough to cut glass.

"I . . . I had a dream last night. About the body."

You pause. Dead silence.

You forge on, your stomach a tight ball of dread. "I've been having dreams about the children for weeks. I've had these crazy kinds of dreams all my life; I see things, and there's no way for me to know if they're true, but they always turn out to be real. I know it sounds crazy, but I think . . ." You pause and stand up on tiptoe to peer over your cubicle. "I think I even know who the killer is."

More silence; when he finally speaks, his voice is clipped, businesslike. "I need to talk to you right now. In person. Don't you fucking dare move. I'll be right over."

What happens next?

- You attempt to talk some more with Hawking; for some reason, you really, *really* don't want to see him at the moment. *Turn to Option 9 (below).*
- Hawking hangs up and you put the phone back in the cradle, feeling anxious about the daunting task of convincing him that you're speaking the truth. *Turn to Option 10 (page 218).*

Option 9

As you attempt to talk to Hawking in a way that doesn't make you sound like a completely crazy person, you strangely find yourself growing dizzier and dizzier, and the last thing you see before things go black is the sight of the floor rushing up to meet you.

When you wake up, your whole body is screaming with pain and a huge weight presses against your back. Your head, in particular, is pounding, as if your brain were a demon and your skull a portal to hell. You attempt to lift your hand to touch it, to check to see if it's bleeding, but you find that you can't. In fact, you can't move at all; your hands appear to be tied or cuffed behind your back. Dark red smears mar the floor, and you have a horrible suspicion that it's blood.

The question is: Whose blood is it?

"What . . . what happened?" you manage to croak out.

You feel somebody lean down even harder against you, and you groan in pain. Hawking's voice growls into your ear, and you wince reflexively. "So you're awake. I always knew you were a crazy bitch back when I dated you, but I guess I didn't know exactly how crazy. I should've killed you when I had a chance, you sick fuck, but I think I'll enjoy seeing you fry for the murders of those children even more."

"What are you talking about?" you ask, a heavy ball of dread forming in your chest.

"You really are nuts, aren't you?" he says. "Maybe I hit you harder in the head than I thought. Don't pretend you didn't confess to the kidnappings and murders just now. Don't pretend you didn't try to run, and don't pretend you don't remember killing your boss when he tried to stop you."

As his words wash over you, you suddenly realize that the dreams of the murdered children weren't really dreams after all. Your reality fractures and re-forms, and you are suddenly aware that the killer of the children, the repulsive man who kicks at puppies when he thinks nobody is watching, the brute who drives you too hard when you have a deadline to meet, *is actually you.*

As it dawns upon you that your life is the embodiment of one of the oldest cop-out surprise endings, Hawking drags you up and starts walking you to the door. You hear somebody screaming, even as you once again feel the slow descent into numbing blackness. This time, instead of fighting it, you embrace it and its blissful oblivion.

Option 10

You attempt to get some work done while waiting for Hawking to turn up, but your concentration is hopelessly shot. Rumors swarm the air like flies flocking around a week-old corpse. Every time you catch sight of your boss, you cower a little. Is it your imagination, or is he giving you an especially evil look? Can he possibly guess that you know his secret? You lean your elbows on your desk and bury your head in your hands, a knot of stress forming in your stomach and another right between your eyes.

"Hard at work, I see," a voice rasps over your head. Your head snaps up. Hawking is leaning against one of the partition walls of your cubicle, muscular legs sheathed in sinfully tight denim. Your eye is immediate drawn to his hard, massive, gleaming . . . gun, just barely peeking out from the shoulder harness under his jacket. The thing looked like it could stop a speeding bus cold in its tracks. Small Asian nations probably paid him good money not to point that thing in their direction.

"Hawk," you say, trying to keep your voice cool. It's difficult, though. Hawking, more than any other man you've met, makes it impossible for you to keep calm. It's one of the reasons why you broke up—the volatile cycles became too much for you to take. "Let's go into one of the conference rooms."

"Yes, let's," he says, voice dark and sardonic—as dark and sardonic as his eyes. You're practically sweating under that hot, unforgiving gaze.

Do you:

- Gaze into his dark eyes and start feeling dizzy? *Turn to Option 9 (page 216).*
- Proceed to the conference room? *Turn to Option 11 (page 219).*

Option 11

You open the door to the conference room and flick on the light. Hawking closes the door behind him, and you perch on the edge of the table nervously and lick your lips. His eyes flicker at the motion and his expression tightens.

You draw a deep breath. Explaining this isn't going to be easy. Hawking is surprisingly calm, though. He doesn't interrupt you as you tell him about your dreams, giving him details about the dreams of the missing children, even the ones whose bodies haven't been found yet. Your stomach churns at the recall.

When you're done talking, the silence is heavy, Hawking's face impassive. Finally, he asks, voice hard: "Do you expect me to believe this?"

"No, not really," you say. "Nobody has before, so why should you?"

He explodes out of his chair, and you flinch. His face hardens, and he grabs your arms in a punishing grip. You bite back a cry of pain.

"This kind woo-woo bullshit is what killed my mother," he spits out, "And I'll be damned if I'm going to let a charlatan like you get away with it."

He lets go of you in disgust and starts pacing. "Slime like you don't understand, do you? You sell us all a line we want to believe in, build trust, rake in the cash, and then run. And when a woman has breast cancer and believes some snake oil salesman when he claims putting a special kind of magnet next to the tumor will make it go away, well, hey, you have just the right kind of magnet, don't you? For a price, of course. And when the woman has so much faith in the magnet that she refuses chemotherapy and dies, well, then, that's just too bad, isn't it? You didn't guarantee a cure, you just said it might help."

He stops his tirade and turns to you, eyes alight with loathing. "You people make me sick."

You feel shaken. The pain in his voice is real, and you figure there's no way for him to believe you now. "I'm sorry," you whisper. "I'm so sorry."

He stalks his way to you. "You better be," he snarls. "Now tell me the truth before I stop treating you with kid gloves. How did you know about the kids?"

As you seethe with misery, an idea strikes you. It might just be crazy enough to work. "I know how to make you believe me."

He snorts. "How?"

"I've had dreams every night about the missing kids," you say. "Why don't you come over tonight and watch over me? When I wake up, I'll tell you what I've dreamed, and you can check the details. You can do this for as many nights as you want."

He stares at you, and a smirk eventually twists his lips. "Is this your way of inviting me over for a bit of fuck-the-ex-boyfriend, kitten? Because really, all you had to do was ask." He runs his eyes over you appraisingly.

You turn beet red, even as your body heats up in response. "Look," you say, "I have no way of proving I'm not some kind of psycho killer, except for this. I'll still be proven right if you put me in jail and continue to find new bodies even with me locked up. This way, I don't have to be put behind bars."

He glares at you, but he doesn't argue.

"Come on," you say, desperate. "Hawk, you know me. I'm not a liar. We didn't work out, but it wasn't because I was less than honest with you."

He still doesn't say anything. Instead, he strides to you and grabs your arms again, the pressure painful on the bruises he left there last time. You wince, but you're soon past noticing because he's kissing you with brutal expertise. You gasp with indignation and slap a palm to his chest in an attempt to push him off, but you're reminded of how very good he is at this. He is rough and forceful at first, but he gentles when you stop struggling; his tongue darts into your mouth and flirts with yours, then runs lightly over your lips. You moan a little in pleasure.

The sound snaps him out of the sensual haze he has fallen into. He raises his head, eyes glittering and dark.

"Fine, kitten. You win. I'll be there at eight. Have dinner ready for me, won't you? I still like my steak rare and my desserts . . . tart."

He lets go of your arms, strides to the door, and opens it.

Turn to Option 12 (below).

Option 12

The jerk hasn't shown up.

The slab of rib eye lies in a puddle of semicongealed fat. The wine hasn't just had time to breathe, it's had enough time to sing a Verdi opera or two. The dessert, at least, isn't languishing. You ate both servings when it became clear that he wasn't showing up.

He didn't even have the decency to call. And it's past your bedtime.

Just as you're brushing your teeth, you hear somebody hammering on the front door. Spitting hastily into the sink, you run downstairs, only to find it open and Hawking standing inside.

"I thought I locked that thing," you say.

He holds up a thin, flat metal bar edged by a series of irregular teeth. "Never leave home without your lock-pick kit."

"You're a cop."

"It's not illegal to own a lock-pick set—in this state."

"It is to pick a lock to gain unauthorized entrance."

"You were going to open the door for me anyway."

"Nice. How does that kind of logic hold up for sex-assault victims?"

"Awww, did I upset you, kitten?"

You sputter and give him a glare that should've singed his skin off. Instead, he ruffles your hair and goes to the table. "Excellent, you haven't put the food away yet. I'm starving. I didn't even have time to get a goddamn sandwich."

You feel angry enough to break his head, but refrain, settling for asking him in a scathing voice, "Where were you?"

"Work," he says around a mouthful of room-temperature steak. You wait for more, but nothing is forthcoming.

"Couldn't you have at least called?" you finally ask.

"Nope."

"Why?"

"Didn't have the time."

"Aren't you going to tell me more?"

"Nope. Can't. Boss's orders," he replies, sounding positively cheerful, and takes a bite of meat.

"Fine. I'm going to bed," you say.

"All right. I'll join you there once I'm done," he says.

"No, you're not. If you want to sleep, you can goddamn well take the loveseat in the bedroom."

His dark gaze is mocking, but there's something more. Anger? Desire? Regret? It's impossible to say with him.

"Go to bed," he says, tone no longer flip. "I'll take the loveseat."

You lie down on your bed and attempt to settle down. For the first time in three years, you'll be spending the night with Hawking. Memories of what bedtime with him used to be like are flooding you and making your body jumpy, sensitive. If there were one problem the two of you never had, it was sexual chemistry.

Part of you hopes you're asleep when he comes in; the other part—the stupid part—hopes you're not.

You finally fall asleep, with no sign of Hawking in your bedroom. As you sleep, you dream. Do you:

- See Hawking in your dream? *Turn to Option 13 (page 223).*
- See your boss in your dream? *Turn to Option 14 (page 224).*

Option 18

You don't realize the dream is a dream at first. Hawking is in it; he's talking to your boss in your living room, an intense look on his face. You strain your ears, but you can't make out what they're saying.

You try to yell a warning to Hawking, but your mouth is leaden. As you attempt to speak, your boss puts a hand on Hawking's chest, a questioning look on his face. Hawking takes his hand, and the two of them hug.

Something is horribly wrong. You know somebody is going to die tonight, and it's not going to be a child.

When they finally pull back, the expression on Hawking's face is familiar. It's the look you've seen on his face in the past, when he was still in love with you. He leans down and kisses your boss, their hands grappling each other with hungry desperation, and you notice that Hawk's sleeves are stained maroon.

The dream shifts, and you see a dark figure entering your room. Hawking approaches your sleeping body, carrying your chef's knife, the one you keep immaculately sharpened. He reaches your bed and caresses your face; you nuzzle his hand in your sleep, completely unsuspecting.

You scream at yourself to wake up, to do something. He gently smoothes the hair back from your forehead, and you arch your neck in response. You curse yourself for a fool; you weep and shout, but still you sleep.

He places the blade right against your carotid artery.

The force of your snapping awake actually presses the knife deeper into your neck. Oddly enough, it doesn't hurt.

You attempt to gasp something to Hawking, but your lips are numb and you feel tired. You try again. There's something he needs to know. Danger. There's danger everywhere. You still love him, and there's danger everywhere. But he's here now. Maybe it doesn't matter, after all. Maybe you can go back to sleep. You close your eyes.

The last thing you feel is Hawking kissing you on the lips. He whispers something. It might have been "I'm sorry."

Option 14

In your dream, your boss isn't torturing a small child, like he has in all your previous dreams. Instead, he's standing still, wreathed in darkness. A chill runs down your spine: he's standing under a tree across the street, and he's watching your house.

The question is: Does he know Hawk is here?

The dream jumps forward, and you see your boss approaching your door slowly and silently, like a fat tarantula stalking its prey. He tries the door, gently, gently, and it swings open on soundless hinges.

Goddammit, you'd forgotten to lock the door after Hawk picked the lock.

You wake up with a gasp, your heart almost leaping out of your chest. Just then, the bedroom door opens and a dark figure steps through.

You yell and throw a pillow at him and scramble off the bed, determined to get to the window and escape. A hard body lands on top of you, and you struggle like a possessed woman; a harsh curse rips the air when you hit an especially tender spot. Despite your efforts, he pins you down so thoroughly, you can barely blink.

"What in the fuck are you trying to do?" an all-too-familiar voice rasps in your ear, and you realize that it's Hawk.

"Hawk," you gasp. "The front door. I forgot to lock it after you came in."

Hawk freezes. "Oh?"

You gulp in air, trying to talk coherently. "I dreamed," you whisper. "My boss. He's outside. I think he's—"

The gunshot rips through the air, hitting the bed right where your head had been moments before.

Hawk rolls off you with a curse; he whips out his gun from his holster, lightning fast, aims, and fires back.

A grunt of pain indicates that he hit *something*. Hawk squeezes off a few more shots, three or four in a row, and is rewarded with another gargling cry.

Hawk slumps down against the bed and pants. From the other side of the bed, you can hear harsh, tearing sobs.

You touch Hawk with a shaky hand, trying to see if he's okay. He takes it in a crushing grip, brings it to his mouth, and kisses it, then leaps to a crouch, all animal grace, and works his way around the bed, gun at the ready.

The rest of the night is a fever dream; Hawk calls for backup, and your house fills with a swarm of policemen and paramedics; dawn is breaking when the last of them leave your house. You're on the couch, desperately wanting to sleep, but too wired actually to do so. Hawking collapses next to you and gathers you into a hug, tucking your head against his chest.

For a long time, you're content to stay in his arms, listening to his heart thud steadily. When he shifts, it's to tip your chin up so he can give you a soft, sweet kiss. Before you know it, you're sitting on his lap, hands tangled in his hair, each of you devouring the other's mouth like you'll die if you stop for breath; you're grinding yourself down against his rigid arousal even as he groans and thrusts himself up to meet you.

When he pulls back and pushes you gently but firmly away, your painfully aroused body screeches in protest.

"Wait," he says. "Wait. I need to talk to you first."

Talking is the last thing you want to do; you have much better ideas for his mouth and tongue. You slump against his chest and say, "What?"

"I didn't believe you before. About . . . that woo-woo crap. The . . . the dreams."

You snort gently. "Thanks, Hawk. Woo-woo crap, indeed."

He sighs. "That's not how I wanted that to come out." He pauses. "I want to apologize. For being such a dick to you. For not believing in you. It's just that . . . I love you, kitten, and I wanted to believe you so much that I overcompensated and acted like an asshole."

You sit up abruptly, and his eyes drop to note the jiggle of your breasts as you do so. "You *what?*" you say, incredulity lending a sharpness to your voice.

"I love you," he says. "Every time I see you, I get a blue-steel boner hard enough to drive spikes through concrete. I've tried dating other women, but they never look right, smell right, or feel right, because they're not you." He snorts and shakes his head. "Shit, why do you think I was so eager to work with you on your feature story? I felt like a motherfucking dog, following you around so you'd drop some kind of scrap for me so I can beg for more."

You stare. You couldn't have been more surprised if he'd stood up and proclaimed he was Elvis.

"You had good reasons for breaking up with me last time," he says. "It's not easy dating a workaholic homicide detective, and I hated losing you that first time, but losing you a second time will kill me."

"Hawk," you start to say, but he puts a finger to your lips.

"What I'm trying to say is, if we're going to fuck, you better damn well understand that it's not just going to be a good fuck— and God knows we've always been able to get the job done with each other—it'll be making love." His mouth quirks up. "I refuse to be your meaningless fling. We're growing old together. I'm dragging you off to City Hall, we're goddamn getting married, we're going to buy a goddamn house together, have a bunch of goddamn kids, and they'll give us a bunch of goddamn grandkids, and we're going to spoil all of them goddamn rotten. And if you can't agree to my terms, then I'd rather get up and leave, just walk out right now, and never see you again. Something's got to give."

He looks down ruefully and grimaces. "And I have a feeling it might be my cock."

You take his hand away from your mouth. "Hawk," you say, "I love you, too, you fool. You goddamn fool. You . . . Yes. I want it all. You *fool.*"

You lean down and kiss him, and he kisses you back, groaning with relief and love and lust and gratitude. And suddenly, you're struck with the certainty that you'll never fear your dreams again, because you've found . . . *The Man of Your Dreams.*

Option 15

Your maid comes in, tea tray laden with breakfast. As you nibble away at toast and sip your tea, she begins to prepare your outfit for the day. What is it?

- A velvet riding habit with a tailored jacket that hugs your supple, sensual curves before sweeping into a long, full skirt made of shocking scarlet, its daring tempered only by the pale lemon yellow collar of softest silk, which the modiste insisted was the first stare of fashion. Accompanying it is a hat, a four-foot work of millinery art replete with six feathers, four rosettes, and a miniature partridge in a small fruit tree with a teeny sateen orangutan. Today is the first day of your father's house party, and it is always inaugurated with a foxhunt. *Turn to Option 16 (below).*
- A fashionable traveling dress sewn of kerseymere trimmed with rouleaux of deep blue crepe, with a pale blue collar, complete with a capelet of the softest fox fur with a matching muff, because while you are to sail to your father's plantation in the Bahamas, you must keep up appearances on the way to the ship. *Turn to Option 19 (page 234).*

Option 16

After your maid dresses you, you go down the stairs, looking forward to the opportunity to dazzle the eligible bachelors. Your sunny mood is dimmed, however, when you notice the dark figure towering at the bottom of the stairs. Beowulf Winthrop, the Duke of Merkinshire, beholds you with a dark and unfathomable expression on his lean, harsh face. Rumored to have killed his wife to secure her fortune, he has never remarried.

He bids you good morning with an insolent gleam in his eye and an even more insolent appraising look at your body. You reply coolly and sweep by him.

At the stables, your groom is saddling your new mare, a spirited chestnut bought only yesterday. You can't wait to test her mettle.

"That's a fine piece of horseflesh you have there, but she needs a firm hand—perhaps a firmer hand than an eighteen-year-old chit can provide," a deep voice says from behind you.

You whirl around and see the Duke of Merkinshire lingering by the doorway. "Your opinion is appreciated, Your Grace, but I think I know how to handle my cattle," you answer, before deliberately turning your back on him.

A hard hand grasps your chin and wrenches your face around. You gasp in indignation, but it is muffled by his mouth, which descends on yours and starts kissing you with punishing sensuality. You struggle at first, but find yourself overwhelmed by heat and a strange lassitude as the kiss goes on. Just as you begin to enjoy it, he withdraws.

"I hope for your sake that you don't bite off more than you can chew, *mon enfant,*" he says, then turns and walks away.

The hunt begins, and your mare proves to be every bit as fast and every bit as difficult as you expected. You quickly outstrip all of the riders, except the duke, which is exceedingly provoking; you'd hoped to leave him behind, a mere speck of dust in your trail.

You approach an impossibly tall hedge at breakneck speed, and your horse sails over the top with so much ease and grace, you could have whooped with joy—which is why, when she stumbles as she lands, you're completely and utterly shocked. The jar shakes you free, and the world goes black as all the air is knocked out of you; you choke for breath, to no avail.

Suddenly, assured hands are holding you up, and the buttons on your dress are undone with fearsome efficiency, followed by the laces of your stays. A warm hand rubs your back, and your breath returns in a painful rush.

"You little fool!"

It's the duke, you realize with a mixture of excitement and fear. You turn your limpid sapphire gaze at him. His face is dark with fury.

"You deserve to be beaten for that stunt," he bites out, and gives you a little shake.

"The devil with you. I . . . hate . . . you," you manage to croak out.

"You do, eh, little girl?" he growls. "Well, allow me to give you a reason for that hate, then."

Before you quite know what happens, he flips you over and begins spanking you. You struggle and pummel at him, seething with rage at the indignity, but it does no good; the blows land on your already-bruised bottom with punishing regularity. Tears sting your eyes, but you refuse to cry out.

Over the roar of the blood in your ears, you hear people approaching.

A scandalized hush falls over the party once they realize what they're seeing. You scramble off the duke's lap, face flaming with humiliation, attempting to keep your dress up. He shrugs off his coat and throws it over you. As he does, the world turns black at the edges, and before you realize what is happening, a velvety darkness embraces you.

When you come back to consciousness, you're back in your bedroom, and your maid is watching you with an anxious eye. "Oh, miss, you're awake again!" she cries out. "What a blessing. We were so very worried, we were. Let me tell his lordship that you're awake."

Soon enough, the word comes back: your father has summoned you to the library. When you get there, Merkinshire is next to him, looking even grimmer than usual.

"I always knew you were impossible," says your father, disappointment lacing his voice, "But I did not credit you with such recklessness. Luckily, Merkinshire here is willing to do the right thing."

Your mouth falls agape. *Surely* he couldn't mean . . .

"I'm obtaining a special license. The two of you should be able to marry by the end of the week," says your father, voice implacable.

"But . . . Father . . ." you sputter.

"Not another word from you!" he barks. "I always knew I should've used a firmer hand with you, or married again after your mother died; at least Merkinshire will take you off my hands now and have the joy of dealing with you."

After this announcement, you spend the rest of the day in a daze. Merkinshire makes himself scarce—he surely wasn't looking to be trapped in another loveless marriage when he accepted the invitation to the party. Still, the proof of his lack of regard stings you more than you would like to admit, as do the speculative whispers and knowing glances that accompany you wherever you go.

When the next day dawns and there is still no evidence of Merkinshire, your peevishness begins to transform into restlessness and anger. By the afternoon, your agitation is driving you to distraction, so you decide to indulge in one of your favorite forbidden activities: you don boy's clothing and sneak off to a ruined tower that lies on the boundary of your father's property. You know the ruins well, and you enjoy the challenge of clambering over the tumbled stone walls.

You are scrambling up a familiar but tricky wall when you hear a shout from below. You look down, and to your surprise, it is Merkinshire, looking travel-stained and utterly furious.

"Get down from there!" he says, voice hard as the granite beneath your fingers.

"If you want me, Your Grace, then you can very well retrieve me yourself," you toss back, and climb your way up even more determinedly.

Does he:

- Catch up with you before you reach the top of the wall? *Turn to Option 17 (page 231).*
- Catch up with you only after you reach the top of the wall? *Turn to Option 18 (page 231).*

Option 17

Merkinshire is strong, and his lack of familiarity with the wall is more than compensated for by his sheer brute power. Before you quite know it, he is beside you, clinging with grim determination, an even grimmer look in his eyes. "You impossible chit," he grinds out, "come down before you kill yourself."

"I won't," you say. "Look, we're more than halfway up. If we go up the rest of the way, there's an old stairway on the other side that we can take."

"I see you'll need some lessons in wifely obedience," he says through clenched teeth, and reaches out one hand to grab you.

"No, don't!" you begin to say, but too late. An astonished look crosses his face as the grip on his other hand fails. You look on in paralyzed horror as he falls several feet to the ground, dashing his head against the rocks.

You clamber down the wall and ride for help as fast as you can, but it's too late: he's dead.

The resulting scandal ruins your prospects forever and exiles you to the Continent. Crushing guilt and shame keep you in isolation for many years, where you turn to poetry and the works of the Enlightenment for solace. Eventually, however, your money, beauty, disregard for convention, and bold intellect lead you to become a hostess of some of the most popular salons in Paris, and the lover of many brilliant musicians and artists, including Frédéric Chopin and Eugène Delacroix. You die at a ripe old age, surrounded by friends; although you have never stopped feeling sorry about Merkinshire's death, ultimately, you regret nothing.

Option 18

The next time you look down, Merkinshire is nowhere in sight. Shrugging off the pang of disappointment, you continue climbing determinedly.

When you reach the top edge of the wall, a pair of dusty Hessian boots greets your sight. Sinewy brown arms covered in a light furring of black hair reach down and haul you unceremoniously over the top.

"So you found the staircase on the other side of the wall, I see," you say, attempting a tone of insouciance but sounding disappointingly breathless instead. The grip on your arms turns brutal, and your heart experiences an unspeakable thrill, even as you toss your head defiantly.

"Witch," he growls, and his mouth descends on yours, the kiss both pain and pleasure. You struggle against his hold, but his hands are iron shackles. More insidious, however, are the chains of pleasure snaking through your body, tying you down, quieting your struggles. As he feels you relaxing against him, he gentles his mouth and begins kissing you more thoroughly, his lips and tongue moving with passion and consummate skill.

When the two of you at last part, you are both breathing raggedly. He traces his thumb against a smudge of dirt against your cheek. You gently push yourself into his touch, positively purring with pleasure. He groans and kisses you again. When he raises his head this time, his eyes glitter with some indefinable emotion.

"Witch," he says again, and pulls your head against his chest, where you can hear the pounding of his heart; if you weren't so utterly certain that it were impossible, you would almost say his voice sounded affectionate.

"Witch and hoyden I may be, but at least I don't abandon my new fiancée to the gossip vultures as I hare off to who knows where, doing who knows what," you retort.

"Ah, that bothered you, did it?" he asks. "I assure you, it was for a most worthy mission." He lets go of you and reaches into one of the pockets of his coat and pulls out a small velvet box, which he hands to you silently.

Filled with a hope you dare not name, you take the box from his hands and gently open it. Inside is the most beautiful ring you've ever seen, a gold band mounted by a single perfect cabochon sapphire, its dark blue depths surrounded by tiny, brilliant diamond chips.

Overcome, you look up at him. "I . . . I had no idea," you stammer out. "I thought you left because you couldn't stand the thought of being forced to marry me."

Merkinshire gives a sharp crack of laughter. "Silly chit. I can't imagine what it would feel like to want something more; as it was, I was relieved when your father told me we would be wed by the end of the week. You're a regular menace to morals, *ma petite,* and I'm not sure my purity can withstand many more of your assaults."

You swat him on the chest. "Yes, I've assaulted your virtue, to be sure—by falling off horses and climbing up walls. I can hardly credit how long you've managed to withstand my debonair charms."

"No," he corrects you, his voice gentle for once, "You have merely enchanted me by being the most magnificent female I have ever seen." His eyes narrow as he looks down at your face. "Though your penchant for endangering your very beautiful neck is less than endearing to me. I'm very fond of that neck, and I can think of any number of much more delightful things I'd wish to do it."

"Fond of my neck, are you?" you say, attempting to sound casual.

"Yes, well, and perhaps other parts of you as well," he says. "I love you, you little fool, and have for all this age. I've merely waited for you to be old enough to court properly. When I saw you fall off your horse, part of me died at the thought that you may have been lost to me before I ever had a chance with you." He drops his forehead to yours. "Please forgive me for striking you," he says huskily. "This apology cannot begin to make up for the pain and humiliation you suffered, but you have to understand that I was frantic over you."

Your very heart and blood are singing with joy at his words. "I forgive all," you whisper back. "For, dear heart, I love you, too, and have ever since the first time I saw you. You were so frightening and distant and arrogant, however, that I didn't know what to do with my passion, and so I told myself I hated you. How foolish I was!"

Overcome by emotion, he says nothing; he merely crushes you to his chest, and you thrill at the firmness of his embrace, the swift beating of his heart. As his head swoops down once again to kiss you, your heart throbs with happiness as you realize you have managed . . . *To Tame the Dissolute Duke.*

Option 19

You stand on the deck of your father's ship, the *Calliope,* as playful winds blow your flaming tresses into a streaming banner behind you. You inhale the warm salty air and grin at the wonder of the beautiful, calm expanse of ocean. Next to you, your companion, Miss Eldredge, leans heavily against the railing, looking a bit green. You, however, are blessed with a cast-iron constitution and haven't been sick even once in the month you've been at sea.

Suddenly, you hear the lookout above you call, "Ship ahoy!" A bustle immediately begins; as time goes by, you see a speck form on the horizon, then become larger with astonishing speed.

The excited murmuring on deck begins to take on undertones of alarm, however, when the strange ship takes down its standards and runs one up that is completely unfamiliar to you: black, with a horrible skull painted on it, and two crossed swords underneath.

Miss Eldredge grasps the import immediately. "Oh, sweet merciful heaven, pirates have found us! Come, my dear, we must hide below!"

Determined to show a brave front, you say, "I have every faith our good captain will successfully fight off these vermin," even as your arm shakes a little when you put it around Miss Eldredge's shoulders as you move to the cabins below with all speed.

The fight is poor, nasty, brutish, and short; the screams of men and booming of cannons etch themselves indelibly in your memory. Locked in a small closet in the cabin, however, you have no idea who prevailed.

After an eternity of silence, you hear knocking on the door. When there is no response, the knocking turns into hard, solid blows that eventually break the door open. Your heart sinks. It does not seem your ship has prevailed after all.

The light from the open closet door dazzles you. "Oho! Look at this tasty little morsel, hiding itself away for a special occasion," cries out a horrible voice. A hand covered in dirt and blood closes around your arm and yanks you out. You scream and struggle, but your cries are silenced when you are struck a smart blow across the mouth.

You see before you a filthy patchwork excuse of a man, his companion equally disreputable. "Oh, the captain is going to love this little treat, isn't he?" the man says, and chuckles. "Come, duckie, let us go find Captain Severin. This was a good haul, a good haul, indeed."

They tie your hands behind your back and drag you to the deck as you weep hysterically at the unspeakable things that will surely await you, then drop you at the feet of an unusually tall man. You don't look up until a deep voice rasps out, "Well, what have we here?"

What does the pirate captain look like?

- He is heavily bearded, with fleshy jowls and small eyes glittering with cunning. When he smiles at you, his few remaining teeth are rotting away horribly. *Turn to Option 20 (below)*.
- His chiseled features startle you with their pure masculine beauty; whatever it was you expected, it wasn't Michelangelo's David made flesh. His gunmetal gray eyes are framed by outrageously long eyelashes, but beautiful though they are, their calculating look strikes terror in your heart. *Turn to Option 21 (page 237)*.

Option 20

"Good job, me lads," says Captain Severin, chuckling with glee. "Take her to my cabin. And mind you, no poaching; I like me girls fresh and lively."

You are brought to the captain's cabin, where you attempt to find something to saw off your bonds, but to no avail. When he enters his cabin several hours later, you instinctively back yourself up against the wall, heart pounding with fear and hatred.

He locks the door behind him and looks at you, the gaze shrewd but, surprisingly enough, not unkind. Finally, he sighs and says, in cultured tones that contrast sharply with the coarse accents of his earlier speech, "I would appreciate it if you put off the hysterics until much later, or avoid them entirely. First of all, allow me to assure you that I am not in the least interested in ravishing you. My taste, to be honest, runs toward comely young men, not girls barely out of the schoolroom. My interest in you, m'dear, is strictly pecuniary. I recognize the name of your ship, and the money I'll be able to recover from returning Lord Hartley's precious daughter intact, not to mention avoiding his wrath should she be returned damaged goods, is of infinitely more value to me than allowing the savages that run my ship to have their fun with you. So if you keep quiet, follow my orders, and don't leave the cabin, I can assure your safety. Disobey me, and I won't be held accountable for what my crew do to you. Do we have an understanding?"

As he speaks, your heart lifts with joy and hope. You can only pray this is not some fiendish pirate's trick. "You have my word," you say, voice trembling.

"Excellent," he says. "So very glad we could come to an understanding. Care for a round of *vingt-et-un*?"

The time you spend on the ship passes uneventfully. Captain Severin proves to be unexpectedly good company; the two of you spend many nights playing cards and talking about poetry, and he regales you with stories of his adventures on the high seas. After several months, you are set down in a port in a strange city, where your father retrieves you, crying for joy. When called upon to recount your experiences to your friends upon your return, your sojourn aboard a pirate ship is so unremarkable that you embellish a little, turning the pirate captain into a handsome, salacious beast who restrains his passion only because he is shamed by your good-ness and purity, and gives you up with the greatest reluctance be-cause he wants you to marry well instead of leading the dangerous life of a pirate's wife. As you tell the story over and over again, you almost begin to believe the story yourself, but always, you remem-ber the gentle treatment from the rough and ugly captain, and thank him silently.

Option 21

"This is a pretty little prize, boys," says Captain Severin. An enig-matic smile quirks his sensual mouth. He leans down and lifts your face to the light. You hiss at him and attempt to shake free; how-ever, this does not deter him in the least, and he merely tightens his grip on your chin. He sees your bruised and bleeding lip, and his expression hardens.

"Take her to my cabin," he says, and straightens up. "And boys? She's mine now; any attempts to poach on what's mine will be, as it always has been, punished most severely."

The looks of fear and respect on the faces of these hardened criminals would almost be comical, but they give rise to even more trepidation in your breast—how depraved is this Captain Severin, if he makes even the most cruel and rapacious pirate quiver in his boots?

You are brought over to the pirate ship and left in the captain's spartan quarters, hands still bound; you are unable to sit still, how-ever, and are pacing the cabin when the captain enters.

"Ah, my captured tigress, prowling in her cage," he says mock-ingly.

You glare at him, too overcome to speak.

"Come here," he says lazily. You back away in response, until your back hits the wall, and he huffs with amusement. "Sweet child, you're in my domain now. Nobody will heed you if you call out or scream—indeed, my crew might find it . . . stimulating. I have no wish to treat you cruelly, but rest assured, I will tolerate no insubordination and will take the kid gloves off if I have to. I assure you that you do not want me to retrieve you."

"I would rather die a thousand deaths than submit to the will of a savage, unfeeling beast like you," you hiss, proud that your voice wavers only a touch.

Severin shakes his head wearily. "The hard road it is, then," he says, and starts toward you.

Your attempts to run are futile, of course; he catches you soon enough and subdues your struggles with ease. Desperate, furious, and fearful of what is to come, you rear your head back and spit in his face.

His eyes widen with fury, and you suddenly realize that he had, indeed, been restraining himself with you. He pins you with one arm and wipes the spittle off his cheek. "Very well, my spitting tigress," he says, "If you hate me so much, let me give you good reason to detest me, then."

He tosses you onto the bed and begins systematically cutting your clothing off with a knife he has retrieved from his boot. You stop moving only when he points out that he will not be responsible should you shove yourself into his blade. A cynical smile slants across his face at your sudden docility. "Death is never preferable, is it, no matter what you tell yourself?" he says.

He looks down at your now-naked body, and a heat sweeps across his expression. "You are indeed quite the tasty morsel," he says, and leans down to suck on your nipples. The sensation races down your body, unexpectedly pleasurable, and a liquid heat begins pooling between your legs. You struggle anew, but now it is to escape the unwanted pleasure, not your bondage. The movements seem only to excite him, however, because he presses his hips against you.

After many moments of similar torment, he sits up and unlaces his breeches. Your eyes widen at the sight of his large, rampant manhood, easily as big around as your wrist, throbbing with potency. You have no idea what is going to happen, but you're quite sure it's going to hurt. As you begin weeping, he changes his position, shoving his body between your legs; he reaches between your legs and touches your secret cove of femininity. It is brimming with unexpected moisture, which mortifies you but seems to please him.

"You may tell yourself you do not want this all you want, my tigress, but your body shows me otherwise," he says. With one hard thrust, he sunders you apart with his fleshy spear.

The pain is searing, agonizing; you cannot help but scream. You attempt to buck him off, but succeed only at seating him more firmly against you. At your vigorous movements, the captain suddenly moans and shoves himself even deeper, every muscle tensed to rocklike hardness. After an infinity, he finally shudders and collapses against you, his weight almost smothering you.

He lifts his head and looks down at your face, glistening with tears and contorted with hatred, and says, enigmatically, "Damme. Unmanned by a mere girl." He rolls off you and unties your arms. Defeated, humiliated, and furious, you curl into a ball. He throws a sheet over you, puts himself to rights, and leaves the cabin without so much as a word.

The sound of the lock might as well have been a death knell.

As you grasp yourself tightly in an attempt to prevent yourself from shivering apart, you're not sure who you hate more: Captain Severin for wrenching your innocence from you, or your body for betraying you so with its pleasure.

The next several weeks fall into a pattern. You are locked in the cabin; the first mate and the captain are the only people you see. Every night, the captain returns to the bed and slakes his lust on your body. The pain fades with time, and the pleasure correspondingly grows. One memorable night, the captain is able to bring you to a frenzied peak of pleasure, the likes of which you have never experienced, and he seems inordinately pleased by this.

The morning after, you are determined to escape.

You choose to slip away on a moonless night. Once you started responding to his caresses and showed no signs of wanting to escape, the captain has become much less vigilant about locking the door. Tonight, the captain sleeps much more heavily than usual, due to an excess of passion and rum.

Unfortunately, your escape is assailed by problems from the start. Although the swim itself presents few problems, you fail to wrap your food securely enough in oilskin, and everything is ruined by the time you reach the shore. You also find that you are not especially skilled at woodscraft, and the pirates, once they realize you've escaped, are able to track you down in no time at all. You're glad to be caught again, at any rate. You're starving and sunburned; the astonishing array of oversize creatures with far too many legs terrify you; and you had to discard your shoes while you were swimming, so your feet are cut and bleeding from stamping around the forest.

How angry is the captain when you're finally unceremoniously dumped back in his cabin?

- Coldly furious. *Turn to Option 22 (below).*
- Blazingly angry. *Turn to Option 23 (page 241).*

Option 22

The hard look on Severin's face when you are brought before him terrifies you. "So, my little tigress," he murmurs, idly flicking his finger against your cheek, "My company is so onerous, is it? My treatment of you too brutal to be borne? Very well, then. Far be it for me to stint on hospitality. I think you should have a taste of the rest of the crew's charms and see how they compare to mine. That was the reward I promised them for bringing you back, after all, and I am a man of my word."

He is impervious to your pleas for mercy and your sobbed apologies as his men drag you off. He's right: they are infinitely more cruel with you than he was, but the complete lack of pleasure is a relief, in a strange way; at least your flesh is no longer a traitor to your spirit. When you are returned to Severin's cabin, limp as a rag doll, you find that you are finally broken. You do not fight him as you used to, but you do not respond to pleasure, either. Severin seems displeased and disappointed at your detached docility, and that gives you a hollow sort of satisfaction.

After a few months, the ship docks at Tortuga, and Severin hands you over to the madam of a bawdy house for a modest sum of money. While the existence isn't exactly happy, you discover the blissful numbness laudanum can provide you, and spend the rest of your life in an opiated haze.

Option 23

You have never before seen Severin so furious. "I've seen some acts of stupidity in my time," he says scathingly. "You have to understand, being a crewmember on a pirate ship is not exactly the most intellectually taxing occupation in the world. But you . . . you could win a blue ribbon at the village idiot parade. What were you going to do, dear heart? Subsist on moonbeams and dew? Gnaw your way through a coconut? Hunt down a wild boar with your bare hands and tear it apart with your teeth? The wild boar is much more likely to kill and eat this particular tigress than the other way around, believe you me."

The lines on his face tighten, and he grasps your shoulders, his grip bruising you. "I was worried sick about what could've befallen you, you stupid bitch. A million fates flashed through my mind, each one worse than the last, and I was helpless to stop any of them. You think you know how the world works, but let me assure you, my pet, you have no idea—none!—about the predators you will encounter out there, most of them with bigger, sharper teeth than I."

"I'm sorry," you whisper, exhausted and dazed.

"Sorry? Sorry? You haven't even begun to be sorry," he bites out before he crashes his lips against yours, ruthlessly plundering its tender treasures.

That night, he makes love to you with astonishing intensity, showing you that what you thought was pleasure was but a pale imitation of what you are capable of feeling. As you start crying from the surfeit of sensation, Severin gentles and buries his face against your hair, stroking away your tears. "Don't cry," he whispers. "Don't cry, my tigress. I'm not sure my heart can stand it. Don't cry."

That night, the two of you sleep the sleep of exhausted children, with your head tucked securely against the beating of his heart.

Your slumber is interrupted, however, by the hammering on the door the next morning. A Royal Navy ship has been spotted, it seems, and is now pursuing them.

Severin leaps out of bed and begins throwing on clothing. You sit up, holding the sheet to your chest, trepidation making your eyes wide and dark. Before he goes, Severin leans down and kisses you lingeringly on the lips. You cling to him with uncharacteristic tenderness.

"Be careful?" you whisper against his lips as you part.

"Of course, my tigress. Prior to this, I had nothing to fear—but now, I have everything to lose."

Your heart swells at his words, and after he leaves, you put on your clothing. You sit and wait for the booming of cannon fire and the sounds of fighting to begin.

But nothing happens. No shock of impact, no frantic scrambling around the deck as the crew man battle stations. Your curiosity finally gets the better of you. You push on the door to the cabin, and to your surprise, it swings open. As you creep along, you see nobody; the ship is eerily deserted at this level, though you can hear the men bustling on the deck. As you pass a door, you hear voices coming from a large room—one of them the distinctive rasp belonging to Severin.

Unbearably curious but also terrified of being caught, you press your ear against the door.

"That was a job well done," says an unfamiliar voice. "We've been trying to track down that confounded traitor for an age, and by Jove, you finally delivered the goods."

"Glad to be of service to His Majesty, sir," says Severin.

"Well, are you retiring after this, Severin? Been playing pirate a dashed long time; time to put down roots, don't you think, with the tidy fee the Service is going to give you for this? Or at least come back to civilization, where the floor won't rock in this abominable fashion unless a man's in his cups."

"I believe so." There was a short pause. "There is a woman, sir. Waiting for me in the only home I've ever known. When we arrive . . ."

You don't catch the rest. You back away slowly, thinking of the sweetheart Severin has left at home, of the lies he has fed you. You've never realized "heartbreak" could be so literal a description. You flee back to the cabin, sobbing quietly all the while, and fling yourself onto the bunk. You ponder another escape attempt, but he has shown you how futile it is; he will always be one step ahead of you.

When the cabin door opens, you look up, eyes still streaming. He immediately rushes to the bed and embraces you. You wish you were strong enough to push him away; instead, you lean into him and burst into sobs yet again.

"Why are you crying, my sweet?"

You push yourself off him and give him a fulminating glare. "Why am I crying? Why, you . . . you toad-pated knave, it's because you have been in love all this time with another woman, and now that your mission is done, you're going back, and you're going to marry her, and forget all about me, and . . . and . . ." It is too much for you; all you can do is break into incoherent sobs.

"Another woman?" Severin sounds genuinely puzzled. "My mission? How on earth . . . ?" He arrests himself, and then starts chuckling.

His laughter is salt on a fresh wound. You start hitting him on the chest. "Pig . . . you are a pig . . . a stinking, horrible, rutting barnyard animal. How could you, oh how could you, I was fool enough to think you loved me, and I was even more of a fool to allow myself to love you back."

His laughter dies down, and he catches your fist. "Will it help your wounded sensibilities if I tell you that this very cabin is the only true home I've ever had?"

You stop struggling and blink rather owlishly at him as realization dawns on you. "Oh," you say in a small voice.

"Oh, indeed. So, the tigress fancies herself in love with me, eh?" he says, a roguish smile quirking the lush curve of his lips.

You attempt to push him off, but you might as well have engaged in a shoving match with an oak tree. "Certainly not. Admitting such foolishness would only make you insufferable."

"Insufferable for love of you," he says, kissing you on the forehead. "What do you say, my tigress? Will you have me? I don't have much yet, but I have a little land in Shropshire, and His Majesty has paid me a pretty penny for my work. Are you willing to be the wife of a former pirate?"

"You fool," you say. "What other possible answer do you think there could be? Yes! Yes! And again, yes!"

As he leans down and drowns your senses with fiery kisses, you can't help but think that though he may have imprisoned you at first with his desire, he is now a true . . . *Captive of Your Heart.*

Option 24

Your body still hurts from the battle yesterday, but you have no choice: you have a task to do, and you have to finish it today. Vampires and a few other Otherworld citizens are being ritually tortured and mutilated in your city, and the Vampire King has hired you to solve the mystery; as the city's best part vampire/part werewolf warrior-psychic, your skills are constantly in demand.

You hop on your motorcycle and make your way to the Vampire King's compound. When you finally reach His Undead Majesty's inner sanctum, you're surprised to see he's not alone. A representative from each of the five Otherworld factions is there, arranged around the throne; when you enter, all their eyes snap to your face. The crackle of energy almost knocks you on your ass. There's excitement, anticipation, fear, and something else . . . something you're having difficulty identifying.

You bow your head to the motley assembly, the only symbol of submission you've ever been willing to show anyone, man, beast, or man-beast.

"*Ma belle*, finally you are here," says the Vampire King from his throne, his French accent lending his voice a seductive lilt. Not that he needs that extra boost; his stern, austere beauty has literally driven people mad with despair and passion in the past, most famously Michelangelo—or so the rumor went, anyway. You yourself have never been immune to his charms, but you've made sure to keep your shields up tightly whenever you're in his presence, because he would have exploited this weakness ruthlessly. "We have important news, and a rather interesting . . . development."

The Vampire King steeples his fingers and leans back. "It appears that the people behind the murders are human occultists who have discovered a portal to a completely new realm, one rumored to be filled with creatures who are powerful beyond imagining. We successfully took care of these humans last night; unfortunately, this was not before they created a weak spot in the portal using the blood and organs they had harvested. The things at the other side have been trying to break through. We, on the other hand, are very much interested in ensuring that the portal stays intact."

Oh, God. This was going to be messy. You don't betray any of your thoughts, however.

"This is, of course, where you . . . come in," says the Vampire King.

The hesitation in his voice raises the hairs on the back of your neck. "I will be happy to provide my services to the best of my abilities, Your Majesty," you reply.

An enigmatic smiles quirks the elegant curves of his mouth. "To be sure. We've discovered that the only way to seal the portal is by putting in a team effort—in a manner of speaking. You see, the portal can only be sealed if the five Otherworld nations set aside our differences and come in the body of a psychic warrior who belongs to at least two other Otherworld nations. The combined energies can then be focused and used to seal the portal shut forever."

You look at him in confusion at first. "What do you mean, come in . . . Oh. *Shit*."

You are now able to identify that energy you had felt when you first entered. It was the sexual arousal emanating from five of the most powerful Otherworld entities in the known worlds. You are, quite literally, screwed. Or soon will be.

"You're joking," you say, voice calm, even though inside you're shaking. "You can't seriously—"

"Oh, but I am not joking, *ma puce*. It would be gauche to jest about something so serious. We *are* going to do this, whether or not you allow us to. You are the only person alive who meets all the requirements, and I can assure you, allowing the portal to open will be even more unpleasant than our attentions. You can make it easy for yourself—and we will give you no small amount of pleasure in the process—or you can resist, and be hurt."

Part of you feels furious at the ultimatum, but, much as you hate to admit it, part of you is also somewhat intrigued. You imagine making love to the Vampire King himself, and part of you goes liquid and shudders in ecstasy at the thought.

Your voice tight with anger and other emotions you have difficulty explicating at the moment, you say, "Fine. I'll do it."

The Vampire King smiles, turning to the assembly. "Excellent, *ma chère*. I am glad you saw it our way. Now, please do strip yourself of all your clothing and pick your first consort."

After you shuck off your clothing, do you:

- Fuck the head of the Werewolf clans? *Turn to Option 25 (page 247).*
- Fuck the chief of the Chupacabras? *Turn to Option 26 (page 248).*
- Fuck the leader of the Tanuki? *Turn to Option 27 (page 251).*
- Fuck the tentacled Elder God? *Turn to Option 28 (page 252).*
- Fuck the Vampire King? *Turn to Option 29 (page 254).*

Option 25

You step over to Evgeny, the head of the Werewolf clans. He is a magnificent specimen, with a beautifully shaped head, a deep chest, and long, muscular limbs. He's still in human form, but you hear that some werewolves involuntarily change at the moment of orgasm, regardless of the state of their Moon Cycle. You've never done it yourself, but then, you're only part werewolf. You are both excited and repulsed at the idea; you've never had sex after you've changed.

"Come, pretty halfling," he growls. He opens his arms, and you step into a very strong, very warm embrace. He starts nuzzling your neck; your nerve endings leap with pleasure, and you moan as he reaches your nipples and begins playing with them, pinching and pulling lightly. Warm liquid pools between your legs.

You can feel the many sets of eyes watching, and it adds an extra edge to the pleasure. You feel but do not see the tips of his fingers sharpen into claws. The change moves upon him from the outside in, the extremities of his body beginning to shift before the center. Where before there had been warm skin, now there was the strangely luxurious sense of fur behind you, and, as his arms pull you closer to him, around you as well.

Suddenly he turns you around so you no longer face him, and your heart seizes a moment with a cold pulse of fear as you catch a glimpse of him as he transforms from a large, powerful man into an even larger, more powerful werewolf. A clawed hand covered with thick dark brown fur pushes your shoulders down as he forces your knees to bend and you find yourself in a truly submissive position, your hands and knees against the cold floor while your backside and thighs are pressed against a shockingly hot, solid wall of hairy, hungry man.

He thrusts himself within you, seating his massive length deep within you to the hilt. You scream as he howls behind you, and as he moves, you realize: he's not done changing. With each thrust he grows larger and fills you to the point where you can't possibly take more, but still he pumps in and out of your heaving body, his claws holding fast to your hips. The last part of him to shift to werewolf form is his cock, which continues to throb and engorge, until it matches the mammoth size of the werewolf who wields it.

With one last deep thrust, he pushes you over the edge into a searing orgasm, your body stretched to its limits with his unholy size. Evgeny follows you into orgasm, and the force of the pulsing jets of his pleasure nearly dislodge you.

With boneless abandon, both of you slide to the floor, his warmth and soft fur covering you as the soft breeze chills the perspiration from your glistening skin. Your rest is momentary, as Evgeny forces himself to slide from your warmth. Realizing what comes next, you force yourself to stand up. You will not meet your fate on your knees.

Do you now:

- Fuck the chief of the Chupacabras? *Turn to Option 26 (below).*
- Fuck the leader of the Tanuki? *Turn to Option 27 (page 251).*
- Fuck the tentacled Elder God? *Turn to Option 28 (page 252).*
- Fuck the Vampire King? *Turn to Option 29 (page 254).*
- Have you fucked everybody? *Turn to Option 30 (page 257).*

Option 26

Xanti, the chief of the Chupacabras approaches you, and you take a moment to study his form.

His arms are muscular, green, with darker green and opalescent blue spots hugging the contours of each hardened curve. His eyes are large, also green, and set deep within his smooth, hairless head. His spines lie back against his skin, trembling slightly with each beat of his eight-chambered heart, a heart you can see beginning to speed through the translucent skin of his chest.

"Chupacabras do not ride their women like cattle," Xanti rasps, his forked tongue giving his words a sinister, sensual lisp.

"They don't?" You are confused and apprehensive, but curious.

"No. We suck the blood from our nourishment, and suck the pleasure from our women." Xanti allows that long, split tongue to caress his lips in a teasing invitation, and you cannot deny that the muscles of your thighs tighten momentarily at the sight.

"How do you come?" Forming words is becoming a challenge. Your arousal must be palpable to everyone in the room who still watches every move of your body, every shiver of your skin.

"Through our spines."

"Oh." A cold grip seizes your arms—but it's not apprehension. It's Xanti. His skin is ice cold, and throbbing. Your eyes meet his large golden gaze. Then his tongue begins to slide out of his mouth, longer, and longer, the forked tip teasing your nipples as you begin to gasp with pleasure. He wraps his tongue around them, squeezing like a python against its prey, dragging sounds of encouragement from your throat.

His spines, which had moments ago lain against the length of his body, are now, each and every one, erect, throbbing with swirls of onyx and cobalt, his unique blood filling them all to a state of complete erection. You feel his claws grip your hips, and your body lifts into the air.

His tongue, oh, God, his *tongue*. It moves within you, around you, until you cannot tell what it's doing, except that it's draining all sensation from your body to reside solely in your dripping, writhing core. The forked ends pinch and twist around your clit, slapping against it, then soothing the sting with long, sliding strokes.

When you cannot take one more moment of the teasing tongue bath, Xanti affixes his mouth against you and begins to suck, pulling the skin of your drenched pussy into contact with the multiple rows of his sharp, razorlike teeth. The orgasm Xanti has built with his tongue and teeth is being sucked out of your core by his powerful jaws, the same jaws that drain sheep of their blood in an instant.

You don't notice that two figures have advanced alongside your body. Xanti's spikes throb and stand erect down the length of his spine, a row of fleshy monuments to his own arousal. Evgeny and Zusan, the Elder God, lift you from Xanti's mouth, only to impale you on the largest and widest of Xanti's spikes. It is hot—so hot, you can hear the moisture in your body begin to sizzle as your sheath is forced down the unyielding length.

Xanti's claws grasp you again, almost desperately, you think, and Evgeny and Zusan step away. What scared you moments ago becomes both soothing and stimulating. Your eyes open to see a glimpse of the spine within you, now solid black, throbbing in time to the deep rocking pressure you feel within you. The sight sends you into an orgasm so intense, you're rendered momentarily blind.

Your screams are echoed by a growing hiss, and you realize that Xanti is coming with you, inside you and against you. The spine shudders, and a hot fluid begins to fill you, sliding down your thighs as his rasp recedes with your scream, echoing in the hall around you.

Xanti carefully lifts you from his spine, and with the assistance of Evgeny and Zusan again, places you on the floor, where you can barely stand. You open your eyes and watch as the spines slowly fold against him, paling as the darkness within them returns to his body. One glistens with the proof of his pleasure, and yours.

Xanti kneels before you and kisses your hand, then rises and steps back.

Do you now:

- Fuck the head of the Werewolf clans? *Turn to Option 25 (page 247).*
- Fuck the leader of the Tanuki? *Turn to Option 27 (page 251).*
- Fuck the tentacled Elder God? *Turn to Option 28 (page 252).*
- Fuck the Vampire King? *Turn to Option 29 (page 254).*
- Have you fucked everybody? *Turn to Option 30 (page 257).*

Option 27

You await Nobu's attention. He is only two or three feet tall, hairy, like a raccoon that stands on two legs. You see his long, bushy tail, striped in gold and brown, curling behind him. He sighs as he straightens and begins to turn around.

They're huge. Enormous. His scrotum drags along the ground as Nobu turns around slowly. He reaches down, lifts the mammoth sac from the floor, and hefts it over his shoulder. His belly is just as round, though not as large as his testicles, and you cannot help but gape as he waddles his way toward you.

"I do not usually mate with humans," Nobu says. He lifts his immense scrotum from his shoulder, and drops it to the floor at your feet. As the others stand and gather behind you, he begins to slap the skin of his balls in a gentle rhythm. You feel a presence close behind you.

It is the Vampire King. "We will assist, *mon coeur*," he whispers against your neck, making you shiver; from beneath Nobu's furry round belly, a long, thin erection reveals itself.

You press back into the Vampire King's hard, cold body, the subtle slapping rhythm of Nobu's drumming echoed in the clenching of your thighs.

"Oh, yes," you hear Nobu whisper, and his glittery brown eyes gaze at your breasts. His erection grows longer, a lance of flesh and bone, quivering in its own rhythm.

"It is time," Nobu whispers. Strong arms lift you from beneath and slowly move your body onto Nobu's long, thin cock. Before you can react, the Vampire King begins to bounce you on Nobu's scrotum, and you feel your breasts begin to bounce, the slapping mirroring the way your backside slaps against Nobu's scrotum, a staccato accompaniment to Nobu's panting.

"Oh, yes, more," Nobu whispers. He lowers his head and gasps as he comes, folding his body forward so you're trapped, impaled on his long cock, his warm and throbbing scrotum behind and beneath you, and the furry solid roundness of his belly against yours. You arch your back in an orgasm that catches you off guard and throws you that much further into oblivion.

"Exquisite," murmurs Nobu. You raise your head. He smiles and pats your breasts. "You are so soft, yet so strong." He straightens, helps you off him, and throws his balls over his shoulder, a twinkling grin in his button black eyes.

Do you now:

- Fuck the head of the Werewolf clans? *Turn to Option 25 (page 247).*
- Fuck the chief of the Chupacabras? *Turn to Option 26 (page 248).*
- Fuck the tentacled Elder God? *Turn to Option 28 (below).*
- Fuck the Vampire King? *Turn to Option 29 (page 254).*
- Have you fucked everybody? *Turn to Option 30 (page 257).*

Option 28

Zusan stands proudly beside you. His body, the human elements anyway, are still, but no stillness ever affects the tentacles that grow from his shoulders, his abdomen, his hips, and his groin. You cannot look away.

"Trust me," he says in his reverberating voice. "It will be good."

You cannot speak. How does he . . . where is his . . . ? For God's sake, which tentacle is it?

You have your answer when you see his rampant cock growing from a curved piece of flesh on top of his lowest tentacle.

Standing an arm's length apart from you, the tentacles from Zusan's shoulders and sides approach you. Tentacles are on your hips, guiding you back against the tapestry hanging on the wall. The rough wool abrades your backside, but then you are lifted by two ropes beneath your arms. Your eyes fly open—no, not ropes. More tentacles hold you upright, against the wall, looping beneath your arms and forming a firm brace in front of your hands.

Suckers attach themselves to your nipples and begin to pull in a seductive rhythm, the sucking and pulling spreading as tentacles attach themselves to the skin of your breasts, your belly, and oh, God, your clit. Sparing no moment for buildup, Zusan has attached a large, round sucker to your clit, and is pulling the pleasure from your body.

You scream as you feel an orgasm that may be larger than you are rising within, blanketed with burning heat. You are on fire, turning into heat itself, panting as the overwhelming pressure and suction, stroking and pulling surround every inch of skin.

"Fill me," you whisper.

"Everywhere?"

"Oh, yes, please."

You turn your head and slide your tongue around the end of the tentacle that hovers, quivering, near your face. You hear Zusan whisper, "Yesss," as you begin to suckle on the tip. His tentacle is dry and warm; you suck harder, drawing more of his firm, undulating tentacle into your willing, hungry mouth.

His arms and tentacles raise you up, and his cock, which has grown to a size that matches the tentacle on which you feast, slowly enters your body. You moan in pleasure.

"There's more," he says.

The tentacle beneath his cock slides between the cheeks of your ass, dipping itself in the incredible wetness that rains from your clenching heat. You feel the tentacle quiver, working slowly back and forth to separate your cheeks, and then, with a subtle prod, it pushes at your tight, puckered entrance.

You tense again, and while your clenching makes Zusan gasp at the sudden tightness that grips his cock, the denial of entry makes his eyes narrow.

"Open up," he says, his tentacle tapping a seductive, slick rhythm against your ass. You feel the tip slide inside you. You gasp. You tense and release, and each time you relax, more of his tentacle slips inside your ass, until you are full of him, so full you can't move at all. His cock in your pussy, one tentacle in your mouth as you suckle upon it greedily, tentacles around and underneath you, and one powerful thrusting peaked tentacle up your ass. You wrap your legs around his waist and hold on.

It's heaven, and hell, this tensing and releasing, and more pleasure than you think you can stand; you cannot stop the relentless acceleration toward an orgasm so big it seems impossible. The throbbing on your mouth, the sucking of your tongue, the thrusting cock deep inside you, the sliding, pulsing fucking of your ass, and the low, vibrating tones of his voice combine to make you shatter. You come, waves upon waves of pleasure, so tight and sharp you scream, "Oh, my God."

"I am," Zusan agrees, as he orgasms after you. You spasm one final time as he slips out from your mouth, your ass, your clenching, greedy, heated pussy, and he lowers you to the floor to stand again.

Do you now:

- Fuck the head of the Werewolf clans? *Turn to Option 25 (page 247).*
- Fuck the chief of the Chupacabras? *Turn to Option 26 (page 248).*
- Fuck the leader of the Tanuki? *Turn to Option 27 (page 251).*
- Fuck the Vampire King? *Turn to Option 29 (below).*
- Have you fucked everybody? *Turn to Option 30 (page 257).*

Option 29

The tension between you and the Vampire King is an almost tangible energy between you, so electrically charged you can almost see it drawing him to you, visually linking your bodies.

"It is long past time," he says. "I have waited for this opportunity for far too long, *ma chère.*"

You don't say a word. You don't trust yourself to speak. He reaches for you, drawing you firmly against him. The curve of your hips fits perfectly with his, as if you were made to be there.

He parts the fabric of the black robe he wears to reveal that he's nude underneath. He is magnificent. Sculpted, muscular, and lean, with curves and shadows your tongue longs to explore, he is truly a work of art, and probably older than much of the art in any museum.

The Vampire King lowers you to the floor, covering you with that magnificent body. "No biting," you say in a low moan.

"Oh, *mon coeur,* you spoil my fun."

"No."

You feel his teeth against your neck; his fingers cup your breasts, slowly kneading them. You can feel the press of his cock against your hip, the only part of him that's hot.

He slides down your body so fast you do not see him move. Then you feel those same teeth stroking over your clit, pressing at the most sensitive spot on your body. His tongue slides inside you. The pressure builds, and suddenly, you want more. You want him inside you.

He moves again, before you can blink, and thrusts deep into you. Then he sweeps back down to taste you. Back and forth, faster than you can see, he moves. He is a blur above you and a solid mass within you. You arch your back, and he rests above you, holding himself deep within you.

"You must let me."

"No," you gasp, unwilling to allow him to penetrate you with his teeth, but so eager for more of his cock.

"*Ma petite,* you will be the death of me a second time."

"Good," you whisper, as the slow, deep movement of his cock brings you closer and closer toward orgasm. You lift your head and look into his eyes. Before he knows what you're about, you bite him where his neck meets his shoulder.

The reaction is immediate. "You dare?" he growls, even as his cock surges.

"Yes," you say, drawing back. Then you feel it. The latent part of your cross-species blood, the werewolf that you've never changed into while mating—it's surfacing. Your teeth are growing, canines stretching into long, deadly spears eager to plunge and tear.

"You must stop, or I will retaliate. It . . . will be beyond my control."

Your mouth curls into a teasing grin, showing your gleaming fangs.

You bite him again, this time plunging one sharp point into the base of the thick vein in his neck, tasting the flood that emerges. With a hiss, the Vampire King latches his teeth onto your neck, drawing that same spurting flood from your neck that you're sucking from his.

Suddenly the quest for orgasm becomes a battle of wills. Your mouths refuse to move away, while his cock and your clenching cunt rock closer and closer together, trying to move even closer. You flex your fingers, feeling your nails sharpen into deadly points, but the Vampire King is too fast. He grabs your arms, pinning them above your head. He's still fastened to your neck, still tilting his hips deeper into the curve of your own.

What began as an explosion of lust hovers at the edge of bliss in a stalemate, two warriors with impossible power head-to-head, unwilling to back down. The Vampire King lets go of your neck. He begins thrusting, deeper, harder, driving you to the edge. Your head falls back away from his neck and you stare up at him.

"Oui."

"Oui," you echo. At that moment, you both arch and yell, pouring passion into each other.

With a show of limitless strength, he lifts you both to stand, separating his body from yours. He leans down to lick one stray drop of your blood from your neck, then steps back and bows, a sardonic smile on his handsome, chiseled face.

Do you now:

- Fuck the head of the Werewolf clans? *Turn to Option 25 (page 247).*
- Fuck the chief of the Chupacabras? *Turn to Option 26 (page 248).*
- Fuck the leader of the Tanuki? *Turn to Option 27 (page 251).*
- Fuck the tentacled Elder God? *Turn to Option 28 (page 252).*
- Have you fucked everybody? *Turn to Option 30 (page 257).*

Option 30

Pick your way through all your options again. That's right: there's no end. All good paranormal series end in nonstop, round-robin nookie. You didn't know? Now you do. You've chosen your own fate: the fate of the never-ending fuckathon, paranormal style. Enjoy! For now you are *The Licking Fucking Sucking Dripping Drumming Darkness.*

Color by Numbers

Colors are never ordinary in romance novels. Love is a many-splendored thing, and the color palette on a heroine alone could make an interior designer swoon with envy. And now, we Smart Bitches are more than happy to provide you with a chance to have a chance in re-creating the glory yourself. That's right: a coloring book page. Feel free to get creative, but here are our suggestions for the colors to use:

THE HEROINE

Hair: Pick among Golden Champagne, Burgundy Spice, Sultry Auburn, Coffee-Kissed Chocolate, or Velvety Raven's Wing

Eyes: Pick among Rain-Drenched Emerald, Rain-Drenched Topaz, Rain-Drenched Sapphire, Rain-Drenched Amethyst, Rain-Drenched Mist, or Rain-Drenched Cocoa

Skin: Honey-Kissed Cream, with hints of Seashell Pink along cheeks

Glove, shoes, and dress: Lucent Lavender

Petticoat: Magnolia Bloom

THE HERO

Hair: Pick among Lion's Mane, Mahogany, or Coal Black

Skin: Bronze Battle

Eyes: Pick among Granite, Gunmetal, Aquamarine, Brandy, Green, or Brown

Breeches: Doeskin brown

Spats: Ivory

Shoes: Leatherine Black

SCENERY

Sky: Blend together Crepuscular Salmon, Sunset Shimmer, and Ravishing Robin's Egg

Grass: Very, Very Verdant

Rose petals: Scarlet Surprise

Rose leaves: Hunter Green

Ship sails: Eggshell

Ship proper: Oaken Solidarity

Ocean: Aegean Summer

Write Your Own Romance

Write Your Own Paranormal Romance

Fill in the following, then read aloud for fun and absurdity, Smart Bitch style.

Sharp thing: _____

Quiet thing: _____

Animal: _____

Body part: _____

Foreign term of endearment: _____

Body part: _____

Animal: _____

Supernatural being: _____

Invertebrate animal: _____

Organ: _____

Noun: _____

Noun: _____

Animal: _____

Verb: _____

Country: _____

Adjective: _____

Job or avocation: _____

Character trait: _____

Noun: _____

Number: _____

Number: _____

Spice: _____

Noun: _____

Verb: _____

Animal: _____

Organ: _____

Noun: _____

Killian drew her [*sharp thing*] and crept, silent as drifting [*quiet thing*], down the hallway. The Chalice was down here; she could feel it. As she reached the ornate iron door at the end and cautiously turned the knob, she wondered what sort of [*animal*] guarded it in the room beyond. Almost definitely a hellbeast of some sort, or, if she were lucky, merely a three-headed demonspawn, each with three rows of needle-like [*body part*]. If she weren't lucky, however . . .

"[*Foreign term of endearment*]."

The word floated out from the blackness of the room beyond. Damn. Seemed like tonight wasn't her lucky night.

She straightened and gently pushed the door open. No use for subterfuge now; Azuriel had beaten her to the Chalice. She walked into the room, trying to keep her body relaxed, [*body part*] loose yet ready, like a(n) [*animal*]'s.

He glowed at the edges like the fallen [*supernatural being*] he was, and his beauty pained her and terrified her at the same time. She knew how deceptive that beauty could be, how it could turn like a(n) [*invertebrate animal*] and sting her unexpectedly.

"I have missed you, dear [*organ*]," he said, his voice musical as [*noun*], soft and soothing as [*noun*]—and every bit as implacable.

"How nice," she said, trying to keep her voice light, trying not to let her love show, nor her ultimate intention. She should never have fallen in love with a(n) [*animal*] like him in the first place, and she should certainly not still [*verb*] him now, not after what he had done to her in [*country*]. She approached him, sword held down to her side. "I haven't missed you at all. Haven't given you a second thought, in fact."

"You were always a(n) [*adjective*] liar," he said, amusement showing in his face. "A magnificent [*job or avocation*], but a terrible liar. This, however, is a poor showing, even for you."

She was close now. Almost close enough. She shrugged her shoulders. "You know me too well." Closer. Almost. Almost. His [*character trait*] always was his biggest [*noun*]. "I may have thought about you every now and then, but let me assure you, the memories of you have inspired me to homicide no more than a dozen times. Well, not more than [*number*]. Okay, fine, [*number*] on the very outside."

She could breathe in his scent, [*spice*] and [*noun*], and his face was right in front of hers. His mouth was quirked in a half-smile. He reached out to [*verb*] her.

She moved, quicker than the reflexes of a hunting [*animal*], faster than thought itself, aiming for his [*organ*].

The jar of her shattering [*noun*] indicated that he'd moved faster still. *Well, shit*, she thought, *This is going to be more interesting than I'd bargained for.*

Write Your Own Regency Romance

You know the drill: grab your pelisse and your wrap, fill in the blanks, and read aloud your lush Regency romance, now made 300 percent more awesome with your input and brilliance!

Name of British food, spaces omitted: _____

Adjective: _____

Noun: _____

Adjective: _____

Noun: _____

Plant: _____

Noun, plural: _____

Noun: _____

Verb: _____

Body part: _____

Emotion: _____

Adjective: _____

Adjective: _____

Sexy word: _____

Noun, plural: _____

Noun, plural: _____

Noun: _____

Body part: _____

Organ: _____

Adverb: _____

Adjective: _____

Body part: _____

Noun: _____

Noun: _____

Body part, plural: _____

Name of oil or energy company: _____

Adjective: _____

Verb: _____

Verb: _____

Regency exclamation (see page 273 for ideas): _____

Noun, plural: _____

Organ: _____

Body part: _____

Verb: _____

Verb: _____

Noun: _____

Animal: _____

Emotion: _____

Furry animal: _____

Another furry animal: _____

Noun: _____

Verb: _____

Body part: _____

Emotion: _____

Body part: _____

The ball had become a most dreadful crush, and Miss Chastity Merriweather-[*name of British food, spaces omitted*] slipped past the double doors left ajar in the ballroom, seeking respite from the near-[*adjective*] heat of candles and press of [*noun*]—and a dark, [*adjective*] gaze that had not left her all night. As she stood in the dark and took dainty sips of [*noun*], scented by the [*plant*] bushes that grew nearby, she heard slow, deliberate [*noun, plural*] behind her, and sensed a large imposing presence beside her.

The Devil had found her, it seemed, despite her best efforts at escaping him.

He'd certainly wasted no [*noun*].

She tried to turn around and [*verb*] past him, but too late. His arm wrapped around her [*body part*], and she gave a brief shriek of [*emotion*] when she felt herself being hauled unceremoniously against a very [*adjective*], very [*adjective*] body, but the cry was swallowed when a hard, sensual mouth sealed itself against hers.

She struggled briefly in his grasp, but the [*sexy word*] assault soon overcame her delicate senses. [*Noun, plural*] raced through her blood, and [*noun, plural*] ran up and down her [*noun*]. When his tongue traced the seam of her [*body part*], she gasped; he took advantage of her open mouth and slipped in. His tongue proceeded to flicker and caress her in a most provocative way, and before she quite knew what had come over her, her [*organ*] joined in the love-play, tangling with his [*adverb*].

His abrupt withdrawal was [*adjective*]. His mouth was damp and his [*body part*] tousled; Chastity realized with a mixture of [*noun*] and [*noun*] that she had been responsible. She hadn't even remembered putting her hands on his head. With a sinking feeling, she suddenly realized she could feel exactly where *his* [*body part, plural*] were, and she was quite sure they were in a place no proper lady should allow a gentleman.

The problem, of course, was that Devil [*name of oil or energy company*] wasn't a gentleman.

His [*adjective*] face looked down at hers with an unreadable expression, making it impossible for her to [*verb*]. She attempted to [*verb*] herself, and said: "[*Regency exclamation*], sir, I'm sure I shouldn't be allowing you to take such [*noun, plural*]."

His arms instantly tightened around her. "Chastity, my [*organ*], surely you did not think I could view your furtive attempt to leave as anything other than an invitation," he drawled. His gaze dropped to her [*body part*], and another expression flitted across his face. "And given the way you [*verb*], I hardly think you are a stranger to these sorts of assignations."

Chastity gasped. How *dare* he [*verb*] her [*noun*]? "You . . . you [*animal*]!" she cried out in self-righteous [*emotion*]. "You insufferable [*furry animal*]! You, you . . . [*another furry animal*]! I can assure, you, sir, that never has a person been so outrageously free with my [*noun*]!"

"You can [*verb*] me all you like," he said. "Your [*body part*] may say something, but your lips and tongue say something else entirely."

Chastity's shriek, this time of [*emotion*], was once again cut off by the Devil clamping his [*body part*] over hers.

WRITE YOUR OWN VAMPIRE ROMANCE

It was a dark and angsty night. The wind raged, the trees whispered, a child counted to ten between flashes of lightning and claps of thunder. And the book you're reading is scaring the pajama pants right off you. Fill in the blanks, and hold on to your elastic waistband, because it's Vampire Romance Mad Lib Time.

Hot item: _____

Adjective: _____

Body part: _____

Natural disaster: _____

Noun: _____

Noun: _____

Noun: _____

Noun, with an extra "h" added: _____

Body part: _____

Body part: _____

Adjective: _____

Adjective: _____

Adjective: _____

Noun: _____

Noun: _____

Body part: _____

Word for emotion, but with two extra "h"s added to it: _____

Body part: _____

Adjective: _____

Flavor: _____

Favorite childhood food: _____

Favorite adult food: _____

Astronomical object: _____

Organ: _____

Verb: _____

Verb: _____

Noun: _____

Verb: _____

The dream was the same as it always was, yet different.

He was there in the room with her, like he had been for every night in the past several years. His gaze ran over her body, making her tremble, making her hot, hotter than [*hot item*]. He touched her shoulder, stroked it, pinned her to the bed. And smiled.

His teeth were beautiful and white and very, very [*adjective*].

A hard thrust of his [*body part*], and he was inside her, like he'd been in so many dreams. She screamed in pleasure and pain as the orgasm swept through her like a [*natural disaster*].

He laughed, hard and dark and cruel, her dream [*noun*], her [*noun*], her [*noun*]. He bent his head and scraped his teeth against her neck.

The dream was the same. But different.

This time, he raised himself and looked down at her. "Finally," he said, "You're ready for this, [*noun, with an extra "h" added*]." He smiled, baring his teeth again, and this time, when he lowered his [*body part*] to her neck, the [*body part*] pierced her, [*adjective*] and [*adjective*] and [*adjective*] at once.

[*Noun*] slammed through her body. She could feel her blood pulsing into his mouth, and while a part of her was horrified, her [*noun*] wanted nothing more than to push as much of herself into him as she could.

Something pressed against her mouth. His [*body part*], she realized through the fog of pleasure.

Bite, said a voice inside her head. *Bite as hard as you can, my* [*word for emotion, with two extra "h"s added to it*].

So she did. Her teeth were strangely sharp, almost as sharp as his, and the skin parted easily. A flood of warmth entered her [*body part*]. His blood was [*adjective*], [*flavor*], and utterly delicious; it tasted like [*favorite childhood food*] and [*favorite adult food*].

Then the pain.

The pain caught her unawares. It came from nowhere and everywhere; it was agonizing, searing, impossible; it felt like a(n) [*astronomical object*] was burning her [*organ*] from the inside out.

The pain woke her up. That was when she realized it wasn't a dream. Her body was racked with convulsions of pain and pleasure while the man of her dreams pinned her to the bed, drawing her blood with great gulps from her even as his filled her mouth so fast she had to [*verb*] or [*verb*].

Before the blackness of [*noun*] claimed her, she felt him [*verb*] himself from her, and the last thing she saw was his face, wreathed in a red feral smile.

Spot the Bullshit Regency Term—
It Goes All the Way Up to Eleven

One of the best parts of reading Regency romance is when an author has done her homework. When the research is tight, the reading is right. Let that be your guiding motto as we challenge you—as we have also done our homework, with the assistance of Google-Fu.

There are eleven bullshit Regency words that we totally made up hidden within this mass of what-the-fuck. Find them. All eleven.

alkithole	calf-clingers	mizzlefust
amuse-mouffe	faradiddle	Paphian
antidote	fleeker	parantesson
aristide	fribble	peep-of-day boy
attern goggler	gobble-cock	penny-pated
autem	grigs	piffletosh
axwaddle	ha-ha	scare-babe
Bartholomew baby	herring-top	sham Abram
blashy	hummel-pummel	tap-hackled
bloss	jarrenbill	twiddlefoot
buck fitch	loose fish	wear the willow
bumbleboots	make micefeet of things	

Answers: These are the fake Regency words—
amuse-mouffe, aristide, bumbleboots, fleeker, herring-top, hummel-pummel,
mizzlefust, parantesson, penny-pated, piffletosh, twiddlefoot.

Chapter Heaving Bosom

The Future of the Genre

The End, the Beginning, and the Future

In our attempts to examine the genre, we've looked at the distant past, the not-so-way-back past, the Days of Yore, the present, and the possibility. But now, it's time for us to toss on that sparkly velvet cape and the glittery shoes, grab our crystal ball and our nearest Swanne Chapeau, and *gaze . . . into . . . the future.*

Really, soothsaying on the subject of romance is an incredibly irresponsible thing for us to do because we are not of the publishing industry. We're readers. Really loud readers with a Web site that hosts a loud, gregarious, opinionated, and dare we say, Bitchy community of fellow readers and fans of romance, yes, but just readers. We don't drive industry trends, unless by "drive" you mean pay for them, put them in shopping bags, and drive them home from the bookstore. We don't make publishing decisions or recommendations to editors, and we surely don't have any control over What Comes Next.

Before we move into the reckless and irresponsible musings that constitute two women with absolutely no real applicable knowledge of the publishing industry making sweeping and grand sparkly predictions about the future of romance publishing, let us state that, well, we're two women with no real insider knowledge of the publishing industry. We know romance, and we like to think we know our readers and our fellow romance bloggers, and thus our predictions are for shits and giggles. Don't make any investments based on our blather, for God's sake, and read all instructions in the manual before operating. All rights reserved, no purchase necessary, must be two years of age or older, and void where prohibited except when expressly stated that it's bodacious by law.

Spending all this time looking in the rearview mirror means we have a few predictions about the future. We're betting our last crispy dollar that the romance market remains strong, even as predictions of health in the publishing industry make it sound as if the heroine and the industry both have terrible, life-threatening colds. Yes, there may be too many books on the market, and maybe there is some financial pole dancing that could be done in a different titty bar, but romance readers are always going to want romance, we're always going to want more of it, and we're always going to pay for the pleasure of reading it. Romance readers are a faithful lot, and our genre, we love it enough to keep it going.

The marvelous thing about the romance genre is its flexibility, its fluidity, and its endurance. It's a bendy, twisty, accommodating ho, that romance genre, and because of that, it'll be just fine and dandy while the rest of the publishing world may run about screeching to the skies about the end of the world as they know it. In our world, the ending is always happy, if you know what we mean, and we think you do.

Ready to take a glimpse into the future? Let's break it down.

ONLY OLD LADIES READ ROMANCE. THE READERSHIP IS DYING OUT.

HEY! We'll pretend you didn't say that, and you can pretend Sarah's not wearing mom jeans. Romance's readership isn't going anywhere, for two very distinct reasons. First, the youth of the Internet and the youth of publishing. The Internet has created a large, powerful voice for readers, and we're not just talking about us, though we are plenty loud. The Internet is the worst and the best thing that ever happened to publishing. Worst because feedback is instantaneous, and reviews are everywhere. Feelings are hurt, snappy accusations are made, and minor flame wars break out with the least bit of tinder when someone's tender pride gets a swat in the backside. All that instant feedback can be tough, and we know it.

But the Internet is also among the best things that's happened to publishing, in our opinion, because the Internet allows readers and writers and publishers to interact in ways they haven't before, and that interaction lends a clarity to determining what it is that readers want, like, and, most important, will buy. Plus, the industry of publishing has a huge number of young people working within it, young as in "hopelessly and utterly wired at all times," and therefore the Internet and its cranky denizens have more editorial assistants quietly watching and reading—more than one might think. Youth and the Internet will save publishing, specifically romance publishing, from the dire predictions of "fail, fail, epic, fail."

The other element working in romance's favor? The letter "e," as in e-books. Harlequin's decision to release every book as an e-book as well as a paperback was so brilliant we might need to genuflect. Harlequin could have been dismissed as a dying concept in romance publishing, because, really, who subscribes to book clubs like Harlequin anymore, or CD clubs for that matter? The readers who would happily immerse themselves in a selection of books each month that they personally didn't choose is definitely on the wane, if it hasn't reached endangered status already. With that pesky Internet came the desire to customize every last purchase to the point where some people take any removal of autonomy as a personal affront. So the idea of a publisher shopping for books for you? Not likely to appeal to the younger, wired audience, in our opinion.

But the same desire for new entertainment that kept the mail-order-romance business in healthy vigor is now flourishing in a younger audience that haunts the e-book library at Harlequin. Instead of falling into antiquity, Harlequin is reinventing itself with the same product: short, satisfying novels for people who read often but for short amounts of time. The only differences now are age and possession of an e-book reader. The fact that other publishers of romance have begun to offer most if not all of their titles in e-book format underscores the major act of smart forged by Harlequin with their e-library.

But aren't all e-publishers skeevy? Nope. Not at all. But some e-publishers might be. The only thing standing in the way of the limitless success of e-publishing is some of the e-publishers themselves. There are sites all over the Internet that show you cute pictures of people's cats. And there are other sites that discuss the more mercenary, scary, and economically clever machinations of some very shady e-publishing institutions. The former is fun; the latter, if you're a writer, should be required reading. The Internet is a marvelously busy place when keeping track of salacious rumors that might indicate that something is wrong in a publishing operation, particularly one that's new or doesn't have much of a track record. What do you need to look out for? What's the difference between a shady e-pub, a legitimate e-pub, or a print publishing house? Let us help you.

Shady e-Pub	Legit e-Pub	Print Publishing
Your editor is very forthcoming about every detail of her life, and how her recent bout with hemorrhoids has affected the company's book production.	You know your editor's name, and a few details about her personal life. Maybe you read her blog.	You know your editor's name, and a few details about his or her personal life. You've had drinks. At a conference. Far away from your actual home.

(continued on next page)

Shady e-Pub	Legit e-Pub	Print Publishing
Cover art is drawn by a basement full of elves kept under deplorable conditions and forced to create using only brown, black, blue, green, and white, and Poser.	Cover art can be questionable, but there's an art "department," or at the least an "art director." Or a person who asks about the story and then downloads and alters stock images.	Cover art might involve a multithousand-dollar illustration, hand painted by an artist. Or stock photography. But there's a whole crew of art folks doing the art thing. On Macs. Which are awesome. Note: No one, regardless of publisher, is immune to bad covers. It happens.
Pays you royalties with checks that bounce like the slapping ball sack of a very humperating man on top of a woman who is on top of a mechanical bull situated above a jackhammer.	Pays you royalties.	Pays you royalties.
E-mail to the editor bounces like that man and his jackhammer, with a reply, "Due to extended inactivity, new mail is not currently accepted for this mailbox."	E-mail to the editor receives a response within twenty-four to forty-eight hours.	It takes five or six e-mail messages to the editor, and you might get responses only when the book is due for publication.

Shady e-Pub	Legit e-Pub	Print Publishing
The covers portray characters whose sexual identity is in question, even when the book is not meant for the GLBT market.	The covers feature real men and women in sexual poses.	The covers feature the same woman's legs on eight different books. Recycling stock images is for professionals only! Do not try this at home!
The publisher's Web site features falling stars and music upon launch, plus those irritating things that trail your cursor and crash your browser.	The company's Web site loads fast and is easy to navigate.	The company's Web site is updated but every page has uniform look for each book, plus a link to the publisher's lawsuit against Google.
The publisher asks you to pay a fee to list the book on its Web site.	Listing the book for sale on the Web site is part of the publication deal.	Your book is for sale in as many places they can stock it, from Amazon to the bookstore in the mall.

MORE FEARLESS PREDICTIONS!

Not every reader will embrace e-books, and we don't think that paper publishing will die a woodsy death any time in the near future, but e-books will byte their way through more of the market in the next five to ten years. E-book readers will become as ubiquitous as text messaging on cell phones. Whether it's a stand-alone device like a Kindle or a Sony eReader, or an integrated program housed on cell phones, more people will jump into the e-book market, and, as Jane from Dear Author has said to us on a few occasions, there's no better readership for e-books than romance readers. We're gluttonous, and we put our credit cards in the hands of our desire for more reading. Digital consumption and having a buffet of books to choose from on one device is as heady for some romance readers as a stack of brand-new uncreased paperbacks is for others.

THERE'S A PLOT AFOOT!

When it comes to predicting the future of a subgenre, we're not so brave. Because it takes between eight to eighteen months for a book that's sold to appear on the shelves, what's being purchased now by editors won't show up for a while, and thus what's on the shelves now isn't necessarily an accurate measure by which to gauge what's coming down the turgid pike of romance. Today's books are what someone thought would be a great idea over a year ago. However, we can make a few more sweeping, irresponsible generalizations about the plotlines of upcoming romances.

The population of werewolves and vampires will level off and chill the fuck out already. There's more undead and hairy on the shelves now than there are people in Los Angeles, New York, and Omaha combined, and that's a lot of damn people. Paranormals will continue to be the hottest things since the sultry shadows of Nathan Kamp's abdominal musculature, but they'll move away from the undead and hairy and more into the territory of fantasy, alternate realities, and use of space as a new frontier for the what-what, butt optional. Urban fantasy will be the next overplayed trend, and people in a year or two will think of urban fantasy as they think of vampires now.

Jane from Dear Author tells us she thinks that authors will do the hokey pokey and switch themselves around by moving away from the romance genre in favor of other genres where the happy ending and courtship resolution therein are not mandatory. She points to the progression of the J. R. Ward Black Dagger Brotherhood series as evidence that Ward is headed to more urban fantasy, less romance, while authors like Patricia Briggs are moving toward romance readers with emphasis on the romantic coupling.

The line between urban fantasy and romance will continue to

blur, especially as series become more and more popular and readers want to revisit the same constructed world in multiple novels.
But the balance between gritty apocalyptic narrative and Happily
Ever After will be a tough one to maintain for too long. Ultimately,
we think, urban fantasy and romance will do the dance as old as
time for a while, become more urban, more gritty, more scary and
more lethal, then go their separate ways.

And while we're talking about scary and lethal, have we really
explored the true possibilities of the paranormal genre and the possibilities of REALLY NOT AT ALL REMOTELY HUMANOID in-
terspecies love? For example, giant blob of protoplasm heroes. No,
really. He's literally a hero you can mold into your own image. And
let us not forget the variety of openings and appendages that can be
attached to an alien species: with no real prototype to prejudice the
reader's imagination, the sexual adventures of plasma-based alien
life forms are potentially explosive. Literally.

Then there's the paranormal creatures who have been ignored
until now and should receive their due. We predict the arrival, the
rise, and the fall(ing to literal pieces) of the zombie hero and heroine. The reanimated and vacant-eyed protagonists, who may or may
not be stereotypically wrapped in tattered bandages and old clothing, can dry-hump with the best of them, and their love should
definitely see the light of day—unless the light of day sets them on
fire, in which case, even better. Hot fiery love is the best kind.

In historical romance, Victorians will be the next big boom,
partially because of the more modern concepts that are possible
within that time period, such as the arrival of newer technologies
and the possibility of divorce, and partially because the Regency is
tired and needs a rest. Jane from Dear Author agrees: the success of
writers like Sherry Thomas, who set her first two novels, *Private Ar-
rangements* and *Delicious,* in the late Victorian era, means that more
writers will think outside the Regency box and spill over into ad-
joining historical eras. A new set of social rules and standards, with
the same emphasis on wealth and exclusivity, means that readers
will have their history lessons and their opulence in scorching pas-

sionate love stories set in an era that was about as sexually con-flicted as our own. That right there is the lacy thong icing on the cupcake of repressed desire. We'll take a baker's dozen.

While there was a brief blip of Harlequins in Roman settings, the toga-toga-toga romance will probably remain limited. But the arrival of the Harlequin Blaze historical line could mean some hot, hot sexing in some very cool historical settings. Our preferences? Is there a historical setting that hasn't really received enough love and affection from the romance crowd? Not really. But reader prefer-ence for specific historical periods points to another prediction that we do feel rather confident about: the world of the series, and the series set in the same world, will continue without any signs of withering. Whether there's multiple books set within the same constructed world, or within the same period of society, or there's novels that follow one another in a specific timeline, readers love to revisit and writers certainly seem to enjoy indulging in multiple forays into the worlds they spent so much time and so much re-search constructing. The power of that revisit is overwhelmingly attractive, especially from a profit sense, because if readers get hooked on a world, whether it's slang-slinging vampires or other-worldly detectives, supernatural athletes or boarding schools for the paranormally inclined, they'll keep looking for the next install-ment.

And while we're talking trends that affect all genres, let's talk about the Gheys. Gay romances will hit the mainstream. Count on it. There will be a boom, like it or not, as publishers realize that all those heterosexual female gay erotica and slash fanfiction writers exist on the Internet with great popularity because they, and the people who follow them, are hungry and eager for a type of story they can't get anywhere else. Never doubt the power of the Internet to indulge the fantasies and sexual interests of everyone and any-one, and if publishers don't get on board the *Good Ship Buttsecks* soon, they will miss out on the fun and profits of the Hershey High-way Love Stories.

But(t) while e-publishers have satisfied a very horny market that was after more outrageous and adventurous erotica, the erotica e-market has probably and likely leveled out. E-book writing for an e-publisher won't necessarily be the path to mainstream publishing that it once was, especially as more taboo sexual subjects become standard fare in erotic romance. The last and final frontier of sexual exploration isn't so much the sexual congress itself, but the sex of the protagonists. Two men, and after that, two women, will be embraced by romance readers as valid protagonists of romance fiction, as will the writers who craft their stories.

Which leads us to our last and final prediction: the warping of what Happily Ever After really means. Happy endings will not just mean heterosexual monogamy, though the readers who hanker for exactly that will not go away. The future conclusions of romances will include multiple partners and varying definitions of family, not to mention the variations of sexuality. Bisexual heroines and heroes? Bring them on. Homosexual happy endings, in the narrative and literal sense? Word up. Ambiguous endings that don't spell out in alphabetical order the marriage, the 2.5 children, and the merry blissful future in the epilogue with the whole family hale and happy forever? That, too. It may be the most controversial part of the future of romance, but we envision endings that allow the reader to play more of a role in interpreting the future. The writer may provide enough evidence that the protagonists can live together in blissful cohabitation for the rest of their lives, but it won't be explicitly stated, allowing the readers to presume whatever future they like. It won't be popular, but it'll happen, particularly on the border between Mainstream Taken Very Seriously Fiction and the Romance Genre.

Finally, our Top Five Wish List for anyone who is dreaming of the perfect romance plot that's never been done before:

1. Werefish. Wereamphibians, really. Wereslugs. Werefish. Weresquid. That whole kiss-the-frog thing has really not been appropriately visited.
2. The Vampire Motivational Speaker's Bureau. They've got fangs

and Mighty Wangs, and everyone should hold hands, rub one another's backs, and chant their way to O-positive thinking.

3. Erotic inspirational romance: Oh, God, Oh God, Oh God. End of story.

4. If NASCAR fans got their own line, and historical romance fans who love Blaze got their own line, we want us some atheist romance. Candy suggests, "God is dead, but our love isn't."

5. And while Candy is making wishes: hipster romance, please. Intelligent, thin, toned, and confident dudes—the opposite of the overmuscled alpha Thor model—who like concerts, bands you've never heard of, and staying up all night arguing about the economic analysis of food consumption in first- vs. third-world countries, then going out for big-ass pancakes at 5:00 a.m.

Here's the part where being bloggers by nature presents a real and massive problem. There's an end, and we've come to it. On-line, our site grows in all directions. Old entries get new comments, even entries that are two or three years old. New entries get comments. Entries inspire new entries, or a contest in which we write haikus about boobs. The discussion spreads out like back fat in a too-tight corset. A book, alas, comes to an end, and we know we're going to be assaulted by the *"But wait!"*s for at least a few months as we think of one more thing we wanted to tell you about romance and how awesome and awesomely hysterical it is. But all good things come to an end, and while we hope you've had as good a time reading as we have had writing, we propose that all things ending yield more good, which is to say: come by and visit us. We're still talking online, and if you want to dish romance, we're always around at smartbitchestrashybooks.com.

Thanks for reading, and thanks for loving the Luuuuurve™ as much as we do. May we all live Happily Ever After.

WORKS CITED

Barlow, Linda, and Jayne Ann Krentz. "Beneath the Surface: The Hidden Codes of Romance." *Dangerous Men and Adventurous Women*. Pennsylvania: University of Pennsylvania Press, 1992, 15–31.

Beau Monde. www.thebeaumonde.com/about/. May 2, 2008.

Botts, Amber. "Cavewoman Impulses: The Jungian Shadow Archetype in Popular Romantic Fiction." *Romantic Conventions*. Bowling Green, OH: Bowling Green State University Popular Press, 1999.

Collins, Nicole. Personal interview conducted via e-mail. August 13, 2007.

Crusie Smith, Jennifer. "Defeating the Critics: What We Can Do About Anti-Romance Bias." *Romance Writer's Report* 18, 6 (June 1998): 38–39, 44. Also: www.jennycruisie.com/essays/defeatingthecritics .php/. June 1, 2008.

———. Personal interview. May 11, 2008.

DeSalvo, John. Personal interview conducted via e-mail. May 4, 2008.

Duffy, Kate. Personal interview conducted via phone. May 21, 2008.

Ferrer, Barbara Caridad. Personal interview conducted via phone. May 2, 2008.

Gold, Laurie. *At the Back Fence* 91 (March 15, 2000). www.likesbooks .com/91.html/. June 7, 2008.

Gorlinsky, Raelene. Personal interview. May 29, 2008.

Holly, Emma. Personal interview. June 4, 2008.

Hughes, Kalen. Personal interview conducted via e-mail. May 30, 2008.

Kastner, Deborah. "Heart of Denver Romance Writers." Description of Inspirational Romance. www.hodrw.com/inspire.htm/.

Kinsale, Laura. "The Androgynous Reader." *Dangerous Men and Adventurous Women.* Pennsylvania: University of Pennsylvania Press, 1992, 31–45.

———. E-mail. May 15, 2008.

Kleypas, Lisa. Personal interview conducted via e-mail. June 5, 2008.

Krentz, Jayne Ann. "Trying to Tame the Romance: Critics and Correctness." *Dangerous Men and Adventurous Women.* Philadelphia: University of Pennsylvania Press, 1992, 107–15.

Langan, Ruth Ryan. Personal interview conducted via e-mail. March 31, 2008.

Lim, Jennifer. "Cassie Edwards." http://mrsgiggles.braveblog.com/entry/30574/.

Litte, Jane. "Millenia Black Settles Lawsuit with Penguin over Race." DearAuthor.com. http://dearauthor.com/wordpress/2008/05/13/millenia-black-settles-lawsuit-with-penguin-over-race/.

———. Personal interview. June 2, 2008.

Low, Gennita. "Uber Kick-Ass Heroine Has No Front." http://roofer author.blogspot.com/2007/08/uber-kick-ass-heroine-has-no-front.html/. May 24, 2008.

Lynne, Robin. "Your Scandalous Ways by Loretta Chase." DearAuthor.com. June 15, 2008. http://dearauthor.com/wordpress/2008/05/08/review-your-scandalous-ways-by-loretta-chase-2/.

March, Selah. Personal interview. May 7, 2008.

Moviefone.com's Worst Action Movie Clichés. http://movies.aol.com/worst-movie-cliches/action/. June 7, 2008.

Mussell, Kay. *Fantasy and Reconciliation: Contemporary Formulas of Women's Romance Fiction.* Westport, CT: Greenwood Press, 1984.

Osborn, Heather. Personal Interview. September 21, 2007.

Regis, Pamela. *A Natural History of the Romance Novel.* Philadelphia: University of Pennsylvania Press, 2003.

Roberts, Nora. Personal interview. December 11, 2006.

———. "Fun Facts." www.noraroberts.com/funfacts.htm/.

Romance Writers of America. Romance Literature Statistics 2006. www.rwanational.org/cs/the_romance_genre/romance_literature_statistics/.

————. RITA Award Category Descriptions. www.rwanational.org/cs/contests_and_awards/rita_awards/category_descriptions/.

Saintcrow, Lilith. "Half of Humanity Is Worth Less Than a Chair." Nothing But Red. www.lulu.com/content/2323443/.

————. Personal interview. May 1, 2008.

Segal, Francesca. "M&B Writer Who Saved Jews from Hitler." *The Guardian.* http://www.guardian.co.uk/books/2008/jan/27/fiction.features. January 27, 2008. Accessed June 8, 2008.

Stone, Todd A. *Novelist's Boot Camp.* New York: Writers Digest Books, 2006. (Used with permission.)

Vivanco, Laura. "Romance and Sex Education." Teach Me Tonight. http://teachmetonight.blogspot.com/2006/08/romance-and-sex-education.html/. June 1, 2008.

ACKNOWLEDGMENTS

Candy's Acknowledgments

I'm not sure I would've been able to finish this book in one piece and with my sanity (largely) intact if it hadn't been for the support of a whole lot of people. Here are the primary culprits, then:

Ben, thanks for plying me with silly dancing, food, and coffee when I needed it most. Also for taunting me hilariously when things got tough and hugging me tight when things got even tougher. You, more than anyone else (other than Sarah), ensured I made it through the first year of law school *and* the writing of this book more-or-less coherent.

Laurel and Michael, thank you so much for talking to me when things got scary-hairy and sending me off with a power inverter so I could work in the car during the road trip.

Many thanks to Ben Klusman at Enko Photography for the excellent author photos and for being an excellent person in general.

Carol Main: thank you for creating amazing illustrations on a tight deadline. You rock like a rocking thing who rocks a lot.

Schwern: Dude, thank you for proofreading the manuscript and helping to fix the flowchart. You're the best fuzzy boy in all of Portland.

To all my friends: thanks for not allowing me to forget about you when I went into full-on hermit mode.

Dan, Sulay, and Shawna: I've never published a book before, but you guys have made the process remarkably painless. If I were a Care Bear, I'd be showering you with warm, rainbow-colored love right now.

I also want to point out that this book never would've existed if Rose Hilliard hadn't e-mailed us and said "Hey, are you guys interested in writing a book about romance novels?"

To the amazing community of romance readers and authors we've connected with thanks to Smart Bitches: hot damn, I had no idea I'd have so much fun or meet so many amazing people when we started the site. Jane and Robin, in particular, deserve extra special gold stars and pretty ponies.

And most of all, to my coauthor, Sarah, without whom this wouldn't have been possible. Dude, you're a motherfuckin' force of motherfuckin' nature. High fives!

Oh, and just so you know: my good friends Jess and Schwern concocted the greeting card idea with me a couple of years ago, over an epic session of Thai food. Pad kee mao and rape: two great tastes that taste great together.

Sarah's Acknowledgments

(I should not have let Candy go first. Dammit).

This book was made possible by the letters S and B, and by the number 2, with special thanks to the following people:

All the writers of romance who have given me endless happy reading: thank you for continuing to do what you do.

The authors of romance who gave us their thoughts to include in this book: thank you. Seriously, every time I got an e-mail back from one of you, I squeed like I was ten.

All the readers of romance who visit our site and who love the genre as much as we do: thank you. Neither of us knew when we started the site that we'd find so many women who loved romance novels and who were so clever and wickedly funny we want to have a beer with all of you. We are profoundly glad we've met you.

Kate Duffy, for meals, commiseration, and making me snort pasta up my nose from laughing too hard. Thank you for your encouragement, advice, and support.

Jane, Robin, and the crew from Dear Author: thank you for making the Internet a better place for all us romance readers. You guys are awesome.

Joanne Renaud: for the amazing illustrations, and particularly for the creation of Mavis.

Secret Agent Dan, his Super Awesome Assistant Stephen, the Superbly Excellent Maja Nikolic, and the folks at Writer's House: thank you. And Candy is right: Rose Hilliard is to blame. It is all her fault.

Sulay Hernandez and Shawna Lietzke: thank you for patiently decoding the mysterious process of publication. I still don't understand it, but that's probably a good thing. Also, many thanks and piles of sparkly brilliantly colored pencils to the proofreading and copyediting team at Simon & Schuster. You're so good I'm embarrassed to read over what I'm writing this minute.

Candy for being smart and bitchy: thank you. I had no idea any of this was going to happen, but I am so glad it did. You're amazing.

My family, who made time for me to write this: thank you. Biggest thanks go to my husband and children, who make every day a happily ever after.